Reading
WOMEN
Writing

a series edited by Shari Benstock and Celeste Schenck

Women and Romance: The Consolations of Gender in the English Novel
by Laurie Langbauer

Women and Romance

*The Consolations of Gender
in the English Novel*

Laurie Langbauer

Cornell University Press

ITHACA AND LONDON

First published 1990 by Cornell University Press.

International Standard Book Number 0-8014-2421-6 (cloth)
International Standard Book Number 0-8014-9692-6 (paper)
Library of Congress Catalog Card Number 90-55116

Printed in the United States of America

Librarians: Library of Congress cataloging information appears on the last page of the book.

♾ The paper used in this publication meets the minimum requirements of the American National Standard for Permanence of Paper for Printed Library Materials Z39.48–1984.

Contents

Foreword

As the editors of *Reading Women Writing*, we are committed to furthering international feminist debate. To that end, we seek books that rigorously explore how differences of class, race, ethnic background, nationality, religious preference, and sexual choice inform women's writing. Books sensitive to the ways women's writings are classified, evaluated, read, and taught are central to the series. Of particular interest to us are feminist criticism of non-canonical texts (including film, popular culture, and new and as yet unnamed genres); confrontations of first-world theory with beyond-the-first-world texts; and books on colonial and postcolonial writing that generate their own theoretical positions. Dedicated primarily although not exclusively to the examination of literature by women, *Reading Women Writing* highlights differing, even contradictory, theoretical positions on texts read in cultural context.

Laurie Langbauer's *Women and Romance: The Consolations of Gender in the English Novel*, the fourth book in the series, examines the traditional connection between women and the literary genre "romance." Her study questions this seemingly appropriate and "natural" linkage of gender and genre to discover a new relation that is held not in the content or subject matter of romance but rather in its structure. Romance fiction articulates an economy of desire that resists genre definitions (it is a site of disorder), and in so doing it represents what must necessarily be repressed in order for the genre as a system of representation to exist. The implications of this discovery are at least twofold: the dominant social and literary culture derides, and thereby joins, women and romance; romance is the (false) consolation held out to the oppressed gender whose desire moves within—but also reaches beyond—an economy of (false) hopes that the dominant culture both offers and denies. In short, romance represents the Other to the novel: the novel "scapegoats" romance.

The observations that romance has been excluded and derided by the novel form and that women's desire has been denied or derided by patriarchal culture are not, in themselves, surprising. Langbauer, however, examines an unremarked relation among these figures: Why and how does the system that excludes and derides also continually invoke romance, all the while denying that it does so? That is, how do women and romance represent the cultural system's own repressed desires? Her answers are compelling. Informed by the work of Freud, Derrida, and Foucault, Langbauer's book focuses on texts that reveal an awareness of the tensions between the genres of novel and romance. These tensions are always (although not always self-consciously) articulated in gendered terms. Analyzing works by George Meredith, Charlotte Lennox, Mary Wollstonecraft, Charles Dickens, and George Eliot, Langbauer demonstrates how suppressed forms—women, romance—return within the novel to deconstruct its hierarchies.

More provocatively, she speculates on *why* this return of the repressed occurs and what forms it takes. *Women and Romance* also challenges literary theory and criticism to examine how their own anxieties about the genre "romance" repress (but also invoke) anxieties about gender divisions and hierarchies. Even the most sophisticated analysis cannot help but replicate the repressive order of the forms it investigates and (as with feminist criticism) challenges. Langbauer warns us of "the danger of wishful satisfactions, the consolations offered us by totalizing systems that . . . neat images of women represent in miniature and draw us back into." She subjects to radical critique the assumption that a system—any system—can be totalizing. Her book thereby opens an important question: Can a genre or gender represent total Otherness? Struggling with this issue, Langbauer urges feminism to recognize its implication in the systems—literary, social, cultural—it tries to dismantle.

SHARI BENSTOCK
CELESTE SCHENCK

Acknowledgments

I am grateful to the American Association of University Women, the American Council of Learned Societies, the Swarthmore College Faculty Research Fund, and the National Endowment for the Humanities for supporting my research on this project. I also thank Cynthia Baughman, Margaret Berg, the Cornell University Graduate Feminist Reading Group 1982–85, Terrence Holt, Elsie Michie, Beth Newman, Andrea Sununu, and Melissa Zeiger for all their help and support. I offer my sincere gratitude to Bernhard Kendler of Cornell University Press and the series editors, Shari Benstock and Celeste Schenck, for their ongoing assistance and consideration. I am especially indebted to Neil Hertz, Mary Jacobus, and Harry Shaw for their guidance in the early stages of this project and to Deirdre David, Susan S. Lanser, and Mary Poovey for their careful attention to the final drafts of my manuscript.

Chapter 2 appeared, in an earlier version, as "Romance Revised: Charlotte Lennox's *The Female Quixote*," in *NOVEL: A Forum on Fiction*, 18, no. 1 (Fall 1984). Copyright NOVEL Corp. © 1984. Reprinted with permission. A portion of chapter 3 appeared as "An Early Romance: Motherhood and Women's Writing in Mary Wollstonecraft's Novels," in *Romanticism and Feminism*, ed. Anne K. Mellor (Bloomington: Indiana University Press, 1988). A portion of chapter 4, which came to substantially different conclusions, appeared as "Dickens's Streetwalkers: Women and the Form of Romance," in *ELH* 53 (1986), copyright © 1986 by Johns Hopkins University Press; another portion appeared as "Women in White,

ix

Men in Feminism," in *The Yale Journal of Criticism* 2 (April 1989), copyright © 1989 by Yale University.

LAURIE LANGBAUER

Swarthmore, Pennsylvania

Abbreviations

AB   George Eliot. *Adam Bede*. Edited by Stephen Gill. New York: Penguin, 1980.

BH   Charles Dickens. *Bleak House*. Edited by Norman Page. New York: Penguin, 1971.

DC   George Meredith. *Diana of the Crossways*. Vol. 16 of *The Memorial Edition of the Works of George Meredith*. 29 vols. New York: Scribner's, 1910–12.

DD   George Eliot. *Daniel Deronda*. Edited by Barbara Hardy. New York: Penguin, 1967.

E   George Meredith. *The Egoist*. Vols. 13 and 14 of *The Memorial Edition of the Works of George Meredith*. 29 vols. New York: Scribner's, 1910–12.

EL   Mrs. Henry Wood. *East Lynne*. New Brunswick, N.J.: Rutgers University Press, 1984.

FQ   Charlotte Lennox. *The Female Quixote; or, The Adventures of Arabella*. Introduction by Margaret Dalziel; Appendix by Duncan Isles. New York: Oxford University Press, 1970.

GE   Charles Dickens. *Great Expectations*. Edited by Angus Calder. New York: Penguin, 1965.

"I&S"   Fredric Jameson. "Imaginary and Symbolic in Lacan: Marxism, Psychoanalytic Criticism, and the Problem of the Subject." *Yale French Studies* 55/56 (1977): 338–95.

M   Mary Wollstonecraft. *Mary, A Fiction*. In *Mary and the Wrongs of Woman*, edited by James Kinsley and Gary Kelly, 1–68. New York: Oxford University Press, 1976.

MF   George Eliot. *The Mill on the Floss*. Edited by A. S. Byatt. New York: Penguin, 1979.

MM   George Eliot. *Middlemarch*. Edited by W. J. Harvey. New York: Penguin, 1965.

OCS   Charles Dickens. *The Old Curiosity Shop*. Edited by Angus Easson. New York: Penguin, 1972.

OT   Charles Dickens. *Oliver Twist*. Edited by Peter Fairclough. New York: Penguin, 1966.

OWT   Arnold Bennett. *The Old Wives' Tale*. Edited by John Wain. New York: Penguin, 1983.

PU   Fredric Jameson. *The Political Unconscious: Narrative as a Socially Symbolic Act*. Ithaca: Cornell University Press, 1981.

RN   Ian Watt. *The Rise of the Novel: Studies in Defoe, Richardson, and Fielding*. Berkeley: University of California Press, 1957.

VRW   Mary Wollstonecraft. *A Vindication of the Rights of Woman*. Edited by Miriam Brody Kramnick. New York: Penguin, 1975.

WIW   Wilkie Collins. *The Woman in White*. Edited by Julian Symons. New York: Penguin, 1985.

WW   Mary Wollstonecraft. *The Wrongs of Woman; or, Maria, A Fragment*. In *Mary and the Wrongs of Woman*, edited by James Kinsley and Gary Kelly, 68–204. New York: Oxford University Press, 1976.

Women and Romance

Introduction

Women and romance: in the tradition of English fiction, as well as in popular culture, these two terms seem inextricably intertwined. Women supposedly dream of romance—or so Freud tells us when he distinguishes between erotic and ambitious fantasies (women have, or should have, only the former);[1] they certainly seem to read and write romances—Scudéry-like romances constituted the light literature of English circulating libraries and continue today, as Harlequin romances, to stock supermarket racks.[2] Women also star in them: Little Nell, Hetty Sorrel, and countless other eighteenth- and nineteenth-century heroines figure the yoking of women and romance, as much as the heroines of Harlequin fiction, or more mainstream books such as Margaret Atwood's *Lady Oracle*, do still. Whether conceived as a mode of erotic wish-fulfillment, or as a prose form auxiliary to the novel, romance is thought somehow proper to women and usually derided accordingly. In fact, the connection between women and romance seems so appro-

[1]Sigmund Freud, "Creative Writers and Daydreaming," in vol. 9 of *The Standard Edition of the Complete Psychological Writings of Sigmund Freud*, trans. James Strachey, 24 vols. (1953–74), pp. 141–67; this edition hereafter abbreviated *SE*.

[2]Most of the current standard feminist work on romance, in fact, treats just such romances; see for example Janice A. Radway, *Reading the Romance: Women, Patriarchy, and Popular Literature* (1984); Leslie W. Rabine, *Reading the Romantic Heroine: Text, History, Ideology* (1985); Tania Modleski, *Loving with a Vengeance: Mass-Produced Fantasies for Women* (1982; 1984); Ann Barr Snitow, "Mass Market Romance: Pornography for Women is Different," *Radical History Review* 20 (Spring/Summer 1979): 141–61.

priate that it has been considered almost natural—not requiring, or even open to, interpretation.

But why this yoking? The various meanings of "romance" attest to without explaining it: as my book shows, different critics, in suggesting different answers, define "romance" (and "women") differently, while preserving their connection. Their connection is a constant underlying all these meanings, which serve to uphold this yoking but not to question it. I approach the question of their connection not by offering another definition of these terms but by examining the motives behind their definitions, looking at how they work rather than what they mean. I argue that writers link women and romance, and the meanings of these terms change (and can even contradict themselves), according to a certain economy: the subtle, continuous shifts in what they mean are precisely what make their connection a real yoking, precisely what keep it an ever useful ploy of a dominant system, which maintains its positions of privilege—staked out by those attempting to define themselves as "men" and "novels"—by taking its meaning from women and romance. Women and romance are constructed within the male order and the established tradition of prose fiction that grows out of and upholds that order; they are constructed as marginal and secondary in order to secure the dominance of men and novels. The yoking of women and romance results from their similar function: they are blank counters given whatever meaning establishes the priority of the privileged terms.

Yet the privilege women and romance reflect is a consoling illusion. Since Simone de Beauvoir's *The Second Sex*, feminists have been explicitly aware of the pitfalls and compensations in the construction of woman as man's other (a dynamic also subsequently highlighted by deconstruction's attention to the interplay of supposed opposites).[3] The status quo defines itself by gesturing to its (debased) mirror opposite, whose lacks and problems seem to point to its own completeness and strength. Yet it actually constructs this other out of elements within it that threaten its position, projecting them outward in hopes of escaping them. Because

[3]Simone de Beauvoir, "Introduction," *The Second Sex*, trans. and ed. H. M. Parshley (1968), xiii–xxix; see especially xvi–xviii.

these elements are part of the status quo, it can never elude them, and in its very denial is even able to dwell on without admitting them.

Romance as the novel's other becomes just such a(n ultimately ineffective) scapegoat; as I argue in this book, the first English novels, attempting to define their form, use "romance" (a convenient term at play at that time in the lexicon of prose fiction) to refer to whatever the novel (hopes it) is not, deploying the term in an attempt to draw off contradictions and problems of coherence that undermine the novel's incorporation. The debate between the novel and romance endures beyond this early historical predicament because such scapegoating is necessary to the attempt to define and delimit any integral form.[4] The novel's definition of romance points to its own problems, to problems of representation that it cannot escape. By pointing to these, it also points to the impossibility of its autonomous identity; the novel needs romance in order to give it the appearance of identity and meaning, as well as of privilege, but such identity and privilege are already sabotaged by the very problems that prompt their defensive formation.

In this economy, woman is a scapegoat too, a counter given value by the system in which it circulates. Like romance, she is constructed in opposition to a standard—man—and (circularly) seems to uphold that standard by deviating from it. Yet, just as the definition of romance points to problems of representation, the definition of woman points to problems of (gender) identity. "Men" and "wom-

[4]Recent theorists, such as Tzvetan Todorov or Jacques Derrida, argue in fact that such contradictions unsettle the firm establishment of *any* genre. Todorov argues that "the fact that a work 'disobeys' its genre does not make the latter nonexistent; it is tempting to say that quite the contrary is true. And for a twofold reason. First, because transgression, in order to exist as such, requires a law that will, of course, be transgressed. One could go further: the norm becomes visible—lives—only by its transgressions. . . . But there is more. Not only does the work, for all its being an exception, necessarily presuppose a rule; but this work also, as soon as it is recognized in its exceptional status, becomes in its turn, thanks to successful sales and critical attention, a rule" ("The Origin of Genres," trans. Richard M. Berrong, *New Literary History* 8 [1976]: 160). Jacques Derrida in a sense augments or qualifies Todorov's claims, when he suggests that "every text participates in one or several genres, there is no genreless text; there is always a genre and genres, yet such participation never amounts to belonging" (in "The Law of Genre," trans. Avital Ronell, *Glyph* 7 [1980]: 212). For a discussion of the debate between structural and poststructural definitions of genre, see Adena Rosmarin, *The Power of Genre* (1985).

en" are not fixed categories, essential entities, but constructions that rely on each other for their meaning and position within a hierarchy.

The male order constructs woman as man's contradiction, and at the same time often constructs her *as* a contradiction—incoherent, mercurial, nonsensical. The other is what allows the subject to construct a self at all, to seem to resolve its own incoherence and contradictions. Lacan calls the pattern of projection and construction "the imaginary," and this category is helpful because it relates the play of mirrors within the strategy of the other precisely to problems of character and gender. Through the other, the subject reflects back an image of itself, creating the very illusion of *a* self. For Lacan, the constructed self is necessarily gendered: the subject is subject to a sexual system and appears precisely at the moment it recognizes (its inadequacy within) that system, precisely when its lack puts into play an unassuageable desire.[5] Let me bracket for the moment whether Lacan's (so-called) description of that system in terms of the Name-of-the-Father and the Phallus wittingly or unwittingly re-enforces the sexual biases that construct the subject; readers need not even accept such a strictly psychoanalytic grammar to agree that the questions of identity and gender are inextricably related. Feminist analyses that differ from, or are even opposed to, psychoanalysis, such as those that focus on an individual's social and economic role, agree that that role and the identity that arises from it are conditioned (and perhaps even determined) by gender.[6]

In this study, I consider women and romance in terms of their

---

[5]For a discussion of the imaginary, see Jacques Lacan, "The Mirror Stage as Formative of the Function of the I," "Aggressivity in Psychoanalysis," and "The Direction of the Treatment and the Principles of Its Power," in his *Ecrits: A Selection,* trans. Alan Sheridan (1977), 1–7, 8–29, and 226–80; for the relation of the subject to gender, see Jacques Lacan, "The Agency of the Letter in the Unconscious, or Reason since Freud," in *Ecrits,* 146–78, and "The Meaning of the Phallus," and "God and the *Jouissance* of The Woman," in *Feminine Sexuality: Jacques Lacan and the école freudienne,* trans. Jacqueline Rose, ed. Juliet Mitchell and Jacqueline Rose (1982), 74–85, 137–48.

[6]Even when directly denying the usefulness of psychoanalysis to feminism and arguing for the need to ground ourselves in theories of social change, a critic such as Elizabeth Wilson, for example, assumes that an account of the construction of sexual identity remains necessary to feminism; see her "Psychoanalysis: Psychic Law and Order?" *Feminist Review* 8 (1981): 63–78.

utility within an imaginary dynamic, one that serves seemingly established positions—the male order and its literary tradition—enthroned within the system of power. I chart the various ways the constructions of women and romance are put to use and argue that such a dynamic ultimately defeats its own ends, although such defeat does not necessarily empower women—on the contrary, may even redound on them. Women and romance cannot rescue men and novels from a system of relations whose constrictions these latter hope desperately to elude. Subordinating women and romance grants those ranked above them at best local (although effective and destructive) power, for total control resides in the system of construction and representation in which *all* terms are determined. At the same time, it seems worth stressing that the male order has no *essential* connection to those who are biologically male but simply demarcates this uneasy position of privilege in the system of power. This privilege is most often, though not necessarily, assumed by those who are male, however, and even bolstered by references to that maleness (the familiar arguments about strength, brain size, and so on); hence the feminist shorthand, "the male order."

This system of power is something more than the male order, representation, language, the unconscious, ideology, or culture, although all these terms have at different times and places been used as synonyms for it, and I fall into such shorthand in this book too. The controlling system, however, is what enables these, the governing paradigm that permits and gives shape to our world, the solvent or glue—invisible as ether—that holds our understanding of it together. Derrida's phallogocentrism, Lacan's symbolic order, or Foucault's network of power have been recent attempts to describe this system, and I rely on their suggestions about it, whatever their disagreements. My concern with identity in this study profits from the work of Lacan and Foucault, from their analyses of how the individual subject conforms to and props up the system producing it. I am especially indebted in these pages, however, to recent feminist literary theory and its emphasis on how gender is constructed so that the category of woman in particular underwrites and ensures that system.

I examine in this study eighteenth- and nineteenth-century English novels, but I would argue that the pattern I consider applies in some degree to any system of power relations that relies on notions of the coherent self and, hence, of fixed gender. Whether such an argument means that (as psychoanalysis might claim) this pattern is transhistorical or that (as followers of Foucault might assert) it emerges historically in the eighteenth and nineteenth centuries because of changes in the definition of the self cannot perhaps be resolved.[7] What is important to my study is that both these theoretical perspectives, despite their radical disagreements, describe a similar pattern within which to examine these novels.

My claims about the construction of gender and genre may seem to risk the charge of functionalism: I may seem to imply that the male order is in control of the functioning of this signifying system in which it is actually itself defined, that it is able to effect its own self-interest by defining the category of woman, for example, according to whatever allows for its own smooth operation. Rather than implying that systems of relations are so simple, however, I explore our wish that they were so and show instead that categories such as "woman" are not transparent but mark precisely those contested sites that make any claim to power, by "men," for example, problematic (that such problems inevitably hinder smooth operations is what actually opens up a space for analysis and makes my investigation possible). My conclusions ultimately put into question claims to power, suggesting that the bid for power may effect its own kind of indenture. The idea that they might (or ought to) control it keeps those within the position of the male order locked within the system of power relations that favors them (but at a cost).[8]

Moreover, the strategy of scapegoating I describe might more specifically be seen as the process Freud called "negation," a rejec-

---

[7]And the differences between such groups lessen considerably if one attends to the redefinition of his historical context that Foucault seems to imply in the last two volumes of the *History of Sexuality,* in which he reverts to the Classical period to discuss the subject, the same period that underlies psychoanalytic and deconstructive discussions of identity. See Michel Foucault, *The Use of Pleasure,* vol. 2 of *The History of Sexuality,* trans. Robert Hurley (1986), and *The Care of the Self,* vol. 3 of *The History of Sexuality,* trans. Robert Hurley (1988).

[8]For another discussion of the relation between feminist methodology (this time Marxist feminism) and functionalism, see Michèle Barrett, "Ideology and the Cultural Production of Gender," in *Feminist Criticism and Social Change: Sex, Class, and Race in Literature and Culture,* ed. Judith Newton and Deborah Rosenfelt (1985), 71–73.

tion that foregrounds crucial material while attempting to protect against it with a shield of denial. By denying that the figure in a dream is his or her mother, for instance, a patient actually indicates that it is (and the following chapter will attempt to account for why the *mother* might be Freud's exemplary figure here): "Negation is a way of taking cognizance of what is repressed; indeed, it is already a lifting of the repression, though not, of course, an acceptance of what is repressed."[9] Although Freud goes on to suggest that, through negation, the mind "enriches itself with material that is indispensable for its proper functioning," the easy and straightforward operations of functionalism are already put into question.[10] As categories that give the male order access to what it otherwise cannot admit, women and romance do more than simply allow it to function; they also embody just what hinders its operations. That they do both at once, however, suggests the problem of determining the valence of contradiction. The undecidability of negation, the problem of whether the subject can ever really say no to what propels it, suggests that one recent approach to contradiction—celebrating it as the locus of subversion—may be too pat. The suggestion implicit throughout Foucault's work—that contradiction can be the very dynamic that enforces an inescapable order by providing the (specious) appearance of dissent from it—usefully qualifies the mystification of contradiction. At the same time, however, such qualifications can become overly programmatic themselves, if imposed on all contexts, presented as truth (as Foucault himself, in holding open the possibility of resistance to power, well recognized).[11]

How then do we as subjects work within systems of signification and power? Let me unbracket here the question of whether our inscription within the dominant discourse is witting or not. This book is predicated on the idea that no one can avoid working within, and so re-enforcing, systems of power, but the understanding that we all must do so is crucial; it allows us to see and to open up, if not to subvert, those systems. As Foucault and Derrida both argue, the notion of subversion is necessary to the ruling order,

[9]Sigmund Freud, "Negation," *SE*, 19: 235–36.
[10]Freud, "Negation," 236.
[11]Michel Foucault, *The History of Sexuality: An Introduction*, vol. 1, trans. Robert Hurley (1980), 95–96.

which enforces itself by deploying the possibility of transgression.[12] But, because, as subjects, we are caught within a system that already seems to inhabit any space outside it we might imagine, we need not stop analyzing the space we are within. It is crucial to recognize our situation in this space, and an important way to map it is to focus on the moments that seem to transgress it, the strategies of sameness and difference that promise different routes to what might be the same end—the consolation of freedom that seems to sustain our struggle.

What distinguishes feminism from the male order is that feminism to some degree has always been aware of the indifference of power, of our painful entrapment as subjects within it, and of the necessity for continuing to resist what we cannot imagine how to overcome, without wishfully denying it. The male order establishes itself precisely by ignoring its own implication within a controlling order; it identifies with and attempts to take the place of that order by insisting on women's subjugation. Feminist theorists such as Mary Jacobus, Margaret Homans, Eve Sedgwick, Gayle Rubin, and Christine Froula have all in different ways described the methods used by patriarchy to cement and assert the bonds between men by forging them on the site of the woman.[13] Whether in the Oedipal triangle or male systems of exchange, the construction of occluded or invisible women gives the laws of male privilege their currency. Her expulsion or subservience is meant to hide that the bonds of patriarchy are shackles that can never be removed, although they may seem to be lessened, through the defensive oppression of others.

Our very division into *gendered* subjects is one way power deploys itself. But even the privileged term within gender division is privileged at a cost, and men's very identification with power is

---

[12]For Derrida's description of this relationship, see "The Law of Genre" and also "Women in the Beehive: A Seminar with Jacques Derrida," in *Men in Feminism*, ed. Alice Jardine and Paul Smith (1987), 189–203.

[13]Mary Jacobus, *Reading Woman: Essays in Feminist Criticism* (1986); Margaret Homans, *Bearing the Word: Language and Female Experience in Nineteenth-Century Women's Writing* (1986); Eve Kosofsky Sedgwick, *Between Men: English Literature and Male Homosocial Desire* (1985); Gayle Rubin, "The Traffic in Women: Notes on the 'Political Economy' of Sex," in *Toward an Anthropology of Women*, ed. Rayna R. Reiter (1975), 157–210; Christine Froula, "When Eve Reads Milton: Undoing the Canonical Economy," *Critical Inquiry* 10 (December 1983): 321–47.

what most threatens to sabotage them, and all of us. The male order's blind identification with ultimate authority is destructive to everyone inscribed within gender (and risks being ultimately so, according to the claims of feminists such as Dorothy Dinnerstein or Carol Cohn who connect gender roles and the scapegoating of women with the danger of nuclear apocalypse[14]). But, at the same time, the male order is also too simply the other for feminism; feminists' unexamined use of that term tends to deny women's implication in authority—to deny the ways we as feminists cannot, in devising our own theories, say no to fathers like Freud but must use their very perspectives in our struggles with them, and also the ways we as women (necessarily) move within and use the language and structure of dominance itself, simply by operating as subjects who use language, for example. I intend to foreground an examination of these vexed relations to the orders that create us by unraveling the particular strategies that invest men and women, novels and romance, with meaning within those orders.

I examine the consolations of gender and genre by attempting to engage with what have been crucial questions for feminist literary theory; my readings question how genre in prose fiction in general, and in certain exemplary English novels in particular, relies on gender division. The attention to the working of power through the conduit of gender in these novels, however, is inseparable from an attention to key issues in recent feminist debate. Working through questions of form, reading certain novels that particularly put the relations between the novel and romance into play, I also engage in and investigate feminist literary analysis, meditating on its problems and strengths.

The first chapter, for example, outlines the formal emphasis of this book. (In doing so, it interrupts the literary history that this investigation constructs too, delaying for a moment the chronological progression of the rest of the chapters in order to introduce the topics and themes crucial to this study.) It considers the ways

[14]Dorothy Dinnerstein, *The Mermaid and the Minotaur: Sexual Arrangements and Human Malaise* (1976); Carol Cohn, "Sex and Death in the Rational World of Defense Intellectuals," *Signs* 12 (1987): 687–718; but see also Foucault's discussion of the relation between sexuality and apocalypse, which he perceives in terms of the power over life, not death, in *History of Sexuality*, 1: 135–59.

representation mediates our approach to the material by examining how the category of history can trade on certain gender assumptions. My reading of George Meredith's fiction, especially *Diana of the Crossways*, engages in the ongoing critical dialogue about the construction of history in literary analysis by focusing on women's role in that construction: her deployment enables the gender consolation encoded into certain uses of the category of history. An investigation of Meredith's treatment of romance reveals some of the pitfalls built into the concept of history as it is frequently used, suggesting as well dangers we need to recognize in our feminist investigations.

In chapter 2, Charlotte Lennox's *The Female Quixote* provides a focus for a discussion of the tradition of women's writing. Lennox's use of the term "romance" puts into question whether the relation of women and romance is as straightforwardly disabling as some feminist critics, such as Sandra Gilbert and Susan Gubar, have argued. Lennox's use of romance demonstrates instead that woman's ancillary and dependent position does not depend on her association with some particular derided form, but that such associations might actually expose the very mechanisms of her derision. At the same time, a reading of Lennox's novel impels us to question the subversiveness that Elaine Showalter suggests inheres in women's writing in the association between women and certain forms such as romance.

An investigation of the debate about essentialism in feminist literary theory organizes a discussion of Mary Wollstonecraft's fiction. The way her work links certain figures—especially the mother and the prostitute—to romance facilitates an inquiry into the contradictions within recent treatment of the (woman's) body in feminist analysis, especially those readings that focus on the social and economic determinants of meaning. This chapter argues that the turn to the material world, pared down and reduced to the figure of the body, rather than simply freeing feminist interpretation from ideological baggage, must itself be determined by particular assumptions that can also boomerang onto feminism.

The fourth chapter explores my own assumptions by exploring the uneasy relation of Foucauldian interpretation to feminist analysis. The divided nature of romance in Charles Dickens's novels suggests the oscillations of power which recent Foucault-inspired critics of Dickens chart. At the same time, however, the treatment of women in those novels exposes how male claims to power depend on but are called into question by the denial of women's oppression.

Chapter 5 considers what feminist literary criticism might attempt in the future, how it might proceed given what seems the current theoretical impasse, the difficulty if not impossibility of imagining resistance. This chapter reinterprets George Eliot's pessimism, the double bind for women within her novels that has troubled feminist critics, as a reaction to just such a dilemma. A reading of Eliot's treatment of romance specifically in terms of the feminist debate about the specular order, about whether or not the gaze is male, suggests feminism's implication within the orders we as feminists wish to oppose and escape. Rather than suggesting that we cease in our attempts to oppose and resist, however, Eliot's fiction suggests that a wishful ignorance of the limits within those attempts may be more destructive to them than recognizing their limits, than admitting the boundaries past which we cannot see. I end with a short conclusion meditating on what those boundaries have been in my discussion.

1

The Romance of History,
or
Ontogeny Recapitulates Phylogeny,
Sometimes

This book is primarily a formal analysis; it focuses on enduring problems of distinguishing and defining form, in this case the English novel, not on the specific and changing historical conditions within which that novel develops. Yet from a feminist perspective one of the material problems in women's relation to the definition of form must be the problem of the material. Many feminist literary critics—such as Biddy Martin, Nancy Armstrong, Cora Kaplan, Mary Poovey, or Gayatri Spivak—have argued that we need to give renewed attention to material conditions in order to understand the role of gender within the novelistic tradition—and, along with that, to analyze our cultural situation properly and perhaps also to change it. That attention would take the form of an attention to history and the historical process, which such critics claim might grant some access to the material, perhaps enough to help us modify our conditions.[1]

These feminist investigations that attend to material context have been invaluable. In this chapter, however, while not denying or refusing the material, I open up the questions I ask later on by

[1]Biddy Martin, "Feminism, Criticism, and Foucault," in *Feminism and Foucault: Reflections on Resistance*, ed. Irene Diamond and Lee Quinby (1988), 3–19; Nancy Armstrong, *Desire and Domestic Fiction: A Political History of the Novel* (1987); Cora Kaplan, *Sea Changes: Essays on Culture and Feminism* (1986); Mary Poovey, *The Proper Lady and the Woman Writer: Ideology as Style in the Works of Mary Wollstonecraft, Mary Shelley, and Jane Austen* (1984) and *Uneven Developments: The Ideological Work of Gender in Mid-Victorian England* (1988); Gayatri Chakravorty Spivak, *In Other Worlds: Essays in Cultural Politics* (1987).

approaching the question of the material more skeptically. Some of the assumptions guiding me throughout this book have to do with the importance of feminist debate: it seems crucial to me that feminist scholarship expand and extend the category of the political, rather than restricting it to analyses that privilege the material or historical in certain ways. Indeed, as Biddy Martin suggests, one of the strengths of feminism may well be the differences and divergences of its approaches. She writes: "What Leftists have criticized in the woman's movement as fragmentation, lack of organization, absence of a coherent and encompassing theory, and the inability to mount a frontal attack may very well represent fundamentally more radical and effective responses to the deployment of power in our society than the centralization and abstraction that continue to plague Leftist thinking and strategy."[2] The political usefulness of feminist material and historical analyses does not, it seems to me, preclude useful feminist analyses that also may wish to question some of the assumptions encoded within recourse to the material and historical.

The material remains an important focus in this study, then, but precisely because of the ways we do not have direct access to it. I want to focus on the material, but on how our textualizations of it give it the very shape we recognize as material. One of the most important of those textualizations might be called "history." Rather than dispense with the category of the historical, in this chapter I emphasize its identity *as* a category, a representation, a form. I am most interested here in the ways our relation to history remains complicated and uncertain, and the way that those uncertainties can expose, if not undo, the codifications of gender.

Rather than seek to trace the historical determinants of women and romance, I argue that looking for such answers hides (and may close off) another question: just what purposes can be served by the recourse to history? Just as I am concerned not so much with the meanings of "women" and "romance" as with the practice that determines them and the uses to which they are put, in this chapter I consider what the recourse to history allows. In what ways can the category of history—when its own status as a problematic form is bracketed—cover over and shore up strategies of dominance,

[2]Martin, "Feminism, Criticism, and Foucault," 10.

specifically in terms of gender? Feminist critics who ground their work in history have been instrumental in exposing the way that category is gendered. I extend their analysis by examining key critics interested in history—Ian Watt and Fredric Jameson—who work instead at times as if history were removed from gender.

I

The "rise of the novel" is often seen as an important development in literary history, for it is explained according to and also seems to confirm the connections between literature and history. The novel's self-definition rests not just on making romance formally marginal (as the rest of this book demonstrates) but also historically prior to it. It sets up romance as an origin out of which it evolves—and evolution implies superiority. Romance supposedly comes first in this scenario because it is seen as incomplete and inadequate; the novel defines its difference from romance by outgrowing and surmounting it. Rather than accepting such historical conventions, and defining the novel and romance as fixed forms in a progressive chain, I examine just how and why this particular convention works and what it tells us about some of the assumptions of (literary) history.

Ian Watt, for example, for all his careful scholarship and sophistication, differentiates the novel from romance using a theory of history that ultimately assumes an unvexed referentiality. His own recourse to the historical facts of the rise of individualism in eighteenth-century England (a historical narrative he assumes without examining it as a narrative, without questioning what purpose this discourse of individualism might serve, in its own historical context, or in our own) parallels the transparent referentiality of language that he argues is a key element in the rise of the novel out of romance. In Watt's argument, the consolation that material fact supplies, especially when equated with the fixed meanings of words or fixed definition of form, is especially underwritten by the supposedly clear and natural fixity of gender. The Oedipal scenario that is the subtext of Watt's formal and historical evolution props up that evolution; at the same time, it defuses, by sexualizing in a clear gender hierarchy, the problems of the dominant discourse it serves and with which it identifies—a discourse that underwrites the unity and autonomy of the individual subject. But Watt's readings, especially of Richardson, uncover gender slippages that not only put his argument into question but raise questions about the subject's autonomy and the resulting male dominance that his argument needs to assume.

Fredric Jameson, in *The Political Unconscious*, more explicitly examines the way our relation to the material is always mediated. Yet, although his argument subtly details the problems involved in history's textualization of events, its use of history still reveals the consolatory function of history. For in Jameson's argument, the historical process, as he defines it when discussing and defining the novel's difference from romance, points to a place of freedom for that very argument—outside the dominant discourse. It does so precisely through its use of unexamined gender biases: in his discussion of romance, Jameson relies on the fantasy of the pre-Oedipal mother, who exists to reflect back the self, convincing the infant that the outside world is actually a sustaining part of him. This fantasy also, however, supplies a wishful figure for the critic's harmonious coexistence with the dominant system in which he works. Jameson's particular method of historicizing, which he claims subsumes all other methods, and his discussion of the novel as the all-encompassing sedimented form attempt to make his particular vision of history not just one more textualization but a vision that merges with the absent ground of the material itself.

My investigation of history ends in this chapter with a reading of literary fictions, setting up my interpretive practice by demonstrating, through the category of history, the novel's connections to the romance it rejects. George Meredith's fiction also plays with and acts out the consoling function of the gender assumptions that I find in Watt and Jameson. Meredith's work is also predicated on a notion of historical evolution, and he explicitly ties it to a progression out of egoism, out of an attachment to the self. *The Egoist*, for example, works from the assumption that man's natural development is out of primitive self-centeredness into decentered community; the book explicitly claims that the realistic account of events, which characterizes the novel, properly leaves behind the sham and sensuality of romance, which are the trappings of egoism. Yet the problems of egoism that Meredith projects out of his novel onto romance actually mask a longing for individualism and for the power it implies. *Diana of the Crossways* demonstrates the contradictions in Meredith's history and the way that gender relations are crucial to exempting men and novels from the harsh anti-individualism of his system. Diana's difference from Willoughby, the difference of gender, is what preserves this patriarchal egoism; her properly feminine loss of herself in Redworth allows that hero, uncriticized, the "marriage with a mirror" that Willoughby seeks.[3] Such osmosis protecting the privileged self also relies on pre-Oedipal fantasies, on the image of the all-encompassing, nurturing mother. The fantasy of merging with this mother is meant to undo the extinction of the individual, to repeal the death of the self that seems the very hallmark of Meredith's modernism. In Meredith's case, in the familiar logic of negation, his history denies what it most desires.

II

Readers of critical studies of the novel know that critics have difficulty defining the novel, difficulty agreeing on just what it is.[4] The multiplication of definitions and the contradictions among them suggest one lesson that deconstruction has taught: the process of definition undoes itself, the articulation of rules calls them into question. Yet something more is common to definition too: definitions are constructed in service of certain assumptions and goals—constructed within what we may still call ideology if we do not conflate that term with false consciousness, if we recognize that our use of it does not exempt us from it. Rather than attempting to define the novel, we might approach it instead by highlighting the assumptions that press us into certain definitions and the systems generating those assumptions—systems within which we operate whether or not we recognize them. The question would be not so much "what is the novel" but "why do we define it as we do?"

One way critics define the novel is to distinguish it from other forms. Beginning with Dr. Johnson and Congreve, and moving

[3]George Meredith, *The Egoist*, vols. 13 and 14 of *The Memorial Edition of the Works of George Meredith*, 29 vols. (1910–12), vol. 14, ch. 37, p. 170; all future references to this book (hereafter abbreviated *E*) will appear in the text.

[4]For a good overview of the problems of defining the novel, see Gustavo Pérez Firmat, "The Novel as Genres," *Genre* 12 (Fall 1979): 269–92.

through Clara Reeve, Sir Walter Scott, all the way to Northrop Frye in the present day, a staple of critical discussion has been to compare the novel to that related form, romance.[5] Any reader of a standard history of the novel, such as Ernest Baker's, is familiar with this comparison. Baker indeed spends the first volume of his *History of the English Novel* locating the novel's roots in various romances.[6] One problem of this approach is that it cannot elude the difficulty of defining the novel by simply shifting the problem onto romance: having the novel and romance describe each other in a tautology of opposition winds up begging the question of definition. Such a move seems to point despite itself to the way meanings are produced within a system of terms rather than resting on some bedrock outside that system. By defining the novel *against* romance, critics inadvertently suggest that the novel has no fixed meaning, no essence, but takes its place within a sliding chain of signification.

Yet one of the effects of a *history* of the novel is to resist such an assertion; by historicizing this chain, it seems to arrest its slide. Within the assumption of such history, romance, rather than being a counter within a grammar of meanings, becomes fixed—claimed as the first prose form, whether located in ancient Greece, seventeenth-century France, or eighteenth-century England. As the point of origin for the novel, what comes before and generates it, romance becomes the bedrock against which the novel takes its meaning and establishes its identity by establishing its difference.

An emphasis on the primacy of romance in defining the novel often slips imperceptibly over into an emphasis on the primacy of history in defining these forms.[7] Yet the turn from the formal to the

[5]For such contrasts between novel and romance, see William Congreve, "The Preface to the Reader," in his *Incognita; or, Love and Duty Reconcil'd*, vol. 1 of *The Complete Works of William Congreve*, 4 vols., ed. Montague Summers (1964), p. 111. See also the contrasted definitions made by Clara Reeve, vol. 1 of *The Progress of Romance through Times, Countries, and Manners*, 2 vols. (1785; 1970), p. 111; Sir Walter Scott, "An Essay on Romance," in *Chivalry, Romance, and the Drama*, vol. 6 of his *The Miscellaneous Prose Works*, 6 vols. (1827), pp. 154–55; Northrop Frye, *Anatomy of Criticism: Four Essays* (1957), 303–9, and *The Secular Scripture: A Study of the Structure of Romance* (1976), 35–61.

[6]Ernest Baker, *The Age of Romance: From the Beginnings to the Renaissance*, vol. 1 of *The History of the English Novel*, 10 vols. (1924–39).

[7]In her representative monograph on romance, for example, Gillian Beer emphasizes the critical role of history in defining it. Her study illustrates how the standard

historical too often signals our desire as critics for a solution (to the problem of the definition of the novel, but also to the problem of our relation to past events) where none exists. The emphasis on origin that characterizes histories of fiction cannot cover over the problem of origin within history itself, a problem well rehearsed by historiographers. As Hayden White has observed, the word "history" has no simple and completely certain reference itself because its meanings are so various. He writes: "['History'] applies to *past* events, to the *record* of those events, to the chain of events which make up a *temporal process* that includes the events of the past and present as well as those of the future, to systematically ordered *accounts* of the events attested by the record, to *explanations* of such systematically ordered accounts, and so forth."[8] The problem with a recourse to history is that the idea of history as account is often collapsed with the idea of history as past events. Dominick LaCapra

---

general comparison of the novel and romance in terms of the real and fictive already appeals to history—the realm of the real—as the uncontested category that determines meaning. She argues that not only is romance concerned with history (past events), but the definition of something as romance depends on historical positioning: the fictive expression of the disturbing, and even revolutionary, desires of a period may seem realistic—novelistic—to it; but later times, for whom the revolutionary situation is past, reinterpret that expression as romantic—fictive—in order to slot those prior desires back into the status quo, against which it may then form its own reaction (Gillian Beer, *The Romance* [1970], 13). A more recent anthology about romance insists on the exemplariness of romance in demonstrating the importance of history: it argues that romance, even more than other genres, is determined by and "inextricably bound up with a complex, evolving, historical situation," attesting to the importance of history (*Romance: Generic Transformation from Chrétien de Troyes to Cervantes*, ed. Kevin Brownlee and Marina Scordilis Brownlee [1985], 1); this emphasis on the relation between romance and history also underlies the approaches within *The Progress of Romance: The Politics of Popular Fiction*, ed. Jean Radford (1986), which is a volume in Routledge's History Workshop Series. In his study of the history of the novel, Michael McKeon also connects romance and history, asserting that a changing understanding of the relations between romance and history was crucial to the rise of the novel (McKeon, *The Origins of the English Novel, 1600–1740* [1987], 25–64). Even Northrop Frye, whose structural anatomy tends toward the ahistorical, temporalizes, if not historicizes, romance, pushing it back toward an origin, arguing that it parallels our first literary experience, "the experience of a child listening to a story" (Frye, *Secular Scripture*, 51).

[8] Hayden White, "Getting out of History," *Diacritics* 12 (1982): 4–5. One of the principal debates within post-structuralism has been just how to maintain "history" as a useful category while at the same time interrogating its claim to truth. For a variety of approaches to this question, see *Post-Structuralism and the Question of History*, ed. Derek Attridge, Geoff Bennington, and Robert Young (1987).

reminds us that as readers we often conjure up history as a "locus for some prediscursive image of 'reality,'" as "an external, extra-discursive ground . . . assumed to solve all basic problems in interpretation, including those that may have been disclosed by one's own reading of a text."[9] The problem with this, White argues, is that it eliminates the interpretive act, translating reading into knowledge, analysis into truth:

> The difficulty with the notion of a truth of *past* experience is that it can *no longer* be experienced, and this throws a specifically *historical* knowledge open to the charge that it is a *construction* as much of imagination as of thought . . . [which] puts historical discourse on the same level as any rhetorical performance and consigns it to the status of a textualization neither more or less authoritative than "literature" itself can lay claim to.[10]

Past events are not immediately available to us; history's documents—the ones it works from as well as its accounts of them—remain texts themselves.

Readers and critics continue to treat history as if, in White's words, it "were a seamless web and told only one story which could be invoked as a way of defining what is only 'fictive' and what is 'real'" because this appeal seems to permit some kind of authority.[11] The desire for a ground from which to speak that prompts this appeal to the past also operates within that basic filter of past events, memory itself. Freud writes of how memory constructs itself as much out of wishes as actual past events (because it cannot actually distinguish between them), reorganizing, reinterpreting, or even inventing those events to fit the script of the subject's fantasies, especially, Mary Jacobus points out, the fantasy of its own integrity and completeness, which provides the ground for its very existence.[12] The problems of memory are the problems of history as well. When not qualified and examined (and even, perhaps, despite our attempts to do so), the belief in some access to reality through a historical account can be similarly a bid for autho-

[9]Dominick LaCapra, *History and Criticism* (1985), 10, 105.

[10]White, "Getting out of History," 5.

[11]White, "Getting out of History," 11.

[12]Mary Jacobus, "Freud's Mnemonic: Women, Screen Memories, and Feminist Nostalgia," *Michigan Quarterly Review* 26 (1987): 117–39.

rizing wholeness, a "dream of 'total history'" that reveals "the historian's own desire for mastery. . . [his project for] control in a world out of joint."[13]

Simply to turn to history—in order to define the novel, for instance—does not solve the problems of definition and meaning readers encounter at the formal level because history is itself a form. The practice of history—literary or otherwise—is not anymore in the service of domination than any other practice, but neither does it provide its own access to a ground of pure fact, outside power. The recent critical movement has been away from questions of "pure" form; proponents of the old and new historicism argue, quite rightly, I think, that form is never pure; it is tied up with, and a screen that hides, ideological positions. A discussion of form divorced from its material context, they argue, allows an apparently apolitical stance that is actually highly political, if not conservative and reactionary, in the consolation it supplies by suggesting that there is a realm outside politics or power.[14] I want to emphasize, however, that the turn to history can also be a consolation which cannot solve (and may not even recognize) our implication as subjects within ideology and systems of power, although it may offer to do so. Neither formal nor historical criticism can be political without an ever vigilant awareness of the complexities of analysis that may well present insoluble problems, such as the always prior textualization of our knowledge. Attempts to solve such problems by closing off or simplifying them act out of unacknowledged wish-fulfillment and may therefore be especially open to appropriation by a regressive status quo.

In some crucial studies that have defined the literary history of the novel, one of the roles given to history puts into play just such covert desires. Ian Watt's *The Rise of the Novel* distinguishes the novel from romance to demonstrate the close relation between literary form and its social context, especially the rise of individualism in seventeenth- and eighteenth-century England that it claims gives shape to and explains the formal characteristics of the novel. Yet because Watt's study acts out the inability to engage with

[13]LaCapra, *History and Criticism*, 25.
[14]See, for example, Mark Seltzer, *Henry James and the Art of Power* (1984), 171–95.

its assumptions that we must all to some degree repeat, within his argument the relations between history and form are often circular. What interests me is where such (inevitable) circularity lies: Watt seems to need assumptions specifically about the gendered individual to prove the relation between literature and history, while at the same time relying on the relation between literature and history to shore up the certainty and privilege on which the very notion of the individual relies.[15]

Watt distinguishes the novel from previous forms by its formal characteristics, what he calls its "formal realism," a mode in service of and upheld by that locus of the real, history.[16] Not surprisingly, one key element of formal realism is its treatment of time: "the distinctive role which the novel has added to" literature, Watt argues, is its portrayal of "life by time" (*RN*.22). This emphasis on time makes the formal and historical dovetail neatly: just as history, as Watt implicitly defines it, depends on causality and evolution, "the novel's plot," he argues, "is also distinguished from most previous fiction by its use of past experience as the cause of present action" (22). Distinguishing the novel from previous fiction is itself a use of past experience; Watt's argument acts out its own assumptions: it asserts the evolution of the novel out of the form previous to it, romance, to distinguish the novel (*it* emphasizes causality and plot, for example; romance does not), circularly to uphold the importance of history (the determining category of causality and evolution), and to clinch its own identity as realistically—historically—informed.

Distinguishing the novel in terms of its formal realism not only privileges history but also seems to lay to rest questions troubling the certainty of the relations between form and reality, word and

---

[15]For a different reading of how Watt's theory of the rise of the novel relies on gender assumptions, which also gives a significantly different value to the concept of history even as it investigates history as a discourse conveying power, see Nancy Armstrong, *Desire and Domestic Fiction*, 28–58; for a further critique of Watt's gender bias, see Dale Spender, *Mothers of the Novel: One Hundred Good Women Writers before Jane Austen* (1986), 115–37, especially 115–18. For a Marxist critique of Watt's history, which also considers questions of gender, see Terry Lovell, *Consuming Fiction* (1987), 19–45.

[16]Ian Watt, *The Rise of the Novel: Studies in Defoe, Richardson and Fielding* (1957); "formal realism" is defined on page 32; all future references to this book (hereafter abbreviated *RN*) will appear in the text.

thing, that get raised in any formal analysis. By seeming to put the emphasis on the formal (the *formal* realism of the novel is concerned not with "the kind of life it presents" but "the way it presents it" [11]), Watt actually strengthens the category of the real in his argument: although he grants that the scientific objectivity the novel claims for itself "certainly cannot be realised in practice," he still winds up implying that there is no significant difference between the "literary work and the reality it imitates" (11). In contrast to romance, by concentrating on the closeness "of words to things," the formal realism of the novel sets up language as "a purely referential medium" (28). In romance, "language [is] a source of interest in its own right"; what Locke calls the "abuses of language" that occur when language is divorced from its referent (which, "like the fair sex," involve a pleasurable deceit)—these abuses are, Watt claims, "a regular feature of the romances" and "much rarer" in novels (28). The comparative here demonstrates that *The Rise of the Novel* knows its linguistic philosophy and, seeking to avoid the simplifications of naive epistemology, is careful in its treatment of referentiality: Watt's discussion of the philosophical skepticism eroding idealism and his use of cautious qualifiers (formal realism "*purports* to be an authentic account of the actual experiences of individuals," for example [27; emphasis added]) concede the impossibility of pure reference. Yet, in arguing that words do not "*all* stand for real objects" and that a gap between word and thing invades "the *great bulk* of literature" (28; emphasis added), Watt implicitly reintroduces the wish for what he has demonstrated "cannot be realised in practice" (11), the possibility of one-to-one correspondence for some special and privileged literature, the object of *his* study, the novel. He goes on to defuse the force of philosophical skepticism by historicizing it; he implies that the "semantic problem" of the gap between word and thing, rather than being an intrinsic element of the structure of language, becomes situated in history, merely one period's view of language (28).

Such historical situating seems to solve the problem of referentiality, to stay the slippage of meaning within words which might otherwise be unmoored by textual bedrock. History is the antidote to the uncertainty of reference throughout Watt's argument: for Watt, historical context keeps in line what Derrida might call the dissemination of the meanings of a word—its drifting, unruly, multiple associations. For example, Watt remarks that words like "realism" or "original"—both key terms in his definition of the realistic novel, differentiating it from its origin, romance—can actually be difficult themselves to define. Their various meanings contradict each other ("realism," which once meant "universals, classes or abstractions," also now means "the particular, concrete objects of sense-perception" [11]; "original," which once suggested "having existed from the first," now suggests "underived, independent, firsthand" [14]). Rather than questioning the way the interplay between such oppositions troubles his own opposition of the novel and romance, Watt instead refuses to acknowledge that interplay. History is the bar with which he attempts to separate and hold open these opposed meanings, implying that the first meanings, used in the past, remain there, without affecting the present senses of the words—an implication not all of us, including Watt elsewhere in this book, can completely accept.[17]

In the same way, history is also the bar Watt uses to separate the novel and romance. Formal realism is meant to provide "a working definition of the characteristics of the novel" that is "sufficiently narrow to exclude previous types of narrative" (9). It is important to Watt's definition that those previous forms must be excluded; somehow the novel must both rise out of them and leave them behind. With a causality that denies the very past it depends on, Watt tells us that the evolution of the novel does not link it to prior forms but depends on "a break with the old-fashioned romances" (10). The facts of history (changes, such as the growth of Protestantism, that prompt the "growing tendency for individual experience to replace collective tradition as the ultimate arbiter of reality" [14]) become the extratextual lever meant to effect and attest to

---

[17]For one discussion and enactment of the way meaning is interdependent and drifting, see Jacques Derrida, *Dissemination*, trans. Barbara Johnson (1981). Watt himself admits that such "semantic reversals" (*RN*.14) are in service of what can be only "*attempted* rejections" of the past (12; emphasis added). In a deconstructive reading of the instability of meaning, J. Hillis Miller argues that it is just such ambiguity in key terms that "tends to break down . . . generic and historical distinctions. If it does not make literary history impossible, it requires a redefinition of what is meant by 'genres,' 'periods,' 'tradition,' 'influences,' 'history,' 'literature' itself" (J. Hillis Miller, "A Guest in the House: Reply to Shlomith Rimmon-Kenan's Reply," *Poetics Today* 2 [1980/81]: 190–91).

"the suddenness and completeness" of the break between the novel and romance (34).

Watt needs to insist on the completeness of the formal break and to attempt to support it with historical fact because his argument does not really establish it in the readings of the novels he supplies. He admits that the very writers he wishes to cast as the first novelists seem unaware of this break. Their structures and language do not mark it: "they did not even canonise the changed nature of their fiction by a change in nomenclature" (10). Without the hindsight of history Watt enjoys, they do not distinguish their novels as novels but continue to call them romances. Fielding, in particular, explicitly aligns his work with the older tradition and because of that poses "something of a challenge to the basic argument" of Watt's study (239) (and may explain why "regrettably," Watt says, his "treatment of Fielding is briefer" than of any other writer [7]).[18] The identification of the novel with past forms such as romance is not Fielding's problem alone. Despite—in fact, prompting—Watt's attempt to differentiate them, the novel and romance keep collapsing into each other in his argument. The problem is not that Watt resorts to a larger context to explain local effects, which might have a function screening or even seeming to contradict their immediate interest. The problem is that Watt repeats—without investigating—the very contradictions he purports to resolve. Watt, like the early writers, cannot keep his terminology straight: he proclaims Richardson's *Pamela* both "the first true novel" (173) and a "romance with a difference" (204), suggesting the impossibility of maintaining any distinct break between them even in his own discussion.

As Watt's discussion of *Pamela* demonstrates, he invokes history as a bar to try to separate more than the interplay of literary form.

[18]Watt claims that "Fielding's celebrated formula of 'the comic epic in prose' undoubtedly lends some authority to the view that, far from being the unique literary expression of modern society, the novel is essentially a continuation of a very old and honoured narrative tradition" (*RN*.239). I might argue that that tradition is the romance as well as the epic, for Fielding also does not distinguish between those two terms; his full formula defining his own works, in the preface to *Joseph Andrews*, reads, "Now, a comic romance is a comic epic-poem in prose." Watt himself underlines this connection, noting that Fielding's treatment of epic is such as to "put all the French romances in the same category as the *Odyssey* and *Télémaque*" (250). Watt concedes that (in some respects) Fielding is "actually following the example of the French writers of romance a century earlier" (258).

For Watt, *Pamela* is the first true novel largely because of the formal realism of its plot, which, unlike that of its predecessors, avoids being episodic by basing its story "on a single action, a courtship" (135).[19] *Pamela* differs from romance too because of the difference of its treatment of courtship, which involves, among other things, "a more complete and comprehensive separation between the male and female roles than had previously existed" (162). This separation of the sexes, Watt argues, is historically determined, part and parcel of the rise of individualism (136), and such historical reality is once again reflected and guaranteed by language. Watt tells us that this change in gender and its effect on language started to become apparent in the late seventeenth century: men and women began to speak different languages. Watt quotes one writer's ironic suggestion of the need for a dictionary " 'to suit our language to the fair sex, and to castrate the immodest syllables in such words as begin and end obscenely' " (163). Although the call for such a text is facetious, Watt repeats it because his argument needs to show that the impulse behind it is not. The novel advances beyond romance in providing just such a text, in recognizing, recording, and maintaining the differences between men and women. The separate sexes are tacitly aligned with the separate forms Watt discusses: he links romance's abuses of language with the deceits of "the fair sex" (28) and charts the way romance appeals to the fantasies of women (204).

Watt uses history to account for what he sees as a change in the relations of the sexes in a way that seems to consider women's subordination carefully and judiciously. He outlines how the convention of elevating women beyond the supposedly lower promptings of sexuality, for instance, may be just another way of enforcing women's oppression:

Exactly why the serpent's invidious connection with Eve should have been forgotten is not clear; one can only surmise that, by a

19See too Frances Ferguson's suggestions about the way such courtship plots in Richardson's work depend on the possibility of rape; she argues that *Clarissa* epitomizes for Watt the rise of the novel in terms of its relation to private experience specifically because rape exemplifies for him (as for culture) the line between the public and the private, and points to the covert gender assumptions within his thought; Frances Ferguson, "Rape and the Rise of the Novel," *Representations* 20 (1987): 88–112, especially on 99–100.

devious process not unknown to the psychologist, the very difficulties in the situation of women at this time brought about a new
concept of the feminine role which masked their actual dependence on attractiveness to the male much more completely than
before, and strengthened their tactical position in courtship by
making their acceptance of a suitor a matter, not of joint personal
satisfaction, but of *noblesse oblige*. (RN.161)

But Watt's attempt here to read representation in terms of strategy
and tactic rather than fact (and note that it is ultimately women
who come to seem the tactical maneuverers in his reading, rather
than the system of power itself) does not go far enough, does not
consider the usefulness of this convention to Watt's own account—
the way the sensitivity of that account to women's position may
also paradoxically enforce her oppression.

Watt may assert a distinction between genders, just as he does
between the novel and romance, precisely because that distinction
may also be in question. He especially insists on clear gender distinctions with Richardson because, both in the biographical history
of Richardson from which he is working and in the novels Richardson writes, those distinctions blur: although Watt claims that attention to domestic detail helps distinguish the novel from romance
through its air of everyday reality, Richardson may know too much
about such banalities, especially about ladies' clothing (153): Watt
tells us that Richardson shared ladies' tastes "to a very remarkable
degree" (152), and the urbane understatement with which Watt
mocks these supposed foibles in Richardson itself may mark
enough discomfort with such cross-dressing for him to need to
distance himself from and joke about it. Similarly, his discussion of
the historical changes influencing Richardson's work, particularly
his relation to the ills of urbanization, returns (perhaps nervously)
to the ills of gender. He identifies Richardson's peculiar talent with
nervous ill health, an "anxiety neurosis" that he sees as particularly
feminine compared to Fielding's "robustness" (184): ventriloquizing through D. H. Lawrence, he directly connects Richardson's
novelistic perspective not just with a change in demographics but
with (supposedly) diseased femininity, "the mean Jane Austen"
and her "old maid" sensibility (185).[20] Richardson's novels con-

---

[20]Watt's comparison of Richardson and Fielding relies implicitly on the ways he
identifies them as feminine and masculine respectively: see Watt's argument about

tinue the feminine perspective supposedly left behind with romance. Watt attempts to explain away this anomaly by attributing it to Richardson's "deep personal identification with the opposite sex which went far beyond social preference or cultural rapport" (153) (which went as far, in fact, Watt notes—again dryly—as a fear of mice). But such identification suggests a collapse of gender which might be more than idiosyncratic, a general tendency that Watt tries to counter (but cannot quite) with historical facts.

Richardson's animadversions against " 'hermaphrodite minds' " (which Watt quotes from the introduction to the second edition of *Pamela*) become Watt's own.[21] The collapse of the sexes into hermaphrodite minds (canceling the distinctions between bodies) might undo the hierarchy implied in the separation of the sexes. Watt notes that the interplay of gender in Richardson's work threatens just such male privilege: *Pamela* "outrageously flatters the imagination of readers of one sex [women] and severely disciplines that of the other [men]" (153–54). Richardson's works demonstrate the ways "feminine sensibility [is] in some ways . . . at a real advantage in the realm of the novel" (298), not just in the realm of romance. In Watt's argument, Richardson's novels reveal how the novel form, like romance, depends on a feminine sensibility, with its detailed observation of "the texture of life" (298)—which Watt despite himself realizes is, according to the logic of his argument, an attention as necessary to the novel's formal realism as it is demanded by its feminine reading public.

Implicit within Watt's argument is the assumption that the separation of the sexes is essential, not just historical; the cultural recognition of this separation marks an advancement, a rise out of less enlightened times. Although Watt states that the role of the sexes is only a changing cultural construction—he quotes Margaret Mead's dictum that "civilization has largely 'relied for the creation of rich and contrasted values upon many artificial distinctions, the most

---

Fielding's masculine spirit, with its deflation of "romantic pretences" (*RN*.278) and its "wholesome bawdy" (284), an argument that (once again despite claims that it is actually more sensitive to women, sympathizing with rather than condemning "whores in rags" [283], for instance) supplies Watt with a tacit justification for the male privilege of the sexual double standard as part of the "expansion of sympathy" (284) necessary to a true moral education (280–84).

[21]The phrase reads "termagant hermaphrodite minds," and Richardson applies it to Lady Davers, suggesting the way both Richardson and Watt in quoting him make the slippage of gender a female problem, the problem of termagants (*RN*.163).

striking of which is sex' " (162)—he claims that he himself has no wish to suggest that gender distinctions are "*wholly* artificial" (162; emphasis added). Throughout his study, Watt's argument, despite its recognition of women's subordination, implicitly indicts the leisured-lady reading public produced by the inequities of capitalism. He refers to "the reading public's uncritical demand for easy vicarious indulgence in sentiment and romance" (290), and such an audience, he implies, accounts for most of Richardson's excesses; the volubility of his devoted letter writers might be explained by a modern parallel, women's "extended" use of the telephone (189). Yet such assumptions rely on an attitude about gender, not just economics.

The problem with the collapse of gender, as with any of the other slippages that Watt's argument tries to counteract, is that it calls into question those "rich and contrasted values" built on the hierarchy resulting from the separation of the sexes. Although Watt ends his study by discussing Jane Austen's novels as the reconciliation of the divergent—Richardsonian and Fieldingesque—strands of formal realism, Watt also attempts to indict, if not undo, the close relation of femininity to the novel that has caused his argument to contradict itself throughout; he asserts that the relation of the novel to women actually enervates the form—"it is surely true that the dominance of women readers in the public for the novel is connected with the characteristic kind of weakness and unreality to which the form is liable" (299). Although Austen's work marks the "climax" in this rise of the novel (298), hers is perhaps only "technical genius" (296), something the more technically faulty male writers Defoe, Richardson, and Fielding rise above, "by expressing their own sense of life with a completeness and conviction" (301). Although Watt's consideration of the social and economic conditions of history allows him a surprising sensitivity to the constraints of women's role, ultimately his covert assumptions make him translate role into essence: the problems of the novel result from the intrusion of women's weakness, and woman's weakness points to man's superiority and power, just as romance, an inferior form, is improved on by the novel. Watt's quotation of the seventeenth-century wit, who associated women with "castrate" language, suggests the ways foregrounding established gender assumptions seems particularly to draw off problems of lack onto women; no matter what their accomplishments, they remain insufficient, incomplete—man goes beyond them to embody a complete whole, just as the novel evolves into a finished totality.

By insisting on the *rise* of the novel, Watt erects its completeness and privilege as a form through relying on and affirming man's as a gender. And by valorizing qualities like completeness (the sentence praising the completeness of the male authors Watt studies completes his own book), Watt winds up endorsing the assumptions of the liberal individualism—integrity, wholeness, and autonomy—that he aligns with the novel. For all his historical savvy, Watt ultimately presents as axiomatic and universal a view of the subject limited by gender (and, other accounts might show, by race, and class). The assumptions behind his history allow ahistorical claims of privilege and perfect unity for individual men.

The sudden break between the novel and romance that Watt highlights in his argument confirms the male privilege tacit in that argument by inserting it in a key feature of formal realism: plot. This unexplained and overdetermined break in Watt's literary history plots a drama of that history Harold Bloom describes as the (male) writer's Oedipal relation to tradition, his break with his strong fathers that is necessary to raise him to their level.[22] As feminists have argued, and as Bloom's argument itself admits, that overt break between fathers and sons is actually just another way of cementing male bonds, admitting a writer into the tradition and linking him with his predecessors, who, for Bloom, can only be male.[23] For Watt, the break is with a feminine origin, figured by romance, but I might argue that this turn from the woman just marks a moment in the drama Bloom describes, when the son relinquishes his claims on the mother to enter the world of men. What makes Bloom's logic similar to Watt's is that for both the privileged position of the male, and all it represents, depends on the expulsion of woman. In Bloom's case, that expulsion is so

[22]Harold Bloom, *The Anxiety of Influence: A Theory of Poetry* (1973).

[23]For a feminist critique of Bloom, see Annette Kolodny, "A Map for Rereading; or, Gender and the Interpretation of Literary Texts," *New Literary History* 11 (Spring 1980): 451–67, and "Dancing through the Minefield: Some Observations on the Theory, Practice and Politics of a Feminist Literary Criticism," *Feminist Studies* 6 (1980): 1–25; see also Barbara Johnson, *A World of Difference* (1987), 32–41, and Janice Doane and Devon Hodges, *Nostalgia and Sexual Difference: The Resistance to Contemporary Feminism* (1987), 79–93.

complete that woman is invisible, her position marked only by her place within the Freudian triangle on which his argument builds, the position of the mother. Bloom's Oedipal scenario completes what I would call Watt's family romance: a fantasy of origins, initially focusing on the mother, that, Freud claims, the male subject must ultimately overcome through the identification with the father that the Oedipal resolution permits. The role of history in establishing this Oedipal plot is not at all surprising, for Freud himself enlists history in its service; his *Moses and Monotheism* and *Totem and Taboo* project onto history the patriarchal precedents of his own theory, establishing a (fantasy of) history that locates the father—and effectively supplants the mother—at its source.

Fredric Jameson, one of literary criticism's foremost theorists of history, certainly recognizes the complications of referentiality; his notions of history are sophisticated and subtle in the attention he pays to its textuality.[24] Yet, in *The Political Unconscious*, Jameson argues that although history is available to us only through our interpretations of it, history is not simply a text.[25] Jameson, following Althusser's revision of Lacan, explains that he

[24]Yet, although Jameson bases his work on recognizing those complications, the gap between word and thing, between textualization and the material, is underplayed in his own use of language. He does admit, in *The Political Unconscious*, that his own "terminology" "remains unavoidably imprisoned" in categories he wishes to unmask (Fredric Jameson, *The Political Unconscious: Narrative as a Socially Symbolic Act* [1981], 286; all future references to this book [hereafter abbreviated *PU*] will appear in the text). Yet Jameson's argument never fully takes into account just what such imprisonment might mean for it. In an interview about *The Political Unconscious*, Jameson seems instead almost to assume a control of language: he smooths over the ambiguities and contradictions within his writing by attempting to limit terms to particular and exclusive definitions, as if that were possible—words such as "politics," "culture," or "reification" ("Interview: Fredric Jameson," *Diacritics* 12 [1982]: 72–91). By examining Jameson's unexamined, and unacknowledged, play of language, several critics have also emphasized the inscription of Jameson's argument in the categories it tries to refuse; see Larysa Mykyta on Jameson's "slippage in terminological usage" ("Jameson's Utopias," *New Orleans Review* 11 [Spring 1984]: 48), and Jerry Aline Flieger on his failure "to provide a clear-cut working definition of his key concept ("The Prison-House of Ideology: Critic as Inmate," *Diacritics* 12 [1982]: 50). The problem is not sloppy thinking on Jameson's part but that his argument presses him into requiring from language an impossible precision and univocacy in order to reflect the univocal truth supposedly within his theory.

[25]Jameson's use of "History" has come in for criticism from those most willing to foreground history with him. Hayden White argues that Jameson's Marxist master

does not at all draw the fashionable conclusion that because history is a text, the 'referent' does not exist. . . . [H]istory is *not* a text,
not a narrative, master or otherwise, but . . . as an absent cause,
it is inaccessible to us except in textual form, and . . . our approach to it and to the Real itself necessarily passes through its
prior textualization. (*PU*.35; see also his discussion on 82)

History, although inaccessible, is *the* ground of interpretation, Jameson argues, not just another interpretation, not simply another
master narrative.[26] By "master narrative," Jameson seems to mean
something like what Foucault calls "discourse," referring to
"strong" interpretations (such as psychoanalysis or Marxism) that
are distinct from history (as the real) but organize approaches to it.[27]
Yet in the very act of explicitly setting up this distinction, Jameson
implicitly sets it aside for his own Marxist approach. That Marxism,
he tells us, provides the only "genuine philosophy of history"
(18)—and is for him therefore more than the supreme master narrative; he substitutes it for history itself. Or, rather, what Jameson

---

narrative of History becomes monolithic, all-inclusive, and imprecise: "the confusion to the reader that is likely to result from the effort to follow Jameson in his
many uses of the term 'history' will be more than justified" ("Getting out of History," 4). Terry Eagleton argues against this imprecision too, finding within *The Political Unconscious* that "the category of history itself may become rapidly drained of
meaning"; for Eagleton, however, such imprecision keeps Jameson's work from
being properly Marxist—Jameson's dictum always to historicize "merely blurs the
specificity of Marxism itself, which is not at all to 'historicize' . . . but, in a word, to
grasp history as structured material struggle" (Eagleton, "Fredric Jameson: The
Politics of Style," *Diacritics* 12 [1982]: 18, 19).

[26]But see Geoff Bennington's critique of what he considers false privileging ("Not
Yet," *Diacritics* 12 [1982]: 23–32).

[27]Yet his emphasis on such a term as "master narrative" suggests the importance
of mastery to Jameson's own argument (for a detailed discussion of Jameson's claims
to mastery, see Flieger, "The Prison-House," 48–49). The different assumptions of
Jameson's critics fall into place around the question of mastery: Hayden White and
Terry Eagleton imply that Jameson's dalliance with post-structuralism has under-
mined his own mastery, in the sense of skill, achievement, and command, as well as
certainty (see White's emphasis on "authority" throughout his essay); in discussing
Jameson's "magisterial periods," Eagleton's conclusion that Jameson"appears master of what, officially speaking, he is mediator" rather wistfully (just) refrains from
openly approving the mastery that his frequent modifiers, such as "powerful,"
already approve for him ("Fredric Jameson," 22). Eagleton also makes the point that
the referent, and the certainty it implies, has—or ought to have—its place ("Fredric
Jameson," 22). Bennington, Flieger, and Mykyta, on the other hand, imply that
Jameson's very need for mastery undermines his post-structural insights.

calls "History" turns out to have a narrative, that particular narrative of economics which Marx supplies. Jameson claims his Marxism does not just account for the "essential *mystery*" of the real in "disguised and symbolic" form in the same way other approaches do; rather, it uncovers that essence, uncovers the "repressed and buried reality" of the past. Jameson argues that such reality corresponds to "a single vast unfinished plot," an "uninterrupted narrative" (19–20) of our steady but painful journey through a fallen world of class conflict and bourgeois individualism to a paradise regained of total collective unity.[28]

The identity between Jameson's particular Marxist method and historical reality means that, for him, his method accounts for all of history and subsumes all other only locally effective approaches: "Marxism is here conceived as that 'untranscendable horizon' that subsumes such apparently antagonistic or incommensurable critical operations, assigning them an undoubted sectoral validity within itself, and thus at once canceling and preserving them" (10).[29] For Jameson, Marxism occupies the same place as the absent real: the

[28]Narrative is especially useful for Jameson's view of history because its very form privileges the evolution and unity Jameson wishes to code into history's structure: "narrativity not only represents but justifies," White writes, "by virtue of its universality, a dream of how ideal community might be achieved" (White, "Getting out of History," 8). That narrative is further unified by the metaphors of Christian teleology that Jameson explicitly enlists to describe that ideal community (*PU*.70). But Jameson's canniness in rhetorically unifying his vision of history makes for an emphasis on unity not necessarily shared by other Marxists. For example, Eagleton, who agrees with Jameson that Marxism "is not one 'method' among others," faults him for his handling of that method, his "occasional 'over-totalising,'" his Hegelian hunt for the master-code which will unlock all others" ("Fredric Jameson," 17, 15).

[29]Other critics point out the impossibility of such subsumption. Flieger argues that certain psychoanalytic insights that contradict Jameson's notion of history are paradoxically essential to his argument nonetheless ("The Prison-House," 55); she argues too that deconstruction must necessarily refuse cooptation to totalizing theories no matter how much Jameson asserts that a deconstructive approach is only a part of a larger whole. Jameson claims that "I have found it possible without any great inconsistency to respect both the methodological imperative implicit in the concept of totality or totalization, and the quite different attention of a 'symptomal' analysis to discontinuities, rifts, actions at a distance, within a merely apparently unified cultural text" (*PU*.56–57). Flieger argues that you cannot have it both ways; you must either take deconstruction on its own or not at all ("The Prison-House," 54). For a more recent discussion of the benefits of totalizing and its distinction from totalitarianism, see Fredric Jameson, "Cognitive Mapping," and subsequent "Discussion" in *Marxism and the Interpretation of Culture*, ed. Cary Nelson and Lawrence Grossberg (1988), 347–57, especially 358–60.

line of the horizon, the asymptote we can only approach but which delimits the world. And the way in which it does so, Jameson argues, allows it to contain all other approaches within its own totality.

Like Watt's, Jameson's argument values (and his Hegelian Marxism rests on) notions of unity and evolution, although his treatment of literary history—the relation of the novel to romance—attempts to deny such values or, at least, turn them against the ideological and consoling purpose they in part serve for arguments like Watt's. Directly to counteract "denunciations of Hegelian idealistic historiography, of evolutionism, or 'old-fashioned linear history' " (136) in his treatment of prose forms, Jameson introduces the notion of the sedimentation of genre (just as he introduces the idea of an overlay of several modes of production within every social period to counteract denunciations of the rigid economic totalization of Marxism [94–95]). The novel, he tells us, does not simply succeed romance, but their relation sketches "a model of the coexistence or tension between several generic modes or strands" (141); romance is both canceled and preserved by the novel and, "thus sedimented, persists into the later, more complex structure" (141).

Yet the theory of sedimentation is difficult to maintain in practice, as are Jameson's distinctions about the textualization of history. Jameson actually presents the novel as part of an evolutionary chain, not simply more complex than romance, absorbing and complicating it, but the very form that is sedimented, the exemplary form that comes to stand for Jameson's idea of genre. It marks for Jameson, in fact, "the end of genre" (151), not just that which puts genre into question but the cumulative form toward which other prose genres tend. As such, it subsumes those other forms sedimented within it, just as Jameson's Marxism subsumes other methods. Like Watt's "sudden break," for Jameson both the novel and his own method grow out of other forms and methods, make use of them while at once canceling and preserving them, but without themselves being contaminated or changed.

Like Watt's, Jameson's argument defends its uneasy privilege to pick and choose this way through recourse to gender biases. His argument supposedly accounts for and subsumes the perspective of gender: Jameson argues throughout *The Political Unconscious* that the problems of feminism are secondary to and included within those of

Marxism: he notes, for example, that "the existence of marginalized or oppositional cultures," including women, must be restored "to their *proper place* in the dialogical system of the social classes" (86; emphasis added).[30] By arguing that class simply subsumes gender, and that class-based analysis will solve its problems, Jameson need not engage with issues of gender, allowing his argument to retain unexamined gender assumptions: his argument's unexamined valorization of "strong" reading, for example, which he defines as "interpretation proper" (60), continues the appeal to mastery and power that underwrites his claims, and he borrows the phrase "strong reading" directly from Bloom, in whose Oedipal system strength depends on the unacknowledged possession and subjugation of women.[31] Jameson's appropriation even of what seems the purely formal Greimasian semiotic rectangle relies on another gendered system: Greimas, like Lévi-Strauss—remember Lévi-Strauss's description of how the exchange of women allows relations among men—initially uses his formula to calculate the permutations of a

---

[30]Also see his discussion of feminism elsewhere in *The Political Unconscious*, 54n, 99–100, 138, and his modification of this discussion in "Interview," 90–91. (Several critics take issue with Jameson's finessing of the question of feminism; see Bennington, "Not Yet," 30, and Flieger, "The Prison-House," 54.) Rather than subsuming the problems of feminism, Jameson's attention to class, I think, largely ignores or even contributes to them. Although sharp, for example, at noting the "ugliness" of certain "class attitudes" (*PU*.198), Jameson himself falls into certain ugly attitudes about gender, or gendered attitudes about ugliness—participating in the disparagement of the (in this case, corpulent) "old maid." In wryly noting "the peculiarities of Balzac's own sexual tastes" for corpulent older women (158), Jameson codifies categories of sexual attractiveness rather than questioning them. Women's attractiveness (to men), or lack of it, rather than being a product of gender assumptions, is, in Jameson's argument, supposed to cause them: it is "comic yet rueful" that Mademoiselle Cormon still ends up de facto an old maid, Jameson implies, because the reader understands without thinking that for a woman to remain unlinked to a man can only be pathetic—such a woman is "a horrible object-lesson" (169).

[31]The gender plot within Bloom infuses Jameson's discussion of "strong rewriting." He writes that "interpretation is not an isolated act, but takes place within a Homeric battlefield, on which a host of interpretive options are either openly or implicitly in conflict. If the positivistic conception of philological accuracy be the only alternative, then I would much prefer to endorse the current provocative celebration of strong misreadings over weak ones. As the Chinese proverb has it, you use one ax handle to hew another" (*PU*.13). Jameson mimics Bloom's exclusion of women here through the metaphor of the Homeric battlefield, obviously not woman's proper place, as well as the "provocative" reference to properly male tools—a sort of below-the-belt critical exchange—focusing on the most salient and interesting part of each other's apparatus, with all its Oedipal *frisson*.

system of sexual relations, which remains a buried part of Jameson's use of that formula as well.[32] That rectangle promotes Jameson's discussion of the class message in Balzac's *La Vieille Fille*, but his discussion is underwritten in terms of "potent" and "impotent" heroes (65), a standard that assumes potency to be an immediately available and commonly valued constant.[33] Although in his reading here as elsewhere Jameson argues that the sexual struggles Balzac charts are just his displacement of more disturbing class struggles (163), the need for gender assumptions to support his argument maintains gender as an insistent subtext in Jameson's reading. Jameson's very method is fueled by this repressed system of the other, which keeps woman in her "proper place," possessed and exchanged by men, and which ensures male potency—his strength and power.

In *The Political Unconscious*, Jameson explicitly discusses the system of the other and does so in terms of romance. Examining and expanding Northrop Frye's work, he points out that the elements of romance "are all arrayed in binary opposition to one another" (113), especially in terms of the supposedly clear-cut good and evil that structure its world. In an earlier essay, Jameson has shown that such an adversarial scheme is imaginary in the Lacanian sense. It recalls the "primordial rivalry of the mirror stage," in which, Jameson argues, the subject constructs as his adversary, evil and different from him, whomever is like him, threatening his autonomy.[34] The logic of the imaginary is, Jameson also argues, the crucial logic of romance (*PU*.118). And he aligns romance with women, maintain-

---

[32]See A. J. Greimas and F. Rastier, "The Interaction of Semiotic Constraints," *Yale French Studies* 41 (1968): 86–105, and *The Political Unconscious*, 46.

[33]I might argue that Jameson's privileging of male sexual power is such that the ideological sign or, as Jameson calls it, "seme," for the male necessarily points to "semen"—potency, power—in his argument. Potency, however ironically Balzac aligns it with class, remains for Jameson throughout his discussion a "positive sexual seme" (*PU*.166), and, hence, something he is implicitly *for*. Even though Jameson criticizes what he calls "ethical criticism"—a system of values particularly structured in terms of the other, of good and bad, for and against (59–60; 114–17)—his argument participates in this system too in ways that his discussion of "dialectical thinking" cannot really take him beyond (286). For more on what Jameson is for and what he is against, see Alice N. Benston, review of *The Political Unconscious*, *Sub-stance* 41 (1983): 97–103.

[34]Fredric Jameson, "Imaginary and Symbolic in Lacan: Marxism, Psychoanalytic Criticism, and the Problem of the Subject," *Yale French Studies* 55/56 (1977): 357; all future references to this essay (hereafter abbreviated "I&S") will appear in the text.

ing his characterization of woman as other: he notes that "the most characteristic protagonists of romance" are women, as well as slaves (PU.113), and links the romantic in a work like I Promessi Sposi specifically with "the feminine victim" (PU.143).

The association of the imaginary with wish-fulfillment, romance, and women, and the rhetoric with which Jameson describes it (referring, for example, to texts of the imaginary as "more degraded, and easily commodifiable" than texts of the symbolic level [PU.183]), suggest an implicit hierarchy within Jameson's explanation of the imaginary, an urge to pass out of it into the symbolic.[35] Just as romance leads to the more complex form of the novel, the imaginary points toward the symbolic: "here, once again," he writes, "the material of the Imaginary serves as a useful contrast by which to define the Symbolic" ("I&S."368). That contrast is one of opposition: Jameson compares the symbolic's fixity, for example, to the imaginary's play (354). Yet part of what is distinctive about Jameson as a critic is his ability to critique his own method: he explicitly recognizes that an adversarial schema that promotes one term over its opposite is "profoundly characteristic of the Imaginary" ("I&S."350). He recognizes too that his own argument "risk[s] falling again and again" back into the imaginary ("I&S."384), suggesting the impossibility of reaching the symbolic register it values precisely because of that valorization.

Despite itself Jameson's argument repeats the mechanism it wishes to avoid: "falling" back, for example, still asserts the very idea of progress that he means to deny, and "risk" implies that Jameson, or anyone, can avoid these dangers (they are just risky but not certain). Jameson *unwittingly* makes the very missteps he warns against here and throughout his work precisely because he thinks he can avoid them. This confusion is in itself a problem of Jameson's use of history, his assumptions about the real, for his argument goes on to suggest that he can avoid the problems of the imaginary by emphasizing the real. Despite Lacan's obscurations of it, Jameson claims, the real can be precisely located: "it is simply History itself" ("I&S."384). Jameson reintroduces the bedrock of reference, the dialogical third term of "the real," as a way to resolve

[35]In this he is only following Lacan, whose writings also, Jane Gallop suggests, "contain an implicit ethical imperative . . . to disrupt the imaginary in order to reach 'the symbolic'" (Gallop, Reading Lacan [1985], 59).

or circumvent the otherwise endless oscillations that keep us within the imaginary. The referential ground implied in the real, he argues, gives us as subjects a basis for our interpretations and a way out of this double bind.

Other critics, however, find the alignment of the Lacanian real with a referential ground, whether or not immediately available, another imaginary projection.[36] Jane Gallop, working from Jameson's own recognition of the unshakableness of the imaginary, and not letting go of that recognition as he does, suggests that the only provisional and tenuous distinction possible between the imaginary and symbolic has to do precisely with disentangling them from the real. The imaginary is imaginary because it "presents itself as an apprehension of the real"; "the symbolic is a glimpse of the imaginary *as* imaginary."[37] Gallop argues that "in the imaginary mode, one's understanding of other people is shaped by one's own imagoes. . . . But, in the symbolic register, the subject understands these imagoes as structuring projections."[38] The only escape—if you can call it that—from the imaginary lies in recognizing its inescapability.

In Jameson's vision of history, the belief that one can transcend the imaginary and escape the system of the other means also and primarily that one can elude ideology; Jameson's refusal to classify his method as simply a form of textualization, and his belief in a once and future "collective unity" aware of and outside the limits of class determination (*PU.*282–83), taken together point to what is ultimately his understanding of ideology as a false consciousness that can be shed (despite his promise that his book will critique this very notion of false consciousness [12]). The supposed ability of his history to present the real—which becomes the truth—and avoid the self-interest and blindness of ideology is reflected and supported by his literary history: romance becomes the locus of ideology and the novel is somehow (almost) outside or beyond it. The wish-fulfillment of the imaginary, "not yet, according to Freud, the

[36]Alice Jardine writes that "this conclusion, if suggestive, is clearly false. For if the Real *is* anything, it is certainly not history—nor 'reality,' nor a text" (Jardine, *Gynesis: Configurations of Woman and Modernity* [1985], 122); yet Jardine's own use of "clearly" and "certainly" here keeps her caught in a similar trap; if the real is anything, whatever that might be seems to me neither clear nor certain.

[37]Gallop, *Reading Lacan,* 66.

[38]Gallop, *Reading Lacan,* 61.

moment of genuine literary or cultural production," aligns the imaginary with that simpler and degraded form, romance. Such wish-fulfillment also points directly in Jameson's argument to the ideology which supports it, for he links ideology directly to the imaginary, through Althusser, who defines it as "'the imaginary representation of the subject's relationship to his or her real conditions of existence'" (181).

That Jameson is caught in the traps he recognizes simply makes his work exemplary of (to me, the best kind of) post-structural criticism; what intrigues me is how he consistently appeals to gender in those moments when he tries to ignore or wish away those traps. Gender becomes crucial to Jameson's vision of history because it is what seems to guarantee a place outside history's constraints and the constraints of ideology. He makes the escape from false consciousness—from the realm of romance and the imaginary—seem natural by relying on developmental myths of the subject, myths based on the subjugation and expulsion of women. Jameson's system, with its structure of origin and evolution, demands a progressive chronology that gets its momentum from discarding and leaving woman behind—demands, that is, fantasies of the mother, whose utility as a point of abandoned origin is implicit throughout his system, as his use of Bloom suggests. She provides, in particular, the point of departure for his literary history. Whereas, Jameson argues, more advanced forms reflect "the genital stage" (142) with its emphasis on the father and realistic social contradictions, romance, as a less developed form, is properly the realm of the mother. Its logic of wish-fulfillment grows out of that regressive "passive and symbiotic relationship of infant to mother" (142), in which the very world around the hero magically reflects him, anticipating his wishes, a realm of "providential or maternal harmony" (143), just as the mother is the world for the infant and seems (or should be) completely attuned to his needs. This is also, Jameson asserts, the realm of the imaginary in Lacan, "an archaic stage in the development of the mature subject" (174), who must pass beyond this pre-Oedipal interlude into Oedipal conflict and identification with the powerful father.[39] In his read-

[39]Jameson introduces a temporal scheme into Lacan's argument, stringing these inseparable registers into a history, an evolutionary development of the subject that reflects his own assumptions about history. For a critique of "the prevailing tenden-

ing of *La Rabouilleuse*, Jameson designates its subplot of "excessive maternal indulgence" imaginary in this sense (173), suggesting that an overemphasis on the mother mires Phillipe within egotism and the text within wish-fulfillment. And this is also the realm of ideology, that which propels the wish and structures the world in such a way as (to try) to ensure the subject's gratification (181–84). By insistently associating these realms with the mother, Jameson makes leaving them behind seem as natural and proper as growing up—or what our culture teaches as the boy's inevitable turn from mother to father, which allows him to enter the world of men (or, in Jameson's terms, the symbolic).

Yet, as we have seen, Jameson is fully aware of the dynamic of the other, of the way the other is simply a projection of the same and must ultimately collapse back into it. Perhaps he makes the other the mother not just to cast her out, which her cultural construction so helpfully facilitates, but also precisely to collapse with her. The fantasy of the pre-Oedipal mother gives a particular meaning to this sense of collapse, figuring it as harmony and plenitude, the infant merged with what is ultimately its reflection. Such a tacit celebration of plenitude is part and parcel of Jameson's Hegelian Marxism, in which our progress at the same time returns us to a lost state. Jameson indeed explicitly uses the figure of the individual's body completed by one larger than itself to reflect not just the infant's fusion with the mother but "the perfected community" (74), "the lost unity of social life" (226).

This is why Jameson's relation to romance seems so double— why he argues for going beyond it, and at the same time explicitly accepts and even celebrates its similarities to his own system. Both romance and Jameson's history assume "the transfiguration of the world of everyday life in such a way as to restore the conditions of some lost Eden, or to anticipate a future realm from which the old mortality and imperfections will have been effaced" (110). Because of such assumptions, Jameson can exclaim that "the valorization of romance has much to be said for it" (104) and that its association with Marxism "does not discredit [Marxism] so much as it explains the persistence and vitality of [romance]" (105). The valorization of

cy to temporalize Lacan," see Naomi Schor, "*Eugénie Grandet*: Mirrors and Melancholia," in *The (M)other Tongue: Essays in Feminist Psychoanalytic Interpretation*, ed. Shirley Nelson Garner, Claire Kahane, and Madelon Sprengnether (1985), 218n.

a lost unity is the assumption fueling his own method, granting it its charter to catch up and complete other methods by incorporating them into itself. The unspoken assumptions of the gender hierarchy encoded within the romance of the pre-Oedipal mother are meant to underwrite the critic's own privilege, the position of his argument outside ideology. The fantasy of the romantic mother is useful because it supplies a wishful figure for the critic's harmonious coexistence with the dominant system in which he works.

Collapse with the mother is desirable because, as Jameson notes about Conrad's heroines, she epitomizes "the relatively ungrateful function of selfless devotion to the male actors" (276)—effacing herself by serving as the reflection of Jameson's argument, which subsumes her as it has subsumed other positions repeatedly, magically neutralizing their problems while preserving their privileges. The mother's seemingly natural effacement and subsumption supposedly clear for him the site of pure totality that she represents, clear it of its regressiveness, of its association with wish, of its status as a delusive trap, all which get purged through *her* scapegoating. As we have seen, this site of pure totality, for Jameson, is also history or the real. The exemption from ideology that Jameson assumes through this strategy of displacement would make his particular vision of history not just one more textualization but would merge it with the absent ground of the material itself. Unexamined gender assumptions promote access to the real and escape from ideology—the very conditions that *The Political Unconscious* explicitly argues are impossible. Jameson's history needs gender to sustain its desires and protect it from its own lessons.

Unlike Watt's, Jameson's system explicitly interrogates the assumptions underlying individualism, indicting the belief in the fixed self as a historically bound concept and a conservative tool that undermines history's necessary progress to a classless and communal utopia (*PU*.281–99). Although, Jameson argues, we cannot yet fully imagine that utopia, he suggests that the dyad of infant and mother stands for the decentering of the subject necessary for it and, as an image of the fragmentary subject completed by a larger whole, becomes an image of the collective. Such a relation is useful for Jameson's argument, however, because it is not really a relationship at all; the fantasy underlying this particular

dyad sanctions its collapse into the individual—its superficial binary relation masks a consoling illusion, confirming the primacy of
the (male) subject.

It is precisely such a dynamic that George Meredith's novels act
out. History is as essential for Meredith as it is for Watt and Jameson, for, as Meredith told Carlyle, "Novel-writing is my way of
writing history," and by that history Meredith too means evolution.[40] Ground-breaking Meredith scholars, such as Lionel Stevenson and Joseph Warren Beach, among others, have long ago pointed out Meredith's Victorian heritage, the ways the positivistic
biological and social evolutionism of Darwin, Comte, and Spencer
pervade Meredith's notion of historical progress and are crucial to
the philosophical system underlying his work.[41] Meredith's poetry
and prose rely on his belief in social evolution, an understanding of
which helps to clarify the idiosyncratic narrative commentary of his
novels. Like most Victorians, Meredith sees the survival of the
fittest as a metaphor for mankind's gradual development into a
perfection we have not yet reached.

For Meredith, the development of the individual determines the
progress of history within this system of social evolution. The

[40]Quoted by Lionel Stevenson, *The Ordeal of George Meredith: A Biography* (1953),
74. For a discussion of Meredith's novels as a way of writing history, see Jane
Marcus, "'Clio in Calliope': History and Myth in Meredith's *Diana of the Crossways*,"
in her *Art and Anger: Reading Like a Woman* (1988), 20–48. Marcus's discussion of
history (and mothers) comes to radically different conclusions from my own about
Meredith's treatment of women. For an interesting reading of Meredith's romance
that I came across while preparing this book for press, and which also reaches
conclusions quite different from mine, see Diane Elam, "'We Pray to Be Defended
from Her Cleverness': Conjugating *Diana of the Crossways*," *Genre* 21 (Summer 1988):
179–201.

[41]See especially Lionel Stevenson, *Darwin among the Poets* (1932), 183–236; Joseph
Warren Beach, *The Concept of Nature in Nineteenth-Century English Poetry* (1936), 470–
99; and George Macauley Trevelyan, *The Poetry and Philosophy of George Meredith*
(1906). To assert that Meredith has a philosophical system that readers can recon-
struct and paraphrase from his fiction, poetry, essays, and letters does not mean,
however, that those writings are merely tracts of this system; what interests me
most about Meredith's writing is the way it strays from or contradicts the system of
beliefs it explicitly assumes and outlines. For a discussion of the assumptions involved in a theory of evolution as it relates to the form of the novel, see Gillian Beer,
*Darwin's Plots: Evolutionary Narrative in Darwin, George Eliot, and Nineteenth-Century
Fiction* (1983). For a reading of how such assumptions motivate Meredith's fiction in
particular, see Carolyn Williams, "Natural Selection and Narrative Form in *The
Egoist*," *Victorian Studies* 27 (1983): 53–79.

primitive self we all have in us is a creature of egoistic desires. With its sensual self-love and desire for self-preservation (what Meredith calls "the gross original" [E.13.1.6]), such egoism seems to work against the progression of the species. But Meredith argues that egoism can be an excellent foundation for our progress if we consider it as the necessary first step in the survival of the fittest.[42] Coming to terms with our egoism is a social as well as a physical challenge, consisting in resigning those desires the flesh has for its physical pleasures and preservation, and harnessing the energy for the spiritual progression of the race as a whole; as Meredith has Diana say: "Spirit must brand the flesh, that it may live."[43]

Meredith believes that the desire for self-preservation, especially the attempt to deny individual death, to cling to a doomed physical self through the dreams of personal immortality that our culture mistakes for the spiritual, mires men in egoism and slows historical progression. Rebutting the Christian notion of the afterlife, Meredith asks a correspondent: "Which personality is it which endures? I was one man in youth and another man in middle age . . . I have never felt the unity of personality running through my life."[44] For Meredith, the evidence of our senses points to the death of the individual and the continuance of the race: we are left with one rational option, to give up such dreams of self altogether, to trust in the evolution of the species itself for our spiritual fulfillment. Physical law seen through the intellect this way, testifying against the self and to the greater good of the race, *is* the spiritual ideal to which we tend. Or, as we are told more bluntly by Vernon Whitford, one of the unpretentious athletic students who begin to represent Meredith's ideal man (as does Gower Woodseer, say, in *The Amazing Marriage*): "the value to the world of a private ambition I do not clearly understand" (E.13.8.85).

Meredith relates this model of social evolution to the progression of literary history, of romance into novel. Willoughby ironically speaks for Meredith's philosophy when he pretends to believe in

[42]He writes, for instance, that "the primitive is not the degenerate: rather is he a sign of the indestructibility of the race, of the ancient energy in removing obstacles to individual growth" (E.14.39.182).

[43]George Meredith, *Diana of the Crossways*, vol. 16 of *The Memorial Edition of the Works of George Meredith*, 29 vols. (1910–12), ch. 1, p. 13; all future references to this book (hereafter abbreviated DC) will appear in the text.

[44]Stevenson, *Ordeal*, 350.

community and self-sacrifice, a view that he recognizes is " 'novel, I should say, and not the worse for that. We want plain practical dealings between men and women. Usually we go the wrong way to work. And I loathe sentimental rubbish' " (*E*.14.47.303). Meredith's own books are meant to act out the difference between what is "novel" and "sentimental rubbish," community and egoism (in the supposedly unsentimental way a novel like *The Egoist* details the shifting points of view of a group of characters, for example, rather than sentimentally valorizing a hero, as do the romances that Willoughby reads and after which he patterns himself). Meredith sees romance as a necessary but primitive stage in our literary development, just as egoism is in our social and personal. He has Diana, who writes romances, characteristically overstate his view of romance, stressing that, when experienced at the proper time, its untutored enthusiasm indicates a yearning toward spiritual perfection: *"The young who avoid that region escape the title of Fool at the cost of a celestial crown"* (*DC*.1.12). But romance unsucceeded by any (supposedly) higher stage of development remains, for Meredith, a regressive realm of egoistic gratification—of characters like Willoughby or Constance Asper, a "true heroine of romance" (*DC*.35.391), who never go beyond its world "of theatrical heroics" (*DC*.30.360) staged solely to puff the ego, as Willoughby's and Constance's histrionics show. Our desire for fiction, if fed by romance alone, would "idiotiz[e]" us and fiction would be "doomed to extinction" (*DC*.1.19).

The advent of the novel on the other hand, Meredith implies, will advance our literature and race out of such idiotic artificiality into the socially useful mode of historical philosophy (as Meredith calls his theory of social evolution). In the first chapter of *Diana of the Crossways,* Meredith discusses the future of the novel, implying that novels up until his own have been contaminated with egoism and romance—or, as an early reviewer interprets him, "Formerly perhaps, when the novel was in its early youth, it might claim to be mainly narrative and romantic. Now it must vindicate its position by being a disguised treatise on mental philosophy."[45] As Meredith makes clear throughout his work, and especially in this chapter,

---

[45]W. L. Courtney, "George Meredith's Novels," in the *Fortnightly Review,* quoted in *Meredith: The Critical Heritage,* ed. Ioan Williams (1971), 288.

philosophy is what characterizes the novel for him.[46] Only an understanding of human life in terms of (his own) historical philosophy, he implies, can move literature beyond the debased romantic; that understanding "raise[s] the Art in dignity on a level with History" (*DC*.1.18). Without this evolutionary perspective, even history itself is but "the skeleton map of events" (1.19). Meredith's own novels attempt to put this philosophic view of history into play. The narrator of *Diana of the Crossways* is not only a social historian, studying the diaries of the time with the air of a "chronicler" sifting his sources (19.216), but one who, by implication, presents his particular history as a lesson to others: "the example might, one hopes, create a taste" (1.18), the narrator writes, thereby furthering the advancement of the race.

The understanding of history that characterizes the novel distinguishes it from romance because part of the sham of romance is to deny historical progression, to believe in its individual—egoist— importance as a "changeless thing" that "defies time" (35.399). The novel goes beyond such romantic, egoistic delusions of permanence, Meredith suggests, especially by identifying historical progression with the development of the subject: "the brainstuff of fiction is internal history" (1.17), Meredith writes, merging the categories of novel and history into that model of psychological development that has become today equivalent to character.

This emphasis on psychological history within the novel does not mitigate the emphasis on the material that underlies Meredith's historical vision, however. What especially puts flesh on the skeleton of history for Meredith is woman seen in her materiality. In his novels, such material facts figure as an index to internal history: Diana's flesh attests to her spirit, her beauty testifies to her wit, and both confirm her virtue (1.2–3). Such symbolization, in which a woman's body is made the index of her character, is nothing new of course—Charlotte Lennox's beautiful Arabella demonstrates the same correspondence, as does Dickens's Little Nell—but this focus on the (woman's) body as something more than body is interesting all the same because it is so often crucial in attempts to distinguish

---

[46]Although, as Judith Wilt points out, "philosophy" means so much for Meredith that it becomes ultimately "scarcely definable," its emphasis on "advancement" (*DC*.1.17) connects it directly to Meredith's theory of social evolution (Wilt, *The Readable People of George Meredith* [1975], 81).

the novel from romance. The supposed transcendence of the novel over the sensuality of romance is made to rest in the woman's transfigured body precisely because it allows the novel to have it both ways.

For Meredith, the novel, as "the summary of actual Life" (1.17), continues to focus on the facts of life but does so in order to elevate them to a higher purpose, just as his historical vision supposedly translates brute Darwinism into spiritual progression. Romance, on the other hand, Meredith implies, gets mired within the material alone, its "point of original impetus being the grossly material, not at all the spiritual" (1.16). In Meredith's system, the cloaking of sensuality as spirituality will always be exposed, through the body, as romantic, "rebuked by hideous revelations of the filthy foul; for nature will force her way, and if you try to stifle her by drowning, she comes up, not the fairest part of her uppermost!" (1.16). Meredith's novels themselves also dwell on the material, but they are supposedly redeemed by the way they point to the ideal: an emphasis on Diana's sexuality, for instance, is not romantic or sensual because it describes her progression out of egoism. Diana is apparently more realistic—novelistic—than Constance not just because her flaws are clearly evident but because those flaws are symbols of her (necessarily faltering) progression toward an ideal. Yet Meredith's own shrewd analysis of the way the spiritual can cloak the sensual makes us suspicious of the exemption he gives himself from this dynamic.

The figure of the *mulier formosa* (the mermaid who is beautiful woman from the waist up, filthy foul below), with which Meredith makes his distinction between the novelistic and romantic, suggests the way the treatment of the self in that distinction depends on assumptions of gender.[47] In *Diana of the Crossways,* the charting of internal history becomes most especially the portrayal of a woman with a history. Meredith suggests that it is precisely Diana's sexual experience that underwrites her internal history—her psychological development—and makes her worth writing about: "Never should reputation of a woman trail a scent! How true! and true also that the women of waxwork never do; and that the women of happy marriages do not; nor the women of holy nunneries;

[47]Meredith refers directly to this figure in *The Egoist;* see vol. 13, ch. 8, p. 86.

nor the women lucky [i.e., undetected] in their arts" (1.8–9). Woman becomes the type and test case for our transformation as a race out of primitive foulness. She must rise above it in herself, work her way through and beyond the primitive desires that are the history of any remarkable woman. Yet, despite the explicit feminism of Meredith's philosophy—as his "Essay on the Idea of Comedy" outlines, part of the point of his comedy is to show women "moving on an intellectual level with men"—the *mulier formosa* suggests that the woman never quite leaves this foulness behind; it is always part of her, hidden below. She comes to stand for the material in what Meredith sees as its sexual brutishness, and her depiction allows Meredith to include this sexuality in his novels.[48]

Her internal development supposedly sets Diana apart from "women of waxwork" by marking her evolution out of romance, out of her artificial romance with Percy Dacier. Diana's evolution out of romance is crucial in defining her novel as a novel. Although she accuses Redworth of "quixottry" (14.146), she is actually herself a female quixote. She acts out the program I will discuss at length in chapter 2, one in which her education out of romance into the world of the novel is meant to confirm the superiority of the novel over romance; here, that education serves the dual function of confirming Meredith's theory of evolution as well. For most of the novel, Diana, "after the fashion of the ardently youthful," is seduced by romance (4.46). She not only writes *The Princess Egeria*, "a sort of semi-Scudéry romance" (18.203), she also acts the romantic heroine Egeria to Dacier.[49] When Dacier finally claims sexual favors from Diana in exchange for his political secret, Diana is compelled to glimpse the filthy foul in her relations with him: she has been a "loathsome hypocrite" (31.364) who should have either run away with or broken from him. Her recognition that Dacier prefers the titillation of doing neither "kill[s] her romance" (39.437) and propels her out of it into the clear, plainspoken world of Redworth, in which she relinquishes "her hope of some last romance in life . . . for in him shown not a glimpse" (40.453). Redworth's

[48]George Meredith, "Essay on the Idea of Comedy and the Uses of the Comic Spirit," in his *Miscellaneous Prose*, vol. 23 of *The Memorial Edition of the Works of George Meredith*, 29 vols. (1910–12), p. 14.
[49]For further references to Diana as Egeria, see 17.200; 19.218, 222; 28.325.

world is also the world of Meredith's novel, "a different world from the one of her old ambition" (39.433).

Although Diana acts like a romantic woman, a Princess Egeria, Meredith writes that "the right worshipful heroine of Romance was the front-faced female picture [Constance]," who is shallow and unchanging ("Poor Diana was the flecked heroine of Reality" [35.399]). The romantic heroine is fixed in her pose, like a dressmaker's dummy or "lay-figure" (42.476)—trapped in what Dacier calls a "rag-puppet's state of suspension" (31.364). Meredith distinguishes himself as a novelist by distinguishing his characters from just such a puppet theater.[50] When struggling to bring together Diana and Redworth, he writes to a friend that Diana "has no puppet-pliancy. The truth being that she is a mother of Experience, and gives that dreadful baby suck to brains."[51] As he states in the novel: "the woman of flesh refuses pliancy when we want it of her, and will not, until it is her good pleasure, be bent to the development called a climax, as the puppet-women, mother of Fiction and darling of the multitude! ever amiably does" (40.448). As the woman of flesh and the mother of experience, the novelist's heroine, the heroine of reality, is also the heroine of history, her flesh standing for its material, and her experience for its evolution.

I want to put aside, for a moment, the intriguing collapse of the feminine with the maternal in Meredith's assumptions to follow through another connection between the self and gender within his system, the way women are connected to the subversion of the coherent self. Meredith suggests that the novel advances over romance by giving up the idea of the fixed self: Meredith uses fakes like Constance to suggest that constant images of the self actually are false. Dacier runs after Diana partly to trap her, to make her

---

[50]This metaphor is a useful one, for it also allows him to surpass his novelistic predecessors, especially Thackeray, who was not able to animate his puppets the way Meredith can. Meredith writes: "A great modern writer, of clearest eye and head, now departed, capable in activity of presenting thoughtful women, thinking men, groaned over his puppetry, that he dared not animate them, flesh though they were, with the fires of positive brainstuff. He could have done it, and he is of the departed" (DC.1.18).

[51]"To Mrs. Leslie Stephen, Box Hill, Dorking, August 23, 1884," in vol. 2 of *The Letters of George Meredith*, ed. C. L. Cline, 3 vols. (1970), p. 743; this edition hereafter abbreviated *Letters*.

conform to this idea of a fixed core of self. His pursuit of her is the "pursuit of the secret of a woman's character" (16.177), of character at all, which he suspects that she does not have: "the feminine half of the world was a confusion and a vexation to his intelligence, characterless; and one woman at least appearing decipherable, he fancied it must be owing to her possession of character, a thing prized the more in women because of his latent doubt of its existence" (28.331–32). Dacier's doubts turn out to be correct; Diana never becomes totally decipherable to him, and Dacier settles for Constance's reassuring outline, her false character. Diana is inscrutable, changeable—characterless—to Emma and Redworth too, who have trouble accounting for her moods after her break with Dacier. On her entry into the world of the novel, she has become a "daily shifting feminine maze" (40.457). Meredith seems to use this woman's changeableness to present character proper to the novel, character that is unstable and shifting.

Or so critics have argued. Meredith's alignment of women with the subversion of identity has become important in a larger context than his own theoretical system; J. Hillis Miller, arguing from *The Egoist*, suggests too that the breakdown of "a prelinguistic fixed character" is a lesson which "the female protagonist has . . . to teach us men."[52] His well-known article, an early treatise on the deconstructive subversion of fixed identity, bases its argument on Clara's changeableness; Miller concludes that novelists project the problems of characterization onto heroines because "the assumption that ontologically substantial characters do exist cannot be detached from the logocentrism or phallogocentrism which underlies it and of which it is a version."[53] Applying the Derridean notion of the supplement, Miller argues that men try to make women reflect back a phallic notion of fixity because her lack (of it) threatens and undercuts ontological integrity. They try to cover her lack, to make her into a mirror that reflects their possession, but "the female, that imperfect male, missing one member, introduces the deconstructive absence which means there will always be something left over or something short in this mirror, the per-

[52]J. Hillis Miller, "'Herself against Herself': The Clarification of Clara Middleton," in *The Representation of Women in Fiction*, Selected Papers from the English Institute, 1981, n. s. 7, ed. Carolyn Heilbrun and Margaret Higonnet (1983), 102, 109.

[53]Miller, "Herself against Herself," 109–10.

petual too little or too much which makes it impossible for the balance ever to come right."[54] In Miller's system, just as in Meredith's, woman seems naturally to figure the breakdown of the fixed, ego-bound self.[55]

Diana's loss of ego begins when she leaves behind the world of romance she has inhabited with Dacier and that loss is explicitly figured in terms of breakdown (she takes to her room in nervous collapse) and fragmentation. Her romantic dreams have been for a "benevolent despot" (4.46), but her break with Dacier reveals the dangers of that dream. It hides from her what a realistic appraisal reveals: that he is anything but benevolent. Because his despotism devastates her, she is able to see past his sham, to reach the perspective of the novel. He is "in the dominion of Love a sultan of the bow-string and chopper period, sovereignly endowed to stretch a finger for the scimitared Mesrour to make the erring woman head and trunk with one blow: and away with those remnants!" (35.392). Diana's propulsion out of romance shatters into fragments her romantic vision of herself.[56] Diana tells Emma of her fractured and incohesive new identity that " 'there are wounds that cut sharp as the enchanter's sword, and we don't know we are in halves till some rough old intimate claps us on the back, merely to ask us how we are! I have to join myself together again, as well as I can. It's done, dear; but don't notice the cement' " (39.439). In Meredith's system, Diana's break with Dacier marks her triumph as a character, her ability to recognize and relinquish egoist delusion. Her resulting fragmentation seemingly marks the proper novelistic self because it destroys the ego's despotism that bars spiritual progression. This fragmentation of the self is what Miller

[54]Miller, "Herself against Herself," 119. Miller elsewhere also ties the subversion of the determinable to anatomy. He writes that "the impossibility of reading" has "consequences, for life and death, since it is inscribed, incorporated, in the bodies of individual human beings and in the body politic of our cultural life and death together" (J. Hillis Miller, "The Critic as Host," *Critical Inquiry* 3 [1977]: 440).

[55]And, as with Jameson, woman thereby provides a vehicle by which to reach a revolutionized community (her proper place within it is left unspecified). Miller suggests resisting the breakdown of identity because it has what he calls "unsettling social implications," just as Meredith implies that radical social change must follow the historical progress out of the egoist delusions of the self into true community; see Miller, "Herself against Herself," 121.

[56]A vision shared by the doting Arthur Rhodes and Sullivan Smith, who agree that she is "the Arabian Nights in person" (*DC*.37.417).

celebrates in *The Egoist* as a way to elude and sabotage despotism; Clara, he argues, "cannot be possessed as an object because she has no objective form."[57]

Yet rather than providing a way to elude power, such fragmentation might actually be the means of ensuring it. Meredith's insistent imagery of violence done to the body of the woman—the severed head, the wounded flesh—suggests that gender does more than prop up a progressive de-individualization. Diana here quite literally seems to be a scapegoat, providing theories like Meredith's, or Miller's, with a way to preserve the privileges of the systems they criticize while drawing off their evils. Woman not only props up Meredith's vision of evolutionary history but provides a consolation for it, a fantasy of escape (for men) outside the constraints of the loss of the self. For Diana's egoism, shattered by Dacier, gets canceled suddenly and completely when she finally comes together with Redworth and is overwhelmed by "her loss of self in the man" (*DC*.43.483). Diana's loss of self in Redworth, while figuring the breakdown of (her) egoism, actually preserves his. His view of Diana—that "he owned himself incomplete" (*DC*.37.419) and "she would complete him" (*DC*.37.420)—too closely repeats Willoughby's egoist appropriation of Clara: "she completed him" (*E*.13.5.48). Despite Meredith's understanding of her sacrifice, the woman's loss of self remains the reflex of the man's attainment of it.

Such desires for self, condemned in the egoist Willoughby, are ignored or denied when it comes to Redworth; Meredith's novel emphasizes instead the self-effacing, self-sacrificing character of Redworth's love for Diana. In its first chapter, Meredith aligns his novel with *Vanity Fair*, suggesting that Redworth is meant to be an unheroic hero, modeled on Thackeray's Dobbin, whose unassuming character and natural modesty mark him from self-aggrandizing figures like Willoughby. But, as Dorothy Van Ghent has suggested, Willoughby's monstrous egoism is a brilliant authorial ploy, for it seems to make that egoism aberrant rather than a necessary (but also necessarily unspoken) element of the male world he continues to represent, notwithstanding Meredith's deflation of him ("'Well, I own it, I do like the idea of living patriarchally,'"

[57]Miller, "Herself against Herself," 116.

Willoughby says [*E*.13.11.122]).[58] Meredith's system accounts for (and excuses) any residual hint of egoism in Redworth by insisting that none of us ever wholly escapes egoism: " 'O self! self! self! are we eternally masking in a domino that reveals your hideous old face when we could be most positive that we had escaped you?' " Diana asks. "Eternally! the desolating answer knelled" (*DC*.4.47). What matters, Meredith has Diana learn, is that we recognize our egoism and remain at war with it: "at war with ourselves, means the best happiness we can have" (4.48)—a state Redworth supposedly exemplifies, since, from the start, his sense of reason and honor war with and triumph over his desire for Diana. But by making egoism the province of distinctive romantic individuals like Diana or Willoughby, who draw it off from others—from novelistic heroes like Redworth—Meredith tries in part to undo his insight that none can escape it.

Despite the disclaimers within Meredith's system, the patriarchal Redworth too remains as romantic—and egoistic—as the characters the book condemns, and Redworth's egoism is to a great degree unironized. The novel even seems to go out of its way at the end to valorize Redworth's patriarchal power. That power rests on his ability to attract women; the unexpected revelations of his sexual history prompt from other men admiring testimonies to his physical strength that read (to me) almost like unwitting parody: " 'Have you ever boxed with him? Well, he keeps himself in training, I can tell you' " (41.464). Like Whitford (who wins Clara from Willoughby in *The Egoist*), Redworth is meant to exemplify a true manliness as opposed to Willoughby's patriarchal sham: strong, silent types, they attract rather than coerce. Diana, for instance, sees Redworth as "a fatal power . . . benevolently overcoming" (40.453) and his "paternal benevolence," readers are told, actually bespeaks "the loftiest manliness" (43.489). Diana is ultimately glad to give into his superior force. She admits that she "does not stand firmly alone; her story confessed it" (43.486)—a conviction Meredith shares rather than satirizes; several times he instructs a skep-

---

[58]Dorothy Van Ghent, *The English Novel: Form and Function* (1953), 189. Van Ghent discusses Willoughby's egoism in terms of pre-Oedipal structures, which she finds monstrous rather than consoling: she describes Willoughby as a "fetus in full panoply . . . [a] monster of the womb," who acts "as if society were but one huge placenta designed for his shelter and growth" (187, 188).

tical correspondent that Diana, like all women, needs "a sturdy mate."[59] Redworth's benevolent overpowering of Diana actually supplies just the romantic despotism the novel has earlier critiqued, explaining why, perhaps, the novel goes out of its way to note that there is no hint of romance in Redworth (its distinction of itself from romance becomes explicit and insistent in these final chapters). What Willoughby says about Whitford can be applied to Redworth too: "'The story's a proof that romantic spirits do not furnish the most romantic history'"—those who deny romance do (E.14.38.173).

Such moments in his novels suggest that Meredith too is aware that he cannot avoid repeating mistakes, rewriting old plots, despite his recognition and critique of them. In *The Egoist*, he has Willoughby unwittingly describe his own pathology to Clara, telling her the story of an egoist without (consciously) realizing that the term might apply to himself (13.10.115). Meredith, like Jameson, recognizes the trap of identification that structures any economy of the other, but his fiction remains caught in it nonetheless. Critics have long noted that Meredith's novels do not elude the romance they deny. Judith Wilt, for instance, observes that, despite Meredith's attempt to eject it from his novels, "the spirit of romance, like the child who is the father of the man, dominates his outlook all through his career."[60] And, like Jameson's, his social evolution depends on woman's loss of self to allow, but also screen, its contradictions.

Miller's reading of Meredith repeats woman's sacrifice to theoretical consistency. In Miller's reading of *The Egoist*, his treatment of Clara also has a woman act out his theory while drawing its troubling implications away from his own text: Miller's celebration of Clara's fragmentation, for example, does not undercut but enables his own "stable signature" and consistent argument presented as truth.[61] He deploys her as the "deconstructive absence" that

---

[59]"To Lady Ulrica Duncombe, Box Hill, Dorking, April 19, 1902," in *Letters*, 3: 1438; see also "To Lady Ulrica Duncombe, Box Hill, Dorking, March 31, 1902," in *Letters*, 3: 1432.

[60]Wilt, *Readable People*, 68.

[61]Miller, "Herself against Herself," 122. This critique of Miller seems similar to one that M. H. Abrams makes in "The Deconstructive Angel," when he writes that Miller "does not entirely and consistently commit himself to the consequences of his premises." He adds: "He [has] determinate things to say and . . . masterfully

confirms and receives the thrust of his own theory: the body that attests to but draws off the violations of deconstructive fragmentation. His commiseration with her is meant to spare the body of his text, to ward off comparable violence done to the completeness of its argument, while at the same time somehow clearing that argument of the charge of complicity with the phallogocentrism of sense and unity. What I am suggesting here is more than just that the style and structure of Miller's essay do not self-consciously act out its assumptions because the mutilations of the sign of the woman stand in for that performance; what I want to stress is that, despite their complex understanding of the way we as critics are implicated in what we describe, arguments like Miller's construct woman precisely in order to assert their own autonomy from the constraints they (often quite happily) note operating on her.[62] Miller is right that heroines have a lesson to teach men, but it seems not to be the one they have learned. The lesson the heroine teaches is, I think, the impossibility of exemption and escape.

Meredith's theory of history writes itself onto a woman's body, mutilating her, in order to make history material, visible—to realize not only history but his particular Darwinian vision of its ceaseless battle. "History," as Jameson puts it, "is what hurts" (*PU*.102), supposedly wounding its subjects with such power and immediacy that we drop the fixed selves we hold up like shields against it, forcing us into a collective regrouping for succor and survival. In Meredith's idiosyncratic reversal of the old lesson that

---

exploit[s] the resources of language to express these things clearly and forcibly, addressing himself to us in the confidence that we, to the degree that we have mastered the constitutive norms of this kind of discourse, will approximate what he means" (M. H. Abrams, "The Deconstructive Angel," *Critical Inquiry* 3 [1977]: 437). Yet, as Jonathan Culler has suggested, "deconstruction isn't, at least in the work of Derrida and its other most skillful practitioners, some kind of 'new irrationalism,' as it is occasionally suggested. Though it reveals 'irrationalities' in our systems and theories, it is the most rigorous pursuit of the logic of the text, be it a theoretical or a literary text" (Jonathan Culler, "Semiotics and Deconstruction," *Poetics Today* 1 [1979]: 141). Derrida and its other skilled practitioners do foreground the ways their own texts are necessarily marked with irrationalities, however (often on the level of style, through wordplay and metaphor, for example). My complaints are not really with Miller's attempts at stylistic clarity or logical consistency but with the way he uses the figure of the woman to allow these.

[62] As Barbara Johnson has suggested, the seemingly natural effacement of women has provided the male Yale school with the very slate on which to inscribe its own teaching; see her *A World of Difference*, 32–41.

ontogeny recapitulates phylogeny, which he translates as a moral imperative, Diana's experience is meant to teach that, for the good of the race, the subject should (because he must) give up his individual claims. This is the lesson Diana repeats as if by rote: " *'There is nothing the body suffers that the soul may not profit by,'* " she states. " 'That is Emma's history. With that I sail into the dark; it is my promise of the immortal' " (*DC*.43.492). Yet the spirit of history brands the flesh by branding the *woman's* body exclusively. Meredith's novel recounts, but also repeats, the way the world is "very powerful to brand a woman's character" (14.151), marking Diana with her sexual history. Precisely because romance does not register history, the novel suggests, romance is suspect: its shallow unchanging heroines are unmarked, even "featureless, or with the most moderate possible indication of a countenance" (35.400).

That the brutal stigmatization of women is necessary to Meredith's history and form explains the otherwise digressive scene in *Diana of the Crossways*, in which Andrew Heger admires the dissection of a pig, slaveringly anticipating its consumption. Diana is just such a specimen to be slavered over and consumed (consumption is, in fact, one of the organizing metaphors of Meredith's philosophy as he sets it forth in the first chapter); like this sacrificial animal, Diana is a "fair outstretched white carcass" on which the novelist bids his readers fasten their "intent fond gaze" (8.98), and no amount of ironizing, although this scene tries, can completely distance us as readers from our participation. As we are told time and time again, the world's and Meredith's treatment of Diana, meant to goad her out of self, leaves her a "poor stripped individual" (15.161), "perfectly naked" (11.120).[63] The effect of the woman naked is to point to her gender, to naturalize—through her supposedly natural deficiency—Meredith's practice. Woman's mutilation acts out the logic of her lack; she is branded with her inferiority. (That such essentialism is apotropaic is betrayed by Meredith's revision of Diana's story, having his character hunted and torn apart by her own hounds, who, in the myth, chase Actaeon because he gazed on the goddess's nakedness; the threat of castration destroys Diana here, not Actaeon.)

Moreover, Diana is not merely a passive victim, she is made a

---

[63]For other references to Diana as a victim stripped naked to the general gaze, see also *Diana of the Crossways* 14.147; 27.307; and 34.384.

willing participant in women's mutilation. Meredith makes it the hallmark of her character that she holds Emma down during surgery, when they "cut and hack" her (26.294), and he has Diana later attest: " 'I have learnt to admire the men of the knife! No profession equals theirs in self-command and beneficence'" (26.301). Such confessions of Diana's are meant to confirm the powers that mutilate her, especially to attest to the power of the author. Meredith bemoaned what he called the "hideous mutilation" of Diana involved in creating her character and publishing her story, even as he went right on doing so.[64] His early reviewers attest to his covert identification with "the men of the knife" by discussing Meredith's own method of the "clever . . . dissection" of character.[65]

Confession—the verb used most often in the novel and most often attached to Diana[66]—is particularly consoling for the novelist and the reader. By hearing Diana's confession, we seem to be outside of, or aligned with, the forces that elicit it. Reading, the book notes, is a scourge inflicting violence on and purifying what we read (9.111–12; 12.134).[67] Such a location seems to guarantee power; it identifies the novel's treatment of Diana with the same godlike force that the narrator, discussing a society journal, refers to as "Asmodeus lift[ing] a roof, leering hideously" (7.82). But in taking this omniscient position, the novelist aligns himself with those two characters connected in their assumption of godlike majesty, Willoughby, who feels at one with the Powers above watching over him (E.14.43.244), and Redworth, whom Diana comes to see as "infinitely above the physical monarch" (DC.42.477).[68] Both are,

[64]"To Frederick Sandys, Box Hill, November 8, 1884," in Letters, 2: 753. See also his reference to his own "maimed" state, "To Miss Louisa Lawrence, Box Hill, March 4, 1884," in Letters, 2: 728. Complicating these images of mutilation is the fact that Meredith's own wife herself was undergoing surgery as he wrote this novel; see "To Robert Louis Stevenson, Box Hill, Dorking, September 26, 1885," in Letters, 2: 790.

[65]See, for example, unsigned review of Diana of the Crossways, from the Illustrated London News, in Williams, Meredith: The Critical Heritage, 269.

[66]For just some mentions of "confession" in Diana of the Crossways, see 12.131; 14.157; 18.209; 20.232; 22.252; 23.259; 24.275, 282; 26.297; 27.309, 316; 35.391; 48.425.

[67]The one who is especially scourged is Diana; the blank she presents is scourged by what is written on it. Meredith, for instance, has his wits suggest that "women are a blank to [men]" but "traces of a singular scrawl have been observed when they were held in close proximity to the fire" (DC.28.325).

[68]For references to Willoughby's attendant powers, see for example, 13.11.129; and 13.14.157, in The Egoist.

in fact, transfigured into sun-gods. Willoughby's aunts tell us that
" 'when he was a child he one day mounted a chair, and there he
stood in danger, would not let us touch him, because he was taller
than we, and we were to gaze. . . . "I am the sun of the house!" ' "
(*E*.14.44.256). The narrative irony that deflates Willoughby's pretensions fails to touch Redworth; the novel underwrites and confirms him as "Sol in his glory" or "Sol in his moral grandeur" (as
Diana and Emma come to call him [*DC*.42.477]) by adopting the
solar metaphor and infusing its last chapter with it. Willoughby is
self-aggrandizing, but the novel itself elevates Redworth. Unlike
Willoughby, Redworth is not supposed to be in much danger from
such pretensions. He puts Diana's freedom in danger, instead,
compelling her within his orbit.

Yet that such powerful entities are imagined as sun-gods—specifically, as young Willoughby's pun tells us, son-gods—returns us
to the images of motherhood that underlie such fantasies of sufficiency. The branding of the body, Diana states, is Emma's history—
Emma, Diana's surrogate mother, her "madre" she calls her
(2.32)—which reminds us that the woman of flesh is specifically a
mother in Meredith's system. Diana's loss of self is figured in terms
of rebirth; her break from Dacier and romance returns her quite
literally to Emma's breast, where she embodies the figure for social
evolution she supplies us with at the beginning of the novel, of the
present world "in maternal travail of a soberer, a brighter-eyed . . .
distinguishable as the sickness and writhings of our egoism to cast
its first slough" (1.12). The casting out of egoism is associated with
the maternal flesh, the pangs of childbirth in which she gives birth
to herself in a new form, one that has sloughed off the self. Like
egoistic romance ("The gross original"), the mother, Meredith
writes at the end of the novel, is the exemplary "gross material
substance" (43.493) that can sometimes lead to great poetry: she is
at any rate the material out of which he constructs *his* novel and on
which he constructs his system. The romantic spirit in Meredith's
work is not so much the father as the mother of the man. (The need
for such bedrock makes clear the continuing attraction of the ro-
man à clef for Meredith; to safeguard the assumptions of this
novel, for example, by gesturing outside it to the history of Car-
oline Norton, that famous mother.)

The stripping down to essentialism that supports his history reveals more than just the feminine; it reveals the maternal, the feminine engaged in its supposedly most natural function. Diana's secret, which Dacier chases (not really a secret since her name announces it), turns out to be not so much lunar changefulness revealing a lack of character as her ability to reflect the sun. Redworth, seeing "how charged with mystery her features were," unlocks that mystery by realizing that she is like another kind of reflective virgin blank, "a Madonna on an old black Spanish canvas" (9.104). Redworth clinches Diana's maternal status and his own identification with the gods by literally impregnating her at the end of the novel: the culmination of the history of this novel is the very power over Diana to transform her into a mother.

Meredith assumes the mother's traditional identity as the exemplary nonself that nurtures and re-enforces the infant self, especially the son's. Meredith is aware of the relationships of such a picture of motherhood to the egoism he criticizes; he describes Willoughby's egoism as his "tender infant Self" (*E*.14.29.50) and aligns what one critic calls Willoughby's "mother fixation" with the realm of romance (Willoughby's mother, for example, seconds him in asking Laetitia Dale to be "his Egeria" [13.441]).[69] The romantic behavior Willoughby expects from an Egeria is very much the osmosis proper between mother and infant; she is to be his "balsamic bath" (13.14.158), "Love's very bosom" (13.11.129): "she was expected to worship him and uphold him for whatsoever he might be, without any estimation of qualities" (13.11.129). Willoughby's complaint about Clara is that "she would not, though a purer poetry is little imaginable, reduce herself to ashes, or incense, or essence, in honour of him, and so, by love's transmutation, literally be the man she was to marry" (13.6.54). In *Diana of the Crossways*, however, such self-immolating mother-love is no longer romantic, but natural and legitimating; one critic describes Emma's love for Diana by referring to the highly idealized scene of Diana's rebirth at Emma's breast in correspondingly ideal terms: "it is the feeling of being thoroughly understood, even to every vibration of voice, every shade of word, and, stronger still, the certainty that

[69]Stevenson, *Ordeal*, 228.

here there will always be found rest, trust, and love till the world's end."[70] In what Freud sanctioned as the proper development of the mother-daughter relation, such love, however, rather than reflecting Diana's egoism as it does Willoughby's, makes her into just such a reflector herself, allows her own rebirth out of egoism so that she stops acting like a man, turns away from her love for the mother that surfaces here (for this scene is highly erotic as well), deflecting it into love for the father and his representatives, becoming a mirror for a man's ego.

Perhaps Meredith can have it both ways, rely on assumptions he elsewhere criticizes, not just because that criticism has seemed to purge those assumptions of danger but also because, in this novel, they have gone underground. Willoughby, for part of the book, *has* a mother, however shadowy, who is useful in that context because she can be deemed romantic and blamed for his ills, as well as the ills of the novel. But there are no actual mothers in *Diana of the Crossways;* Emma is not really Diana's mother, about whom readers hear practically nothing at all, and the book ends with only the discreetest of possible hints that Diana herself is to become one. In this novel, Meredith counts on what has become almost a feminist truism, namely, that the mother is unrepresentable, resisting and eluding systems of power—perhaps most familiar in our time in contemporary French feminist discussions of her. If mothers in their unrepresentability supposedly escape dominance, so do the selves they reflect, and it is this fantasy that allows Meredith's novel to maintain his history while exempting itself from it. By covertly celebrating the romantic mother, Meredith's system opens up a loophole permitting access to the very realm of freedom it condemns as Diana's romance: in "the kingdom composed of the shattered romance of life . . . she was free and safe. Nothing touched her there" (*DC*.40.450).

Diana of the Crossways emphasizes throughout that mothers are meant to supply a place free and safe, outside and at the start of history. Emma, in the selfless maternity that calls Diana back to life, literally nourishes her with her own food, coaxing her to eat by telling her " ' "pledge me" is a noble saying, when you think of humanity's original hunger for the whole. It is there our civilizing

---

[70]Unsigned review of *Diana of the Crossways,* in Williams, *Meredith: The Critical Heritage,* 269.

commenced, and I am particularly fond of hearing the call. It is grandly historic' " (36.412). "Emma fed her as a child," Meredith writes, "and nature sucked for life" (36.412). It is here, in the realm of nature, just before and overseeing the grandly historic advent of culture, that Meredith places the mother. Her utility for his system is that, although she leads to history, she provides the realm of freedom that also evades it. Diana claims that it is " 'before the era of the Nursery,' " when we are still with our mothers, that we find " 'Liberty to grow; independence is the key of the secret' " (28.328).

The mother's connection with a realm of liberty outside history—a natural realm—is central to Meredith's philosophical system, which certain poems, such as the suggestively titled "The Empty Purse," and critics responding to them, such as Stevenson and Trevelyan, make clear. Meredith's figure for what compels and controls the evolutionary progress of history is Nature herself, which throughout his writing he calls the great and "Mighty Mother."[71] Rather than question Mother Nature (which only makes her appear "terrible and inscrutable"[72]), man must cheerfully trust in her unceasing protection and nurturance, for "thus alone can man face death without dread," when he sees that personal death is not an end but simply a step in the grand progression nature oversees.[73] In undoing the finality of death, Meredith seems to be countering the personal salvation of Christianity with a mystical self-loss, sustained by another fantasy of the pre-Oedipal, the mother overwhelming and subsuming the self. Yet Stevenson points out that Meredith embraces a Carlylean notion of heroism, a cult of the favored few who, paradoxically, find individual distinction through "divine self-forgetfulness"—who, by trusting in the mother, find immortality.[74] The proper relation with Mother Nature actually grants a privileged individualism that rises above death. The effect of Meredith's system is ultimately the same as that which he rebuts: just as for most of the other Victorians, his reaction against the desire for personal immortality is perhaps so sustained and bitter because he could not completely relinquish the desire himself.

[71]Stevenson, *Darwin*, 205.
[72]Stevenson, *Darwin*, 218.
[73]Stevenson, *Darwin*, 210.
[74]Stevenson, *Darwin*, 230.

The life-giving privilege is ultimately not supplied by the mother anyway in Meredith's system but by the spirit of which she turns out to be only the vessel: "The sole path to God is through communion with Earth," Meredith notes in his poetry, and "by being 'true to the mother with whom we are' we may be 'worthy of Him who afar beckons us on to a brighter birth.'"[75] Meredith's heroes are this spirit's chosen sons. This family triangle supports an arbitrary assumption of power by grounding it in supposedly natural fact. Mother-love spotlights and completes the chosen son; her complete abasement to him makes him the equal of the powerful father by granting him similar prerogatives. An emphasis on the mother suggests a route to power that sidesteps direct confrontation with it, and this might have been what Oscar Wilde had in mind when he wrote of Meredith that "whatever he is, he is not a realist. Or rather I would say that he is a child of realism who is not on speaking terms with his father. By deliberate choice he has made himself a romanticist."[76] But Meredith does not just cast himself in the role of chosen son. Meredith identifies with the totality of power, merging with it first of all by taking on the mother's role: throughout his writing of *Diana of the Crossways,* he insistently identifies himself as her mother.[77] Meredith takes over the father's place too. Diana is a mother at the end because she is pregnant with Meredith's creation—she is the site on which his pen inscribes the story he tells—and this creation is precisely the fantasy of self-creation, the belief that the self can be autonomous from the system that creates it.

The desire encoded here is that the power of writing is power over the history it describes because it eludes the end of the history of the self—it grants power over death. *Diana of the Crossways* begins precisely with Meredith granting the diarists (with whose writing he identifies his novel) "power to cancel our Burial Service"

---

[75]Stevenson, *Darwin,* 220.

[76]Stevenson, *Ordeal,* 273.

[77]See, for example, his wish for the time "when I am delivered of this Diana," "To Miss Louisa Lawrence, Box Hill, March 4, 1884," in *Letters,* 2: 727; his desire to "have her out of me," "To Robert Louis Stevenson, Box Hill, March 24, 1884," in *Letters,* 2: 731; his hope "to finish with the delivery," "To Mrs. Leslie Stephen, Box Hill, March 24, 1884," in *Letters,* 2: 732; and his claim that "my *Diana* is out of hand, leaving her mother rather inanimate," "To Robert Louis Stevenson, Box Hill, Dorking, October 10, 1884," in *Letters,* 2: 747.

(1.9). Meredith's favorite metaphor for egoism in *Diana of the Crossways*—a haunting ghost[78]—points to a desire for the self to last after death. The mother is specifically the means to such power because her traditional role associates her with the creation and extinction of the self. Indeed, Meredith's emphasis on cheerfully choosing the mother's law in order to surmount it is the very mechanism of consolation that Freud, in his essay "The Theme of the Three Caskets," suggests that the mother provides. Man prefers, in desperate hope of "wishful transformation," to choose a disguised form of what he cannot avoid, the last mother, "the Mother Earth who receives him."[79] The utility of romance and the mother in my reading is that they show the way novels and patriarchy construct history precisely in order to (try to) put an end to it.

[78]*Diana of the Crossways* repeatedly discusses the way people are "haunted" by self (see 4.47, 48; 19.214), which adds another level of meaning to the ghost Redworth sees in the churchyard (8.96; it is really Diana, and her identification with such ghosts also identifies her with egoism).

[79]Sigmund Freud, "The Theme of the Three Caskets," in vol. 12 of *The Standard Edition of the Complete Psychological Writings of Sigmund Freud*, trans. James Strachey, 24 vols. (1953–74), p. 301.

2

Diverting Romance:
Charlotte Lennox's *The Female Quixote*

Charlotte Lennox's *The Female Quixote; or, The Adventures of Arabella*, published in 1752, coming, as it does, at the historical moment in England that critics associate with the rise of the novel, demonstrates the way gender underlies our constructions as critics of literary history. In its mockery of quixotism, *The Female Quixote* engages with what had already become a literary convention. It borrows its informing tension between the novel and romance from *Don Quixote* but does so with a difference. By shifting the tension to the story of a young woman rather than an old man, it inaugurates within the English novel tradition the inherent relation between heroines and romance. In this chapter, I examine the way that association is crucial to the tradition.

Lennox's novel both exposes and acts out the association between women and romance. Its heroine Arabella, caught between the novel and romance, becomes the focus for the struggle between genres and comes to exemplify Lennox's own dilemma as a woman writer: the imperative to leave behind the insubstantial world of romance, the only realm in which the woman (writer) is given a place, however illusory. *The Female Quixote* reveals that the novelistic world it strives to establish through a critique of the emptiness of romance has no real place for woman except in repeating her association with romance. The only alternative it can offer her is this revelation, this critique, which exposes the workings of the system of representation and the logic of the tradition, without modifying or changing them, or giving her some other structure in which to operate. *The Female Quixote*'s difference from romance comes to rest on revealing women's dispossession, on exposing the lack of stable ground on which women might situate their own stories.

I

Writing about romance in the eighteenth century, J. M. S. Tompkins concludes: "It was impossible that a word so variously and disapprovingly applied should preserve any exactness of meaning. It was, said Mary Hays [in *Memoirs of Emma Courtney,* 1796], 'a vague term, applied to everything we do not understand, or are unwilling to imitate.' "[1] Romance was then, and is now, a vague term, especially when critics try to designate by it a peculiar prose form distinct from the novel. Yet critics suffer more from these taxonomical difficulties than do novelists. The novelists' concern—one heightened for eighteenth-century writers, especially aware that their novels were not only given shape by, but were shaping, their form—was not to dissect romance but to use it to define the novel. Romance meant different things to different novelists, but for none of them was it exact; none of them needed it to be. Romance was what the novel was *not:* "everything we do not understand, or are unwilling to imitate." The utility of romance consisted precisely in its vagueness; it was the chaotic negative space outside the novel that determined the outlines of the novel's form. To novelists and, they hoped, to their readers, the novel was unified, probable, truly representational because romance was none of these. The contrast between them gave the novel its meaning.

The Female Quixote structures its story on the contrast between the novel and romance. Its heroine, Arabella, is a female quixote— a girl so affected by her reading of romances that they seem to have driven her mad. Yet Arabella's excesses of behavior actually reflect what is wrong with romance. She acts the way she does because she believes in romance and is simply acting out its conventions. Through her, *The Female Quixote* shows that romance is excessive fiction, so excessive that *it* is nonsensical, ultimately mad. The silly

[1] J. M. S. Tompkins, *The Popular Novel in England, 1770–1800* (1961), 211–12.

extravagances of romance that Arabella illustrates are meant as a foil for the strengths of the novel.

More than simply providing a contrast to the novel, romance acts as a displacement of the problems of the novel. Lennox does not explicitly define her novel against romance. Instead, she condemns romance as specious fiction and covers up the fictiveness of her own form, implying by her blindness to it as a form that it is real and true. Yet Lennox's equation of romance and fiction attests to a tacit recognition that the problems of romance are the problems of fiction, and of the novel as well. By deriding romance, construing it as the realm of excess and nonsense, *The Female Quixote* veils its own excesses, tries to appear stable and controlled. One way to read Arabella's madness is as a danger the novelist wants to displace, the novelist's own hidden danger. What takes Arabella over are the powerful forces not just of one genre, romance, but of all writing—forces in excess of meaning, which call meaning into question. Or, more precisely, they call meaning into question for women, who cannot find a voice in these structures of representation.

Even eighteenth-century critics, however, recognized the female quixote's danger was no longer real by the time of Lennox's book, if it ever had been:

> the Satire of the *Female Quixote* [writes Clara Reeve in 1785] seems in great measure to have lost its aim, because at the time it first appeared, the taste for those Romances was extinct, and the books exploded. . . . [T]his book came some thirty or forty years too late. . . . Romances at this time were quite out of fashion, and the press groaned under the weight of Novels, which sprung up like Mushrooms every year.[2]

Readers had lost their taste for romances: there were no Arabellas who would believe in them. For writers, it was a different story; there were Charlottes (and Claras) whose novels, like mushrooms, needed dead wood out of which to spring. Underlying the novel's covert need for romance as a means of displacement is an even more submerged tension: an attraction to romance as the very

[2]Clara Reeve, vol. 2 of *The Progress of Romance through Times, Countries, and Manners*, 2 vols. (1785; 1970), pp. 6–7.

source of writing. Another way to read the mad Arabella is as the novelist's fantasy of wish-fulfillment. She is the ideal reader, completely given over to the sway of the text, attesting to the power of romance, a power the novelist desires for her form too. But because that power resides in "everything we do not understand," the novelist is caught in a double bind; she tries to cast out from her writing exactly that power which she also envies and wishes to usurp. She needs, in fact, to kill off her source, which becomes generative only in its death.[3]

In the act of casting out, Lennox is drawn into what she rejects. What Lennox sees as the themes and conventions of romance give form to her novel, just as do those she adopts as antidote to them. Margaret Dalziel has suggested that, "unlike Don Quixote, Arabella is also created to be the heroine of a serious love-story, a story with the conventional romantic characters and the conventional romantic ending."[4] Ronald Paulson adds: "Mrs. Lennox does not satirize Arabella's romances as much as use this form as a convenient vehicle for introducing romance into the humdrum life of Arabella and her readers."[5] The novel uses romance to define itself, but the opposition breaks down and subverts that definition. *The Female Quixote* both mocks and lauds its heroine's quixotism, and the way it ridicules romance actually exposes the attractions of what that form represents. What the novel locates as the problems of romance—the disorder and rigidity of its form, the ambiguities of its language—become its own. Yet Lennox's novel is unable to do more than show that such romantic qualities haunt it even as it rejects them—to gesture nostalgically to what it constructs as a lost realm, an illusory female heritage it can never forget and can never retrace.

What *The Female Quixote* says about romance is useful because it provides one definition of the novel, one that zeroes in on particular elements that are troubling to this novel because also generative

[3]That women writers especially defined themselves early on in the tradition of the novel in parasitical relation to a dead feminine form suggests that, rather than feminizing that tradition, all those early women novelists seemed necessary to purge it of the taint of the feminine, to affirm that even women recognized the need to kill off its female excesses.

[4]Margaret Dalziel, Introduction to *The Female Quixote; or, The Adventures of Arabella,* by Charlotte Lennox (1970), xiii.

[5]Ronald Paulson, *Satire and the Novel in Eighteenth-Century England* (1967), 278.

of its form and meaning. Romance is troubling in another way as well: it acts as a lightning rod for the anxieties about gender at the heart of every depiction of the sexes. Romance has traditionally been considered a woman's form. The novel's very definition of romance echoes the way patriarchy defines women: they are both seen as marginal, the negative of the defining agents. The derision of Arabella in *The Female Quixote* lends extra force to its subordination of romance, for, as a female quixote, she is already subordinate—a subordinate character in the novel's social world, a subordinate sign in its formal one.

Yet Lennox rewrites the conventional derisive association of women and romance. Although she attacks romance for its feminine excesses, she also tries to disassociate it from women by educating Arabella out of it. Yet the novel ultimately shows that women and romance are so bound that separating the two ends the story. It suggests a positive, although wistful, alignment of them— if romance were available to women unmediated, it might be a source of resistance and a ground from which they could speak. By figuring that ground precisely as the realm her novel cannot admit, Lennox exposes romance as a consolation for the dominant tradition as much as for the woman writer. To take her place in that tradition, to write at all, she must cease to be a *woman* writer, give up the necessarily unreachable dream of alterity and romance.

II

Lennox is well aware that novels borrow from what she constructs as romance. She has Sir George, one of Arabella's suitors, claim: "he was perfectly well acquainted with the chief Characters in most of the *French* Romances; could tell every thing that was borrowed from them, in all the new Novels that came out."[6] Lennox herself seems to exercise exactly the same kind of recognition of and control over romance. The attraction of her novel, in fact, is supposed to be that it contains romance within a new setting. It is like the attraction Arabella has, when dressed for the ball as a

[6]Charlotte Lennox, *The Female Quixote: or, The Adventures of Arabella* (1970), bk. 3, ch. 7, pp. 129–30. All further references to this book (hereafter abbreviated *FQ*) will appear in the text.

romance heroine: "This Story was quickly dispers'd, and for its Novelty, afforded a great deal of Diversion; every one long'd to see a Fashion of such Antiquity; and expected the Appearance of the Princess *Julia* with great Impatience" (*FQ*.7.7.271–72). Lennox wants to suggest that what her novel borrows from romance is just stage dressing. The faded costumes have been brought out to draw a crowd. But Lennox's language belies her; romance isn't simply ornamental. What the previous passage also suggests about her book is that its very novel-ty depends on its relation to romance. Sir George, who makes such confident claims about romance, certainly can neither regulate or restrain it. The romance he tells Arabella about himself to win her love backfires. When he actually tries to stage one, romance gets completely out of his control. His romance plot at the end of the book, meant to discredit Arabella's lover Glanville in her eyes, and staged with actresses, costumes, and a script, becomes dangerously real: it so riles Arabella that she nearly drowns herself; it ends with Glanville running Sir George through.

Instead of being in control of romance, the novel is drawn into and repeats it. It does so especially in its depiction of Arabella. Although presented as a spoof, she is very much a romance heroine herself. Like them, she is an impossible paragon—"the Perfection of Beauty, Wit, and Virtue" (4.3.151). The book actually affirms her identification with romance heroines, an identification that imperceptibly takes over from the mockery. At what should be her greatest public disgraces—the Ball and Vauxhall gardens—the ridicule dissolves. Arabella confronts the "design'd Ridicule of the Whole Assembly," but "Scarce had the first tumultuous Whisper escap'd the Lips of each Individual, when they found themselves aw'd to Respect by that irresistible Charm in the Person of *Arabella*, which commanded Reverence and Love from all who beheld her" (7.7.272). The tone of the book changes, becoming the same tone it had earlier belittled as romantic. Arabella and the crowd are frozen in uneasy, wishful moments—uneasy because the romance within the novel comes out of hiding, wishful because such moments acknowledge a fantasy the novel can't acknowledge elsewhere. In these moments, the line between the novel and romance disappears. Arabella is a romance heroine, and receives the respect and obeisance that are supposed to be a romance heroine's due because Lennox shares the powerful desire for a realm where a woman might command such treatment.

Such moments of collapse between the novel and romance suggest that the answer to Arabella's question—"May not the same Accidents happen to me, that have happened to so many illustrious Ladies before me?" (7.3.261)—is "Yes." Part of the jest of the book, of course, is that romantic accidents happen to its determinedly unromantic characters. For instance, Arabella sees one of her suitors, Hervey, as a prospective ravisher and expects Glanville to defend her. Glanville, angry at Arabella for being so ridiculous, and angry at Hervey for ridiculing her, unwittingly winds up doing exactly what Arabella expects of him—he attacks Hervey and, by so doing, becomes romantic, "the Champion of this fair lady" (4.4.157). This kind of joke is part of the debunking of romance, suggesting that the duels between romantic heroes might have more to do with spleen than with honor.[7] But the reader is meant to take seriously some of the characters' romantic actions. Arabella's sickness (from grief) at her father's death is not supposed to be excessive romantic sensibility but proper filial devotion. Not only is Arabella's behavior here similar to the extravagances of romantic heroines, but even the language Lennox uses to describe the event is almost identical to romance language she mocks earlier. The romantic Arabella explains away the supposedly lovesick Edward's excellent health with "as for his not being sick, his Youth, and the Strength of his Constitution, might, even for a longer time, bear him up against the Assaults of a Fever" (1.7.23). Lennox explains that Arabella recovers from *her* fever because "her Youth, and the Strength of her Constitution, overcame her Disease" (2.2.59). Such romantic language might be the only language in which to explain Arabella's recovery of her health, however, because it wishfully assumes a female self, who possesses the strength and integrity that could outlast and overcome the disease of patriarchy.

The wish for this romantic self seems implicit throughout Len-

---

[7]That the conventions of romance assert themselves even in the face of determined opposition—most of Glanville's anger comes from how hard and how unsuccessfully he tries to defuse Arabella's romantic expectations—also suggests the indivisible shadow relation of romance with whatever tries to disclaim it.

nox's story. Crucial to the book's depiction of Arabella, and its derision of romance, is its assertion of a natural, sensible Arabella, superior to and distinct from her romantic self. Yet this essential self is not very convincing, since the book mostly claims it exists rather than demonstrates it. Access to this Arabella, like Glanville's, is supposed to be through her conversation, which, "when it did not turn upon any Incident in her Romances, was perfectly fine, easy, and entertaining" (2.4.65). Yet readers get very little of Arabella's conversation that does not turn on romance, and the little they do get shows an Arabella no more "real" because less literary than the self drawn from romance. The speeches that are meant to impress Lennox's readers are, if anything, even more artificial—set-pieces modeled on historical writers or moral essays.[8] The most sustained of these is Arabella's discourse on raillery, in which she charms Mr. Glanville with her rationality (7.6.267–69). Yet source study shows that this example of the unromantic Arabella turns out to be very romantic after all: it is taken from a romance, a speech in *Artamenes*.[9] Although ostensibly defined against romance, Arabella's character grows out of it, needs it to give her shape.

Ridicule is the tool the novel uses against Arabella and, through her, against romance. During her climactic renunciation of romance, it is only when Arabella recognizes that *she* can be absurd (and has been in regard to the rules of the debate about romance between her and the Doctor) that her "Heart [can yield] to the Force of Truth" (9.11.381), and she can see the absurdity in romance. What convinces her to give up romance is not so much the Doctor's logic as her own shame, and it is later "Reflections on the Absurdity of her past Behaviour, and the Contempt and Ridicule to which she now saw plainly she had exposed herself" (9.12.383) which clinch her rehabilitation. *The Female Quixote* itself constructs a literary tradition that breaks with an absurd past and saves its (woman) writer from shame: the verisimilitude and commonsensicalness of Lennox's novel reflect on past romances, and are

[8]Margaret Dalziel suspects "that the originals could be found for other speeches made by Arabella, as for example her disquisitions on glory, indifference, and suicide (pp. 303f., 310f., and 318f.), in which the style seems different from that of most of her conversation" (FQ.9.11.414 [n368]).

[9]According to Dalziel, from Madeleine de Scudéry, "The History of Pisistrates," *Artamenes; or, the Grand Cyrus. That Excellent Romance,* 1690–91, 9.3.325ff. Cited in (FQ.7.6.406 [n267]).

meant to keep it from the contempt and ridicule that attend their silly stories.

Yet the function of ridicule in this novel is not as simple as it seems. Ridicule seems to be something the book *does;* it holds up Arabella and romance for its reader's laughter and derision. In fact, ridicule is not so much what the book does as what it is *about.* Over the course of the story, we notice that we're not so much laughing at Arabella, we're watching the other characters laughing. Again and again, just at moments when Arabella causes them great uneasiness, they can barely choke back their laughter at her absurdity. This ongoing laugh track may at first seem like an unsophisticated cue—Lennox telling her readers, laugh here, this is funny. Yet what it does is subtly to change the effect of the laughter. Because the characters laugh first, the author and the readers are slightly disassociated from the ridicule, made perhaps to reflect on it.

Ridicule is set up as an issue rather than used as a tactic; it is something readers consider rather than participate in, starting from the first page, when we learn of Arabella's father's unjustified public disgrace. Ridicule most explicitly stands out as an issue when Arabella lectures about it in her disquisition on raillery. What Arabella says there suggests the way raillery works in this book. She says that "the Talent of Raillery ought to be born with a Person; no Art can infuse it; and those who endeavour to railly in spite of Nature, will be so far from diverting others, that they will become the Objects of Ridicule themselves" (7.6.268). Although Lennox blunts her statement by imagining some ideal of raillery (which obviously doesn't exist if, as Glanville suggests, *Arabella* is meant to exemplify it), this passage suggests that Lennox recognizes ridicule as impossibly tricky and shifting, a form of scapegoating that rebounds on the one who uses it. That ridicule can especially be a form of literary scapegoating she has Glanville tell us.[10] He accuses Sir George of

> Rail[ing] with premeditated Malice at the *Rambler;* and, for the want of Faults, turn[ing] even its inimitable Beauties into Ridicule;

[10]Fielding picks up the same thread in his review of *The Female Quixote.* Extreme criticism of the book, he says, reflects only on the critic: "no Persons presume to find many [faults]: For if they do, I promise them, the Critic and not the Author *will be to blame* " (Henry Fielding, *"The Covent Garden Journal,* No. 24," in *The Criticism of Henry Fielding,* ed. Ioan Williams [1970], 194).

The Language, because it reaches to Perfection, may be called stiff, laboured, and pedantic; the Criticisms, when they let in more Light than your weak Judgment can bear, superficial and ostentatious Glitter; and because those Papers contain the finest System of Ethics yet extant, [you] damn the queer Fellow, for over-propping Virtue. (6.11.253)

If, as Glanville suggests, ridicule works to hide the attractions of a literary form, what are the attractions of ridiculed romance?

Perhaps the answer lies in romance's diversion. "Diverting" is the word the novel uses most to describe Arabella's romantic absurdities, and the word suggests not just that they are funny but that they distract from something else.[11] The Doctor gives us the key to what we are diverted from when he says about romances, "if they are at any Time read with Safety, [they] owe their Innocence only to their Absurdity" (9.11.374). Lennox's mockery of romance allows readers to partake of it innocently in her novel, to feel at a distance from what is actually the source of their pleasure. What readers especially enjoy, the Doctor states, is fantasy. The novel projects onto romance all the wish-fulfillment of fiction: "But who can forbear to throw away the Story that gives to one Man the Strength of Thousands; that puts Life or Death in a Smile or a Frown; that recounts Labours and Sufferings to which the Powers of Humanity are utterly unequal" (9.11.378–79). Fielding, in his review of *The Female Quixote*, sees the attraction slightly differently: "[*The Female Quixote*] is indeed a Work of true Humour, and cannot fail of giving a rational, as well as very pleasing, Amusement to a sensible Reader, who will at once be instructed and very highly diverted."[12] Fielding's emphasis on the rational, sensible, and instructive suggests that what the humor of this novel diverts the reader from acknowledging are the pleasures of the irrational, mocked in the novel as romantic foolery. Figuring fantasy and the irrational as romance, the novel seems safely to encapsulate them, to cast them from itself, while still relying on their attractions.

The novel cannot admit it has such forces in its midst because having them there is dangerous, dangerous because disordering. Disorder is certainly the effect they have had on Arabella. Encountering them in romance has driven her out of her senses, "disor-

---

[11]For examples of the use of "diverting," see 1.9.34; 1.13.52; 4.2.146; and 5.4.195.
[12]Fielding, "*Covent Garden Journal*," 194.

dered" her brain (7.13.301; 8.2.339; 9.10.367), and that mental disorder has disordered all around her: contradicted her father's will,
disrupted the line of inheritance, created such day-to-day havoc
that even her retreat at tranquil Richmond ends in "a Scene of the
utmost Confusion and Distress" (9.10.365). But disorder is also a
formal danger. Arabella is described as being "turned" (1.10.41;
1.13.55; 4.4.156) and "out of the Way" (8.6.325), and those are also
apt descriptions of what the novel sets up as the formal problems
of romance—its loose plots, its digressiveness, its endlessness.
Order is what makes Fielding prefer *The Female Quixote* to *Don
Quixote* as a response to romance: "here is a regular Story, which,
tho' possibly it is not pursued with that Epic Regularity which
would give it the Name of an Action, comes much nearer to that
Perfection than the loose unconnected Adventures in *Don Quixote*;
of which you may transverse the Order as you please, without any
Injury to the whole."[13] It's not just that Arabella is out of her
senses, but that the irregularities and improbabilities of romance
are ravings, "senseless Fictions" (9.11.374).

Yet the formal problems of romance are exactly what Lennox
worried about most in writing her own novel. Length is what she
attacks romance for most effectively (certainly the most quoted
scene from the book is the one in which Glanville, to please Arabella, attempts some romances, but "counting the Pages, he was
quite terrified at the Number, and could not prevail upon himself
to read them" [1.12.50]). And length is what plagued her most in
writing her book. Her letters to Richardson, perhaps not the best
advisor in this matter, consult him about the problem: how to fill
volumes without being prolix?[14] According to her critics, it is a
problem he didn't help her resolve. Mrs. Barbauld is one of the first
to find *The Female Quixote* "rather spun out too much and not very
well wound up."[15] And romance's other formal excesses make
their way into the novel. In having Arabella enumerate romances,
Lennox goes too far. Arabella conjures up too many characters,
cites too many texts, repeats too many similar scenes, so that her
recourse to romances ultimately takes away from the order of the
novel, makes *it* digress. In the end, romance splits the book wide

[13]Fielding, *"Covent Garden Journal,"* 93.
[14]Duncan Isles, Appendix to Lennox, *The Female Quixote*, 418–27.
[15]Quoted by Dalziel, Introduction to Lennox, *The Female Quixote*, xviii.

open: Lennox's attempts to evict romance are loose-ended—she introduces the Countess only to whisk her away—and ultimately fracturing—the Doctor comes out of nowhere and his cure of Arabella jars with the rest of the story rather than smoothly resolving it. The obvious sutures with which the book binds up its attempted elisions of romance suggest not only that it cannot give romance up but that it may not wish to.

That the novel cannot escape what it casts as the madness of romance is already evident in its own treatment of madness. What the novel shows is that Arabella's madness is contagious; part of its threat to Glanville is that it will make him mad: Arabella's confusion and disorder leave him in confusion and disorder. His perpetual cry is "You will make me mad!" (4.4.156). As Glanville's threatened madness shows, to define madness is already in some part to include and reflect it. To repudiate romance may be to subject oneself to its essential disorder.

The disorder of romance, its failure to stay within bounds, is one of the ways the novel figures its madness. But another part of the madness of romance is just how strictly bound it is. Through Arabella, the novel mocks the intricate and unbendable rules of romance. As Ronald Paulson writes: "Quixotism in Arabella means a rigidity of behavior."[16] Arabella's relation to romance is a form of repetition compulsion; she forever re-enacts the same romance conventions in the face of wildly different experiences. The special madness of romance is that its rules are so rigid and yet so empty: that the novel sets it up as a form without sense becomes clear in Arabella's explanation of its special provinces, love and honor: "The Empire of Love, said she, like the Empire of Honour, is govern'd by Laws of its own, which have no Dependence upon, or Relation to any other" (8.4.320).[17] It is an empire "dependent upon nothing but itself" (8.4.321), and it is that kind of empty relationality the novel attacks. Romance is mad because it elevates rules for their own sake—and, in fact, Arabella is attracted not just

[16]Paulson, *Satire and the Novel*, 276.

[17]As unlikely a writer as Jacques Lacan refers to the *Pays du Tendre* of Scudéry as a metaphor for a certain reaction to form—the denial that form generates meaning, a denial that tries to maintain access to some reality, to have form, rather than being empty, seem a kind of map (still tied to the notion of a referential ground, even as it denies it). See Jacques Lacan, "The Freudian Thing," in his *Ecrits: A Selection*, trans. Alan Sheridan (1977), 119–20.

to the laws of romance but to law in any form. It is she who insists and dwells on the laws of disputation in her discussion with the Doctor. Romance's attraction to law is a wish for its own rule, outside the laws of the novel or the male order. Yet romance as example of supposedly empty relationality shows that there may actually be no escape, no pure form dependent only on its own meanings. The laws of disputation show how law itself is already imperialized by the very realms Lennox may wish to escape, as it indoctrinates Arabella into them.

The problem with romance is that it suggests writing can be made up of nonreferential relations, and that rule and form can be attractive in themselves. Lennox tries to get around this suggestion in her own book by foisting it onto romance. Yet what informs the novel is a structure fully as formal as that of romance. Lennox's playful treatment of Richardson's *Clarissa* suggests how much the rules of the novel are on her mind, and suggests too that the novel isn't simply a mirror of the world but, like romance, has rules—conventions. At one point in the story, Sir George, playing at romance, slides easily into the role of Lovelace. Supposedly dying of love for Arabella, he writes to her: "Let my Death then, O Divine *Arabella*, expiate the Offence I have been guilty of!" (4.9.174). At another point, Arabella, about to flee from her home, pauses to consult romance convention: "The Want of a Precedent, indeed, for an Action of this Nature, held her a few Moments in Suspense; for she did not remember to have read of any Heroine that voluntarily left her Father's House, however persecuted she might be" (1.9.35). The joke, of course—and one Richardson might not have appreciated—is that Clarissa, the heroine of a novel, has done what is unnatural, improbable, beyond even romance heroines. Lennox attests to the importance of novelistic convention in her initial plans for Arabella's cure. Duncan Isles has argued that the Countess, whose appearance is such a loose thread in the final version of the book, was initially intended to be the agent of Arabella's cure, and to effect it by having her read *Clarissa*.[18] The conventions of the novel were (perhaps too) explicitly to be the antidote for the conventions of romance—too explicit, because that ending would have demonstrated not just that the novel is, like

[18]Isles, Appendix to Lennox, *The Female Quixote*, 425.

romance, a form, structured according to formal laws instead of reflecting truth or reality, but also that formal laws do not necessarily exempt us from or leave behind the (male) ideology we might associate with that reality; romance may not provide a realm outside it.

The novel suggests that language is most at fault in romance: to halt Sir George's romancing, Glanville admonishes, "Pray, Sir George . . . lay aside this pompous Style" (5.4.196), suggesting that romance *is* its style, that one disappears with the other. The trouble with the language of romance is that it can be downright "injurious" (2.9.90; 2.11.105)—romance had addled Arabella partly because its language is so awry; Lennox makes a point of telling the reader that Arabella has read romance in bad translation. Its effect on Arabella is to make her unintelligible; the other characters simply can't understand what she says. Arabella, for her part, can't make any sense of them either, and the languages of romance and the novel are so foreign to one another that Arabella and the others often mean very different things by the same word—words such as "adventures," "histories," "heroes," "favors," "servants," "fair ones," and "knights." This troublesome diction all belongs to romance because the book insists the meanings of the other characters aren't really mysterious; language is romance's problem. The novel makes a sharp distinction between its own "plain *English*" (5.1.182) and the language of romance, which through parody it establishes as the offender.

The Countess, in reasoning with Arabella, confronts this problem of language: "Tho' the Natures of Virtue or Vice cannot be changed, . . . yet they may be mistaken; and different Principles, Customs, and Education, may probably change their Names, if not their Natures" (8.7.328). Sophistry is what the Countess is criticizing here, the sophistry of romance, which speciously makes distinctions on the basis of names, not natures. When first presented with Mr. Glanville, Arabella employs romance with such (supposed) sophism (and yet it is a sophistry that puts the assumptions of the male order directly into question): "What Lady in Romance ever married the Man that was chose for her? In those Cases the Remonstrances of a Parent are called Persecutions; obstinate Resistance, Constancy and Courage; and an Aptitude to dislike the Person proposed to them, a noble Freedom of Mind which disdains to love or hate by the Caprice of others" (1.8.27). The foundation underlying this kind of irony is the belief that words have easily accessible, stable meanings and are transparently referential to them.[19] One of Lennox's very few discursive footnotes, in fact, objects to romance precisely because it does *not* use language this way: "This Enigmatical Way of speaking upon such Occasions, is of great Use in the voluminous *French* Romances; since the Doubt and Confusion it is the Cause of, both to the Accus'd and Accuser, gives Rise to a great Number of succeeding Mistakes, and consequently Adventures" (9.6.351 n). Romance is especially damned because enigmatic language is not just an element of it but is its very source and impetus, the basis for its adventures. Not only does Lennox wish to argue against the uncertainty of language being the foundation for fictional texts, she even suggests that language regulates, brings multiple meanings and erring associations back into line: chiding Arabella for her cockeyed, extravagant notions, the Doctor tells her, "Your Imaginations, Madam . . . are too quick for Language" (9.11.370), suggesting that the very act of casting into words will organize and rationalize her fancy. The attraction of romance is precisely that, by changing names, it might perhaps change (if not natures, then) the different principles, customs, and education that constrain and persecute.

The novel dismisses the autonomy of language by clever scapegoating, relying on class as well as gender assumptions; stumbling over words as things, being caught up in language for itself is, it notes, something that servants do. By reacting in this way, the servants not only expose themselves but expose Arabella's romance language for the nonsense it is. Arabella's maid, Lucy, listens not to the matter but the sound of Arabella's words: in repeating them, she thinks "Solation" is exactly the same as "consolation" (8.3.315). Yet, although the willingness to divorce words from sense is presented as part of romance and as nonsense, the opposite view is also part of romance and is just as patently nonsensical. This is Arabella's own view, which reads words so literally it allows them only one sense (as when Arabella interprets Lucy's "die for Joy" [5.1.181] to mean just that). When language, whether overly loose or literal, is in

[19]Although Arabella's ability to use language for her own purposes also suggests that meaning isn't as stable as it might seem, that language admits play even though that play might be seen as wrong.

excess of meaning, Lennox stamps it as a problem of romance. But the transparency she assumes for the language of her own book is a mirage. It too spins out rich associations, proliferates beyond contained meanings: Lucy's solecism "solation" is also part of a larger undercurrent of the book's language—a metaphor of fire and light that continually asserts its illogical connections over the sense of a scene. For instance, Glanville, discussing the romances Arabella's father is about to burn, refers by-the-way to "that Incendiary *Statira*" (2.1.56), a connection that is hopelessly muddled when viewed causally but figuratively quite apt. Statira, in a sense, really does cause the flames, which are a reflection of and response to smoldering passions inside the romance.[20] And, like romance, this novel reduces associations to a startling literalness that also calls attention to its language. At one point, in the midst of wild wordplay about height—the drunken Glanville, "elevated with the Wine," is displeased at Arabella's pride; he "ris[es] up in a Passion, at seeing her again in her Altitudes"—Lennox's language comes abruptly back to earth; the scene changes to a more literal image of an elevated man: Miss Glanville warns that Glanville will be hanged and swinging from a gibbet if he follows Arabella's bloodthirsty romanticism (3.6.124–29). In both instances such wordplay takes place around images of persecution or constraint (the censored books and repressed passions, the importuned heroine and thwarted hero), suggesting the way the novel borrows a romantic vision of language in order to try to circumvent or ease moments of restriction.

The novel does ultimately endorse this vision, attesting to the power of language by attesting to the spoken word. Just as Arabella makes a firm distinction between being loved and being told she is loved, the novel itself also emphasizes the force of talking. Glanville, for instance, is able to counter Arabella's ravings with words of his own, to talk people into believing her sane (8.1.309). Similarly, he depends on the Countess for her words, trusting that "the Conversation of so admirable a Woman would be of the utmost use to *Arabella*" (8.5.323). And it is ultimately conversation

[20]This metaphor conventionally ties together fire and sexuality, as in Sir George's mock-romantic description of the (sexual) radiance of a fair one's charms kindling a reflected desire in himself (*FQ*.6.1.214). The Doctor also connects fire and sexuality (as well as violence). Romances "give new Fire to the Passions of Revenge and Love" (9.11.380). Seen in this light, Arabella's consuming interest—her "Glory"—is tacitly aligned with her sexuality.

that cures Arabella—the Doctor talks her out of her delusion at the end.[21] With this thematic underscoring of the power of language in its own story, the novel once again winds up confirming what it has initially criticized as romantic, preserving the wish that it encodes there.

III

The novel buttresses its genre distinctions with gender. It associates the dangers of romance with the sins of women and through this association attempts to clinch its derision of the form. Romance's faults—lack of restraint, irrationality, and silliness—are also women's faults. Fielding makes this connection in his review of *The Female Quixote,* in which he finds that novel better than Cervantes's because more credible. A woman *would* be drawn into romances:

> as we are to grant in both Performances, that the Head of a very sensible Person is entirely subverted by reading Romances, this Concession seems to me more easy to be granted in the Case of a young Lady than of an old Gentleman. . . . To say Truth, I make no Doubt but that most young Women . . . in the same Situation, and with the same Studies, would be able to make a large Progress in the same Follies.[22]

To Fielding, the strength of *The Female Quixote* is that it relates something not just about romance or Arabella but about women.[23] Genre and gender collapse into each other, by exposing romance, *The Female Quixote* exposes women:

> tho' the Humour of Romance, which is principally ridiculed in this Work, be not at present greatly in fashion in this Kingdom,

[21]For a fuller discussion of the role of conversation in this novel, see Leland E. Warren, "Of the Conversation of Women: *The Female Quixote* and the Dream of Perfection," in vol. 11 of *Studies in Eighteenth-Century Culture,* ed. Harry C. Payne (1982), pp. 367–80.

[22]Fielding, "*The Covent Garden Journal,*" 193.

[23]Fielding seems initially, in the passage quoted above, to be distinguishing between youth and age as much as between the sexes. He is nowhere in the review interested in young men, however, and his interest in young women reflects the assumption that, because their sexual histories are still open-ended (unlike those of married or fallen women), they have stories to be told.

our Author hath taken such Care throughout her Work, to expose
all those Vices and Follies in her Sex which are chiefly predominant in Our Days, that it will afford very useful Lessons to all
those young Ladies who will peruse it with proper Attention.[24]

In fact, what Fielding identifies as its relation to "those Vices and
Follies in her Sex" is what expressly underwrites romance as unre-
alistic and irrational. As Peggy Kamuf argues, "what a particular
society judges to be logical or probable is always bound up with a
prior determination of what is deemed proper."[25] Romance is associated with women and, as the pun on romance (a love affair)
suggests, with women's sexuality—a sexuality that, because it is
women's, is necessarily "improper," in the sense of the root of that
word: not her own or peculiar to her. Such sexuality is seen instead
as borrowed from men. And so Fielding calls it folly, because it is
ridiculous the way everything secondhand can be ridiculous, and
vice, because it is stolen and therefore illicit and dissipated.

The Female Quixote does in part agree with Fielding's reading; it
equates romance and women's sexuality by focusing on the im-
proprieties of romance, emphasizing how the wildness of romance
offends against sexual decorum. When Arabella asks the Countess
to narrate her adventures, the Countess is properly shocked at the
romantic term. She answers: "The Word Adventures carries in it so
free and licentious a Sound in the Apprehensions of People at this
Period of Time, that it can hardly with Propriety be apply'd to
those few and natural Incidents which compose the History of a
Woman of Honour" (*FQ*.8.7.327). The book affirms that the only
history or adventures a woman can have are sexual ones: when
Arabella *does* hear the adventures of other characters, as she does
about Miss Groves from her maid and about people at the ball from
Mr. Tinsel, what she hears is scandal. The sharp-eyed Miss Glanville points out that the madness romance has caused in Arabella is
definitely sexual. Arabella's romantic behavior is a way of "exposing" herself, of displaying sexual signs. Miss Glanville's jealous
solution is to keep Arabella not from romances but from men. She
observes "that it was a Pity there were not such Things as Protes-
tant Nunneries; giving it as her Opinion, that her Cousin ought to

---

24Fielding, *"The Covent Garden Journal,"* 194.
25Peggy Kamuf, "Writing Like a Woman," in *Women and Language in Literature and
Society,* ed. Sally McConnel-Ginet, Ruth Borker, and Nelly Furman (1980), 292.

be confin'd in one of those Places, and never suffer'd to see any Company, by which Means she would avoid exposing herself in the Manner she did now" (8.3.314). This sexual madness is set up as particularly dangerous. Although Arabella refrains from going to routs with Miss Glanville, romance prompts her to have routs of her own. She creates a scene in the gardens over a woman disguised as a man:

> Mr. *Glanville* almost mad with Vexation, endeavour'd to get *Arabella* away.
> Are you mad, Madam, said he in a Whisper, to make all this Rout about a Prostitute? (9.1.336)

While Miss Glanville indulges her sexuality in the carefully controlled world of London parties, the license of romance makes Arabella's indulgences extreme, links her with a prostitute. Her routs are cast as more than the consoling, appropriated domestications Miss Glanville enjoys; in Arabella's case, the hint of revolution seems back in the word; it implies the power of overthrow associated with any return of the repressed. The construction of romance as a realm of freedom is associated particularly with woman's freedom, the freedom of her sexuality, a freedom so extreme it becomes licentious.

On this level, Lennox seems to accept the derision of romance; her strategy is to separate Arabella from it, to educate her out of romance and disassociate her from its realm. This strategy lends itself to one kind of feminist reading, a kind outlined most clearly in *The Madwoman in the Attic*. There, although they never directly treat *The Female Quixote*, Sandra Gilbert and Susan Gubar accept the traditional derision of romance for much the same reason Lennox does: its negative effects on women through its obsession with love. Gilbert and Gubar argue that romance trivializes women because it reflects a male idea of them; to Gilbert and Gubar, all narrative structures mirror male desires, but romance is the worst offender and emblematizes the rest, because it is the most bankrupt and the one to which women have been especially relegated.[26] In this reading, Lennox would be the madwoman trapped in this male form; she cannot completely escape it, but she can

---

[26]See, for instance, their discussion of romance as "the prison of the male text" (44), "the glass coffin of romance" (68), and so on; Sandra M. Gilbert and Susan

critique it, stand outside it through parody. Gilbert and Gubar advocate a response to this trap that is similar to the one I have been charting—mocking romance in order to leave it behind. Educating Arabella out of romance becomes a symbol of Lennox's own struggle as a writer.

Yet, in *The Female Quixote*, the parallel between women and romance is so complete that a woman can't take herself out of romance without disappearing altogether. The text shows that Arabella's only escape from romance is to stop being a woman. Indeed, Arabella's association with women is tenuous throughout the book. Women are jealous of and reject her; men are attracted and sympathetic. The men view her identification with romance's heroines as something from which they must reclaim her, and that reclamation involves her complete identification with men. The reader is told that Arabella's romanticism reflects very badly on Glanville; he fears that her absurdity makes *him* ridiculous (3.3.116). Instead of casting light on him, he believes, she needs to become sane in order to be his reflection. At the end of the book, Arabella *is* inaugurated into man's realm and becomes indistinguishable from the men in it. She leaves romance by participating in the patriarchal discourse of moral law, and in that discussion loses her voice; her words become literally indistinguishable from those of the Doctor.

Arabella's education out of romance and absorption into the male realm may indeed represent Lennox's own movement; it certainly tallies with the biographical legend that has passed down about her. Her early critics, Austin Dobson and Miriam Rossiter Small, emphasize her contemporaries' feeling that she, too, was a man's woman. Small tells of a "feminine disapprobation which is steadily and impressively cumulative through her life."[27] And Dobson writes:

It is also stated, on the authority of Mrs. Thrale, that, although her books were admired, she herself was disliked. As regards her own sex, this may have been true; but it is dead against the evidence as regards the men . . .

Gubar, *The Madwoman in the Attic: The Woman Writer and the Nineteenth-Century Literary Imagination* (1979).

[27]Miriam Rossiter Small, *Charlotte Ramsay Lennox: An Eighteenth-Century Lady of Letters* (1935; 1969), 10.

A woman who could thus enlist the suffrage and secure the service of the four greatest writers of her day [Johnson, Richardson, Fielding, and Goldsmith] must have possessed exceptional powers of attraction, either mental or physical; and this of itself is almost sufficient to account for the lack of a corresponding enthusiasm in her own sex.[28]

Lennox was especially Dr. Johnson's favorite. Boswell quotes him: "I dined yesterday at Mrs. Garrick's, with Mrs. Carter, Miss Hannah More, and Miss Fanny Burney. Three such women are not to be found: I know not where I could find a fourth, except Mrs. Lennox, who is superior to them all."[29] The most complete story of her relation to Johnson comes from Sir John Hawkins's *Life* and concerns expressly her relation to writing as a male institution. After the publication of her first novel, Johnson held a party for Lennox in which he initiated her into the fraternity of male letters by crowning her with laurel.[30] Just as Arabella, once in this sphere, loses her voice, when Lennox calls on the male sphere in the penultimate chapter of *The Female Quixote*, so does she. Like Arabella's voice with the Doctor's, Lennox's blends with Dr. Johnson's, so much so that it is impossible to know who really wrote the chapter—but whether Dr. Johnson wrote it or whether he influenced a most faithful pastiche is immaterial. What is important is that Lennox herself, literally or figuratively, must disappear; despite the persistent dreams in the book of romantic freedom for women,

[28]Austin Dobson, *Eighteenth-Century Vignettes* (1892), 59, 60.

[29]James Boswell, vol. 4 of *Life of Johnson*, ed. George Birkbeck Hill, revised and enlarged by L. F. Powell, 6 vols. (1934–50), p. 275. The slightly ribald talk that follows this passage suggests that, talent notwithstanding (for Johnson quoted from Lennox under "talent" in *The Dictionary*), a woman's position (in male eyes) in regard to letters is always sexual: "BOSWELL. 'What! had you them all to yourself, Sir?' JOHNSON. 'I had them all as much as they were had; but it might have been better had there been more company there.'"

[30]Sir John Hawkins, *The Life of Samuel Johnson, LL.D.* (1787; rpt. as vol. 20 of *Johnsoniana*, 1974), pp. 286–87. The sexual undertones of a woman's relation to the male enclave of literature continue here. Johnson refers to Lennox's book as her "first literary child" (286) and Hawkins is mildly ashamed of the party "on the resemblance it bore to a debauch" (287). That a male order sexualizes every aspect of a woman's experience *The Female Quixote* bears out, for Glanville finds Arabella's very rationality titillating: "Mr. *Glanville* . . . fancied to himself the most ravishing Delight from conversing with his lovely Cousin, now recovered to the free Use of all her noble Powers of Reason" (*FQ*.9.11.382).

power and authority can enter the text only as a man. Only a man can dispel romance.

In *The Female Quixote*, there is a price for renouncing romance and acceding to male order. With Arabella's foreswearing of romance and her rehabilitation by the Doctor, the story—abruptly—ends. That the story must end with the end of romance is something the book has consistently foreshadowed. The reader learns, for instance, that Arabella prefers the heroines of romance to the women of her day because the heroines at least have a story to be told:

> What room, I pray you, does a Lady give for high and noble Adventures, who consumes her Days in Dressing, Dancing, listening to Songs, and ranging the Walks with People as thoughtless as herself? How mean and contemptible a Figure must a Life spent in such idle Amusements make in History? Or rather, Are not such Persons always buried in Oblivion, and can any Pen be found who would condescend to record such inconsiderable Actions? (7.9.279)

The insubstantial Countess confirms this conclusion; her presence in this book is only in proportion to how much she retains of the romances she once read. Unlike the adventures of heroines of romance, her unromantic story can be told in a very few words:

> And when I tell you . . . that I was born and christen'd, had a useful and proper Education, receiv'd the Addresses of my Lord—— through the Recommendation of my Parents, and marry'd him with their Consents and my own Inclination, and that since we have liv'd in great Harmony together, I have told you all the material Passages of my Life, which upon Enquiry you will find differ very little from those of other Women of the same Rank, who have a moderate Share of Sense, Prudence and Virtue. (8.7.327)

Arabella, with a moderate share of the same virtues, wishes for more of a story than this, and she recognizes the greatest curtailment of a woman's adventures in that other union with patriarchy, marriage. Lennox figures the effects of marriage on writing and women early in the novel. Book 3 ends with some of Arabella's words which forecast the end of the novel: explaining the laws of romance to Glanville, Arabella tells him that a heroine puts off marrying the hero about twenty years, for when "she at last condescends to reward him with her Hand . . . all her Adventures are at an End for the future" (3.8.138). This wishful romantic realm offers a dream in which women elude more than simple constraint; it allows them to dream of being able to elude the total feminine annihilation that makes any position for women already a coopted one, to inscribe female structures and stories into a male order that actually has no room for them. Curing woman of romance, rather than giving her voice as Gilbert and Gubar suggest, ends her story and ends *the* story.

In fact, the book suggests the conventions of romance are what might give women voice. Arabella, defending her romance expectations, asks Glanville:

> And may I not be carried into *Macedonia* by a Similitude of Destiny with that of a great many beautiful Princesses, who, though born in the most distant Quarters of the World, chanced to meet at one time in the City of *Alexandria,* and related their miraculous Adventures to each other?
>
> And it was for that very Purpose they met, Madam, said Mr. *Glanville,* smiling.
>
> Why, truly, said *Arabella,* it happened very luckily for each of them, that they were brought into a Place where they found so many illustrious Companions in Misfortune, to whom they might freely communicate their Adventures, which otherwise might, haply, have been concealed, or, at least, have been imperfectly delivered down to us. (7.3.261).

Glanville here is jesting with Arabella about how unreal romance conventions seem, how obviously they exist for their own sake, even in contradiction of the probable. But he suggests something else, too, something to which Arabella immediately responds— that the conventions of romance are important because they allow women to tell their stories, which are otherwise lost or altered. Beautiful princesses come together in Alexandria, spinning tales— with this image of a woman's convention establishing itself right at the library of antiquity, Lennox suggests how the collusion of romance and women could be a generative one, providing a meeting place for women, a ground from which they might at one time have spoken, from which they might sometime again finally speak.

The entire novel is about Arabella's conviction that romance would be an appropriate sphere for her. The reason it is attractive is because it is empowering, not imprisoning. No matter how much the novel travesties romance, it also presents romance as what gets Arabella out of the boredom and seclusion of her father's house, and when she abandons romance at the conventionally happy ending, she is trapped again, into marriage and submission. Ellen Moers has looked at the association of romance and female power; she suggests that women writers and readers see romance not as a male prison but as a woman's form and find in that recognition a source of feminism. It is *male* writers, reacting to the association of women and romance, who have degraded the form, identified its heroines as passive, and erotic in their passivity.[31] Nancy Miller, too, looks at the way women's fiction rejects the passivity and eroticism conventionally read into them. A repressed content underlies eroticism, a content with all the customary charge and evasiveness of an unconscious desire. Miller sees that content as "not erotic impulses, but an impulse to power: a fantasy of power that would revise the social grammar in which women are never defined as subjects; a fantasy of power that disdains a sexual exchange in which women can participate only as objects of circulation."[32] *The Female Quixote* quite clearly makes fun of romance's emphasis on the erotic. Not so clearly, however, it is compelled by an underlying emphasis on what Miller calls "disdain." Arabella is obsessed with the disdainful ladies, the lordly ladies, of romance not simply because she is obsessed with sex but because even more deeply she yearns for power. As Arabella's routs have illustrated, the association of women and romance touches on revolution, and it hints at a rebellion of the oppressed as well as the repressed, at women's ambitious as well as erotic fantasies. Lennox makes clear, however, that romance remains a fantasy, gestured to but never realized.

One part of the fantasy of romance is its emphasis on individual power, the will unchecked and omnipotent. For example, Arabella

---

[31]Ellen Moers, *Literary Women* (1976; 1985), 137.
[32]Nancy K. Miller, "Emphasis Added: Plots and Plausibilities in Women's Fiction," *PMLA* 96 (January 1981): 41.

tells of Artaban, "disposing the Destinies of Monarchs by his Will, and deciding the Fates of Empires by a single Word" (6.1.210). Arabella, who feels "I am not allowed any Will of my own" (1.11.43), is especially drawn to such a fantasy. What she most often cites from romance are instances of heroines' power—the preeminence of their every gesture, their absolute authority over their lovers, their mastery over life and death. The greatest threat to the heroine's power is the threat to her will that love poses—although love may seem to be the motive force in romance, its dangers are also very present; it is figured throughout romance as chains and fetters. Schooled by romance, Arabella's first thoughts of Glanville are that his "Aim was to take away her Liberty, either by obliging her to marry him, or by making her a Prisoner" (1.9.35). Instead of love being the sole business of romance, as the Doctor, spokesman for the male order, contends, it is at odds with the power Arabella craves, and her first impression of Glanville, although extravagant, shows how her ultimate love for him requires a painful submission of her will.

Female power is an issue from the opening of the novel—it is the Marquis's loss of power, his disgrace at court and subsequent withdrawal, that allows the story to begin. The Marquis indeed falls "Sacrifice to . . . Plots" (1.1.5), especially to the plot of this novel, which gets its impetus for its story about a woman from this symbolic diminution of male authority, an authority seen as exclusive, as precluding any woman's power. Although Arabella's first adventure, with Mr. Hervey, seems tacked on and unrelated to the Glanville plot, it is important precisely because it sets up this ratio of male/female power. Arabella's history begins with this adventure because in it she bests Hervey. Aware of his attraction to her, she deprives him of any erotic power, she forces him to surrender to her his "Hanger," his short sword, and with this symbolic castration can leave him at perfect liberty; instead of preying on her any more, he escapes to London in humiliation. Her triumph over Hervey confirms her as a heroine because with it she defeats the conventional male appropriations of women's stories: by humiliating Hervey, she is neither seduced by him nor marries him, and her story can continue. But such a story can proceed only through Lennox's mockery of it; it must be set up as something unnatural, a

disruption of the normal order. It finds a place in a male structure—a conventional marriage plot that ends with the male order
curbing and correcting what seem to be subversive impulses—
because it ultimately enables that structure, allows it emphatically
to reassert its power: at the end of the book, Arabella becomes a
willing cipher, no longer even sensing in Glanville the male domination so visible in Hervey or her father.

That father, the disgraced Marquis, is Lennox's wishful symbol
of an ailing patriarchy. Although he continues to exercise power as
a petty despot in his retreat, his main function in the novel is to be
ailing: he appears twice on his sickbed, and he is dead before a
quarter of the book is done. Almost all the other male characters
are also ailing: Hervey suffers from headaches; Glanville nearly
dies of a fever; midway through the novel Sir George has a violent
cold and at its end lies in danger from his wound. Although Lennox ridicules Arabella's romantic notion that she is responsible for
these illnesses, in a sense, of course, she really is; Lennox weakens
the men around Arabella in order to give her strength. Glanville,
for example, must sicken in order for Arabella to feel herself
powerful enough to risk admitting him as a lover. It is perhaps a
measure of Lennox's world that in her book female power can exist
only as a delusion;[33] only as long as Arabella sticks to her ineffec-
tual imitation of a romantic ideal and remains blind to the reality of
the novel can she have her own way. Significantly, to make her
abjure this power, Lennox must have Arabella herself eventually
sicken. The last scene of the book depicts the invalid Arabella
renouncing romance, as the rejuvenated men gather around her
bed. Women's power resides in delusion, and although Arabella's
madness does keep her world in an uproar—exposing the hidden
delusions that reside in and undo any seemingly fixed order and
logic, even the male order—such an uproar is only tenuous, provisional, prompting that order to reform itself even more rigidly.

One of the things male contemporaries of Lennox objected to
about female quixotes was their pride, which prompted disobe-

---

[33]Certainly, in the world of her book, the helplessness of women is starkly ren-
dered in a digression, in which the reader is casually told of the fate of Miss Groves's
second child—a girl. Mr. L——has simply disposed of it; how he will not say
(FQ.2.5.76).

dience to fathers and imperiousness with lovers. In a *Rambler* essay written shortly before *The Female Quixote*, Johnson depicts one Imperia:

> She had newly inherited a large fortune, and, having spent the early part of her life in the perusal of romances, brought with her into the gay world all the pride of Cleopatra; expected nothing less than vows, altars, and sacrifices; and thought her charms dishonoured, and her power infringed, by the softest opposition to her sentiments, or the smallest transgression of her commands.[34]

And to a contemporary reviewer of *The Female Quixote*, what is most objectionable about Arabella's romanticism is her pride, her "punishment of [what she considers] presumptuous lovers."[35] Women's pride is the subject of male attack in the novel as well. Arabella's pride is what especially wounds Mr. Glanville; he immediately leaves her when he finds her "haughty and contemptuous" (*FQ*.1.9.33). Arabella's pride hurts him because it mortifies his own; it is unbearable because it usurps a male prerogative, a male assumption of power.

The Amazons of romance come up again and again in *The Female Quixote* and become the symbol for women's usurpation of men's power. Their repeated mention suggests that both Lennox and Arabella find them attractive and noteworthy; conversely, they are what men in the story find most farfetched about romance. Glanville dismisses the hero Orontes's battle with Thalestris the Amazon with "I supposed he scorned to draw his Sword upon a Woman: That would have been a Shame indeed" (3.6.125). Sir Charles later concurs: "O shameful! cried Sir *Charles*, offer a Woman the Command of an Army! Brave Fellows indeed, that would be commanded by a Woman!" (5.6.205). The shame that both men emphasize is sexual; to them, the only way women can share in conventional male strength is by emasculating men. They find the Amazons farfetched because they are threatening. Miss Glanville, wanting to

---

[34]Samuel Johnson, "*Rambler*, No. 115," in *The Rambler*, vol. 4 of *The Yale Edition of the Works of Samuel Johnson*, ed. Walter Jackson Bate and Albrecht B. Strauss, 15 vols. to date (1969–), p. 252.

[35]Unsigned review of *The Female Quixote*, *Monthly Review* 6 (April 1752): 255.

expose Arabella's romantic delusions, knows the most damning way to do so is through a reference to the Amazons, for they point out the battle of gender underlying the battle of genre. Hoping to embarrass Arabella before the men, Miss Glanville asks "Whether in former times Women went to the Wars, and fought like Men?" (5.6.204). And it is this Amazonian power that Arabella, to a degree, inherits from romance: her refutation of the false pedant, Mr. Selvin, is comic because founded on the lies of romance rather than the facts of history. But the readers' sympathy in this context is mostly with Arabella, our laughter at Selvin's expense; the reader is meant to enjoy "the Shame he conceived at seeing himself posed by a Girl, in a Matter which so immediately belonged to him" (7.5.265). This battle of words is the closest Arabella gets to an Amazonian rout. Yet it suggests that Lennox too sets up women's power as whatever they can seize of the matter properly belonging to men. Her own battle of words in attempting to find a woman's form simply engages with and tries to operate within male literary structures.

Arabella's romances are an inheritance from her mother. Such an inheritance seems to be an indictment of women; in the innocent retreat the Marquis has tried to provide, corrupt culture and sexuality intrude through the (even absent) mother; it is she who introduces Arabella into the realm of language and convention through the romances she passes down to her daughter. But underlying this indictment is a wistful picture of romance as a women's form, providing a bond between women. The depiction of the Countess—Arabella's surrogate mother—grows out of this same longing. When Arabella talks to the Countess, it seems surprising to realize that she simply hasn't had anyone to whom she could really *talk* (which also explains Lucy's importance to her). She and the Countess can understand each other because they have both read romance; it gives them a common language. In this bond between Arabella and the Countess, Lennox's mockery of romance disappears. For a moment she explicitly values romance: Arabella and the Countess, alike because they have read romance, are also similar paragons of virtue. Those outside the influence of romance, like Miss Glanville and the women of London, are empty-headed, selfish, and ordinary.

Yet Lennox's positive alignment of women and romance is wistful because she recognizes how tenuous that position is. Her treatment of romance reflects her feelings about the possibilities of the novel. By locating a women's form in romance, she is placing it in what her form, the novel, cannot admit and so casts out. This placement recognizes that women have no real place, and Lennox's novel figures their ostracism repeatedly: women precursors are largely absent—Arabella's mother is dead, the Countess almost immediately leaves her, called away by her own mother's "Indis-position" (8.8.330) (from the Latin, the state of placelessness), and the literary precursors Lennox calls on are all male: Young, Rich-ardson, Johnson. Not only are women exiled to romance, but even that possibility, when not derided, is appropriated by patriarchy: when the book opens, the Marquis has taken his wife's romances out of her closet and put them in his library; the writers of ro-mance, Calprenade and de Scudéry, are men;[36] even though Len-nox herself makes up a romance in this novel, she puts it into the mouth of Sir George.

The Female Quixote needs romance to set itself up as a novel, but, when prodded, romance deconstructs and merges into the novel. Gender categories in the book are just as shifting and soluble. The novel uses romance to try to stabilize gender—in romance, women are beautiful and men are brave—but the world of the novel shows that formula is too simple. When attempting to apply it, Arabella is especially posed by fops like Tinsel: "Nor can I persuade myself, added she, that any of those Men whom I saw at the Assembly, with Figures so feminine, Voices so soft, such tripping Steps, and unmeaning Gestures, have ever signalized either their Courage or Constancy" (*FQ*.7.9.279).[37] What is troubling about such men is that they tamper with sexual definitions; their attention to beauty gives them the affect of women. By ignoring sexual rules they also subvert the power structure; they seem to take on the inconsidera-ble status of women. Arabella goes on to say that "such Trifles are

[36]De Scudéry was, of course, a woman, but she believed it necessary to assume a male persona as a writer. She pretended her books were her brother's, and Lennox believed her.

[37]Arabella also meets masculine women—interestingly, they are the overtly sexu-al women she meets: Miss Groves is "masculine" (*FQ*.2.5.71), and the prostitute is dressed in man's clothing (9.1.334–39). Lennox's alignment of these two qualities underwrites her recognition that in the status quo sexuality is structurally masculine.

below the Consideration of a Man" (7.9.280). But what is more troubling is that, stripped of conventional gender markers, such men ultimately can't be read—their gestures are "unmeaning," they no longer "signalize"—and by being outside Arabella's signifying grammar, they call it into question.[38] They suggest the ways the male order is itself a problematic category. Precisely because it is not monolithic or totalizing, it needs to use women to assert its integrity, to ventriloquize through them its assumption of order.

Although romance seems to provide clear-cut gender distinctions, as the Amazons demonstrate, those distinctions aren't really fixed—women go to war, men think only of love, Orontes even unabashedly dresses up as a woman (FQ.2.5.72). Sir George's romance also feminizes him, not just because Glanville and Sir Charles see it as unmanly, but because he takes on conventional female gestures in it—for instance, he swoons in his story at least three times (6.5.232, 236; 6.10.247). And the effect of romance on Arabella's sexual image is contradictory. On the one hand, the effect goes against what is seen as the very essence of woman, who should be silent, submissive, invisible. Arabella believes instead that a lady's reputation depends "upon the Noise and Bustle she makes in the World" (3.6.128). But, on the other hand, that effect makes her especially womanly, not just because it allows her to play up her sexual attractions, but because its influence distinguishes her as the best of women. The relation of romance to the dominant order remains double: although the fantasy of romance supports it, romance also gestures to an autonomous realm outside that order, in an oscillation ever prompting new defenses.

Whether Lennox is emphasizing the link between romance and women's sexuality or romance and women's power, the structural parallel between romance and women remains. Each is the name for qualities the status quo finds transgressive and threatening, and attempts to dispel by projecting into a separate genre or gender. By doing so, the novel or patriarchy shores up its stability, emphasizes its boundaries—romance and women are in the no-novel's no-man's land outside; their very exile is what gives the others shape. Yet such distinctions are consoling fictions. Women

[38]The signifying agent of Arabella's grammar is herself. Her nonverbal signs, for example, reflect her fantasy of an absolutely transparent language, given meaning by her desires.

and romance also collapse back into the male order, repeating and confirming it. What *The Female Quixote* ultimately shows is not what romance is and how the novel differs from it, or what woman is and how the male order is opposed to her. Lennox uses romance to try to imagine some realm of freedom for women outside the constraints of male power. As the next chapters will demonstrate, what remains basic to women and romance as categories in a system of power relations is the way they are used to try to gesture to this unfigurable realm.

3

An Early Romance: The Ideology of the
Body in Mary Wollstonecraft's Writing

Like *The Female Quixote*, Mary Wollstonecraft's fiction has an ambivalent and uncertain relation to romance. On the one hand, her novels set up romance as what they especially, as women's work, must transcend; on the other, her work redefines the romantic as what might unsettle or elude the control of the male order. For Wollstonecraft, the very difference within the term itself reflects one of the problems of difference: whether such uncertainty unsettles or conserves, whether romance can provide (or even gesture to) an alternative to the world of the novel or can only repeat that world. Wollstonecraft's fiction, like Lennox's novel, does not solve this problem; what distinguishes between these two women writers is that, while Lennox's work emphasizes the necessary illusions of romance, Wollstonecraft's work instead investigates the price paid when the figure of the woman becomes the site for these double binds.

I

Let me begin this chapter with a gossipy anecdote about Matthew Gregory Lewis that Mrs. Oliphant tells in her *Literary History*. Lewis, you remember, was the author of that scandalous romance *The Monk* (1795). Yet the scandal Mrs. Oliphant recounts is not about *The Monk* at all, but quite other. After *The Monk* was published: "The family history of the Lewises [she writes] was . . . disturbed by an incident which plunged them into unimaginable

93

terror. . . . [The mother] wrote a novel! When this terrible fact was known, her son, with a panic almost beyond words, rushed to pen and ink, to implore her to suppress it."[1] Lewis warns his mother of the injuries publication of her novel would cause: his father would be shattered, his unmarried sister left an old maid, his married sister disgraced in her husband's family, and Lewis himself would have to flee to the Continent. Mrs. Oliphant suggests that Lewis objects to his mother's authorship because he fears it would coopt his own. He hears rumors that *she* has written *The Monk* and writes, "This goes more to put me out of humour with the book" than the critics' fury over it.[2] But authorship is not alone at risk; Lewis fears his mother's writing would threaten her identity as a mother, and his own as her son (Oliphant depicts Lewis, in fact, as a mama's boy, whose relationship to his mother is central to his life). "I always consider a female author as a sort of half-man,"[3] Lewis writes to his mother, and his attempt to suppress her novel becomes an effort to avoid the gender uncertainties into which her writing would cast him: what would it mean if one's mother were half-man?

I present Monk Lewis here as an extreme example of a pervasive attitude. Although he is contemporary with Mary Wollstonecraft, he represents a view that is more than just locally and historically bound—more than the quaint prejudice of a certain class of the eighteenth-century that Oliphant, herself a famous nineteenth-century writing mother, attempts (but too overdeterminedly) to argue that it is. Rather, this view points up some enduring structures of the unconscious and writing. That the greatest horror Monk Lewis could imagine was his mother writing provides the background for the discussion in this chapter of romance and women's writing. As a consideration of the relation between women and writing in Wollstonecraft's novels will suggest, such fears have to do with the horrors of uncertainty. A figure for this horror, woman in Wollstonecraft's fiction gets caught in a series of double binds—between novel and romance, motherhood and prostitution—that write themselves over her in an attempt to resolve

---

[1]Margaret Oliphant, vol. 3 of *The Literary History of England in the End of the Eighteenth and the Beginning of the Nineteenth Century*, 3 vols. (1882), pp. 167–68.
[2]Oliphant, *Literary History*, 3: 169.
[3]Oliphant, *Literary History*, 3: 169.

themselves, to find a bridge for their uncertainties, but instead only mark her with this horror.

How do motherhood and women's writing figure in Mary Wollstonecraft's work? Certainly in her novels—*Mary, A Fiction* (published in 1788) and *The Wrongs of Woman: or, Maria, A Fragment* (1798)—Wollstonecraft presents those two rarities of fiction— mothers and women writers—side by side. *Mary* opens with the story of the title character's mother; *The Wrongs of Woman* tells of Maria's mother, among others, and Maria's own motherhood is the focus of its story. Mary and Maria both write, and their lyrical effusions, as well as Maria's extended autobiographical narrative, are included in the texts.

Wollstonecraft's views on the problems of women's writing have seemed to her critics to appear most clearly through her treatment of romance. Mary Poovey argues that Wollstonecraft's novels set out to critique "romantic expectations" but get caught in romance despite themselves.[4] Poovey condemns this collapse of Wollstone- craft's novels into romance because of its ultimate effect: by suc- cumbing to romance, Wollstonecraft's novels fall into the pa- triarchal traps that Poovey thinks she is able to escape in *A Vindication of the Rights of Woman* (published in 1792, it falls in between the two novels). "Finally," Poovey writes, "[in her nov- els] . . . what Wollstonecraft really wants is to achieve a new posi- tion of dependence within a paternal order of her own choosing."[5]

I read Wollstonecraft's treatment of romance differently: I see romance aligned not with the paternal but with the maternal. Wollstonecraft explicitly thematizes this association in *The Wrongs of Woman*. She moves literally from what has come to be called the Name of the Father to the Name of the Mother by repeating, but significantly altering, a scene. Midway through her story, Maria, whose husband has stolen her baby, recounts the separation of a parent and child—in this case, an infant son, who lisps "Papa" to an absent father.[6] Yet one ending of the unfinished *Wrongs of Wom- an* closes Maria's story with the restoration of her baby daughter,

[4]Mary Poovey, *The Proper Lady and the Woman Writer: Ideology as Style in the Works of Mary Wollstonecraft, Mary Shelley, and Jane Austen* (1984), 98.

[5]Poovey, *The Proper Lady*, 67.

[6]Mary Wollstonecraft, *The Wrongs of Woman; or, Maria, A Fragment*, in *Mary and the Wrongs of Woman*, ed. James Kinsley and Gary Kelly (1976), ch. 7, p. 131. All further references to this novel (hereafter abbreviated WW) will appear in the text.

who utters instead "the word 'Mamma!'" (*WW*.Conclusion.203). In Wollstonecraft's fiction, mothers and daughters supplant fathers and sons. In this romantic ending (romantic in the traditional sense that it unrealistically fulfills a wish) mothers and daughters enjoy a union and happiness denied the men. Wollstonecraft goes on in her novels to link the maternal with romance even more securely, drawing on more senses of romance than just this traditional one. Yet we as readers still need to ask whether doing so makes any difference at all, especially for the woman writer.

In order to answer that question, I shall consider the other senses of the word "romance" that inform Wollstonecraft's collusion of the maternal and women's writing. Women as writers are linked to romance in another traditional sense of the term. Everyone is familiar, I think, with a common usage of the word "romance": immature writing, lacking the novel's complexity of form and sophistication of content—in its most generous usage, pure, artless, simple, naive writing. Traditional—especially eighteenth-century—constructions of *women* sound very similar to this sense of romance: women are immature too, which makes them at best pure, artless, simple, and naive. As *The Female Quixote* has shown, this is one reason why romance as a form is usually considered proper to women; it is all that they are fitted to read or write.

On one level, Wollstonecraft seems to accept this equation between women and romance, and the derision it implies. Writing as an anonymous reviewer—presumably male—for the *Analytical Review*, she several times accounts for books that are "romantic unnatural fabrication[s]," as she calls them, marred both by bad writing and inexperience of life, by attributing them to the pen of "a *very* young lady."[7] She also distinguishes between romances and a different, better form, the novel, writing tongue-in-cheek of one "insipid, harmless production" that "we should have termed this a romance, if it had not been called a Novel in the title page."[8]

Yet Wollstonecraft does not consistently accept the traditional definition of woman, or of romance. In *A Vindication of the Rights of*

---

[7]Review of *The Cottage of Friendship: A Legendary Pastoral*, By Silvania Pastorella, in *A Wollstonecraft Anthology*, ed. Janet Todd (1977), 223; see also Wollstonecraft's ironic deflation of another "*very* young lady" in her Review of *The Vicar of Lansdowne; or, Country Quarters, A Tale*, By Maria Regina Dalton (in Todd, *Wollstonecraft Anthology*, 221), and her query, "Why will young misses presume to write?" in her Review of *The Fair Hibernian* (Todd, *Wollstonecraft Anthology*, 224–25).

[8]Review of *Albertina: A Novel*, in Todd, *Wollstonecraft Anthology*, 224.

Woman, she radically redefines woman, especially in relation to traditional assumptions about her maturity. Men treat women as if "they were in a state of perpetual childhood,"[9] and confuse that state with "innocence" (*VRW*.4.153). Yet innocence is a "specious name" for ignorance, an enforced ignorance that is the cause of women's ills (2.100): they are not naturally childish; they are kept that way to bar them from a better state. After exposing this male sophistry that confuses and enslaves them, Wollstonecraft offers women a way to redefine themselves. She substitutes for the innocence they have been urged to cultivate its very opposite, "the treasure of life, experience" (2.114).

For Wollstonecraft, experience in general means education and exposure to the vicissitudes of life, a position of knowledge if not of mastery. But, more than that, the experience she values—the experience that the male authorities she criticizes in *A Vindication* think is implied in any other, which is why they feel women must be kept ignorant/innocent—is especially sexual experience. In *The Wrongs of Woman*, Wollstonecraft suggests that "freedom of conduct has emancipated many women's minds" (*WW*.10.156), and it is her advocacy of women's sexual experience that immediately made her an anathema to an enduring critical tradition. Wollstonecraft argues that ignorance never equals sexual innocence: women barred from direct experience are actually the most corrupt for they debauch their minds reading romances (as Mary's mother is in danger of doing[10]), while the maid who falls can still remain mentally pure (*VRW*.8.241). Granting women sexual—bodily—experience is a way of protecting them from imaginative impurity, from the contagion of romance. In this interest, Wollstonecraft dispels the myth of woman's essential ignorance and immaturity in order to dissolve her seemingly natural connection to ignorant, immature romance.

In the development of her own fiction Wollstonecraft seems deliberately to move beyond romance. In its very opening, *The Wrongs of Woman*—meant as a novelistic continuation of *A Vindica-*

[9]Mary Wollstonecraft, Author's Introduction, *A Vindication of the Rights of Woman,* ed. Miriam Brody Kramnick (1975), 81. All further references to this book (hereafter abbreviated *VRW*) will appear in the text.

[10]Mary Wollstonecraft, *Mary, A Fiction* in *Mary and the Wrongs of Woman*, ed. Kinsley and Kelly, ch. 1, pp. 2–3. All further references to this novel (hereafter abbreviated *M*) will appear in the text.

tion[11]—proclaims itself an antiromance: Maria is in a madhouse, a place that is really horrible, not some silly haunted castle of "romantic fancy" (WW.1.75). This comparison is particularly telling, for Wollstonecraft's own less experienced work, her first novel, *Mary*, written before *A Vindication*, has just such a castle, where its heroine loves to go and muse (M.4.9). Wollstonecraft seems aware that this first work is immature, naïve—traditionally romantic. Although in her preface to *The Wrongs of Woman* she deliberately calls it a novel (WW.73), the editors of the Oxford edition of *Mary* point out that "both title and preface [of that book] . . . carefully avoid the word novel"[12]—no proclaiming a romance a novel in the title page for Wollstonecraft. While writing *The Wrongs of Woman*, Wollstonecraft admits in a letter that *Mary* is "a crude production . . . an imperfect sketch,"[13] and Emily Sunstein, in her biography of Wollstonecraft, *A Different Face*, speaks for the majority of critics who indeed find *Mary* a "sentimental romance."[14]

As a novel, *The Wrongs of Woman* seems to take up where the romance, *Mary*, leaves off; Maria's situation critiques the deluded naïveté of the earlier heroine. Whereas *Mary* ends with the heroine living with her husband, *The Wrongs of Woman* opens with a heroine who has broken away from hers. Maria is older, savvy, and worldly-wise in a way Mary never is: Mary never sleeps with her lover, for instance, while Maria does. Wollstonecraft inscribes the triumph of experience over romance into the very plot of *The Wrongs of Woman*. As a wife, Maria has been treated as an "idiot, or perpetual minor" (WW.11.159) to the extent that her husband has wrongly imprisoned her in the madhouse, kidnapped their daughter, and stolen her inheritance. In order to oppose the view of women that makes such treatment seem right and natural, Wollstonecraft has Maria write a narrative of her life, a story of her own painful road to experience, in which she sheds traditional—"romantic" as she calls them (7.128)— notions of her duties and abilities as a woman. Maria writes in order to aid and instruct her daughter, to help her also "gain experience— ah! gain it—" (7.124).

Maria's book takes the place of—in fact, becomes—the experi-

[11]Kinsley and Kelly, Introduction, *Mary and the Wrongs of Woman*, xvi.
[12]Kinsley and Kelly, Introduction, ix.
[13]"To Everina Wollstonecraft, March 22d [1797]," in *Collected Letters of Mary Wollstonecraft*, ed. Ralph M. Wardle (1979), 385.
[14]Emily W. Sunstein, *A Different Face: The Life of Mary Wollstonecraft* (1975), 153.

ence she wishes to hand on to her daughter. By making Maria a writer, and collapsing her text and her experience, Wollstonecraft underscores her new—unromantic—view of the possibilities for women's writing. The depiction of Maria necessarily reflects on Wollstonecraft as a woman writer: through Maria, she bolsters her own position as experienced—a position she certainly takes in *A Vindication*—passing that legacy through her writing on to her readers, who fill in the place of Maria's lost daughter.

Where does motherhood fit into all this? For Wollstonecraft, maternity is crucially linked to women's sexual experience—maternity is sexuality's sign, what makes it manifest: the sexually experienced Maria is definitely a mother, though Mary never is. And Maria's (sexual) experience, which leads to her maternity, collapses into it, and becomes what enables her writing. Maria is a much more experienced and accomplished writer than Mary (she can give us a complete narrative rather than just Mary's fragments) partly because she is a mother. Maria's maternity provides the ability and occasion for writing: she writes to pass along her experience. But she also writes to maintain her very identity as a mother: she dedicates her narrative to her daughter, apostrophizing her in it, as an attempt to secure her (for that daughter may actually be dead, and Maria no longer a mother). Motherhood is not only the emblem of the woman writer in Wollstonecraft; Maria may be a mother only *while* she is writing.

Yet the mother, through her connection with writing, does not only move beyond romance in Wollstonecraft's fiction. The titles of her novels, by their repetition of variants of "Mary" (Wollstonecraft's own name, of course, as well as the name of the most renowned mother in European culture), suggest a continuity as well as a contrast between the books. While working on *The Wrongs of Woman*, Wollstonecraft, responding to her lover William Godwin's accusation of a "radical defect" in her writing, acknowledges an "original defect" in her mind, a sort of mother defect—a tendency toward romance.[15]

---

[15]For the defect in her writing, see "To William Godwin, [London] Sunday Morning [September 4, 1796]," in *Collected Letters*, 345. For the defect in her mind, see "To William Godwin, [London] Saturday Morning [May 21, 1797]," in *Collected Letters*, 394. The pertinent text there reads: "There is certainly an original defect in my mind—for the cruelest experience will not eradicate the foolish tendency I have to cherish, and expect to meet with, romantic tenderness."

Romance does invade *The Wrongs of Woman* as much as it invades *Mary*. Maria, like Mary, is romantic: she confesses to her daughter peculiarities of temperament "which by the world are indefinitely termed romantic" (WW.7.128). In *The Wrongs of Woman*, it is the world surrounding Maria, particularly her husband, who more often than the narrative itself denounces Maria's romance (11.161; 12.167, 169). Because it is Maria's brutish husband who dismisses as romantic all of her best qualities—Maria notes that "romantic sentiments . . . was the indiscriminate epithet he gave to every mode of conduct or thinking superior to his own" (12.167)—romance also becomes a sign of the narrative's approbation.

This instability in the attitude toward romance in Wollstonecraft's writing grows out of an instability within the term itself. Wollstonecraft elsewhere writes of "romantic wavering feelings"; she collapses the "romantic and inconstant" (VRW.4.169). Romance takes on a new meaning, aligned with those qualities of indeterminacy; it comes to stand for instability itself and hence becomes what Wollstonecraft calls "tantamount to nonsensical."[16] Romance as nonsense becomes a valorized term in Wollstonecraft's novels, one associated, as is its more traditional and derisive meaning, with the maternal. Wollstonecraft directly connects the romantic and nonsensical, for example, in her own paean to the imagination: the "mother of sentiment."[17] Although romance and motherhood can stand opposed—the mother, through her experience, breaking away from the romantic—within this second sense the two are inseparable. This connection again leads away from experience: Wollstonecraft insisted on keeping her inexperienced "romantic" feelings in the face of the wiser experience and "judgment" of her first lover—Gilbert Imlay—because "they resemble the mother more than the father"[18]—that is, experience and judgment come more from the imagination, the province of romance she has earlier criticized.

Romance, nonsense, motherhood, and immaturity: to understand their connection in Wollstonecraft's writing we need for a moment to consider these terms in another context, for they also demarcate the category of the semiotic in the early writings of the psychoanalytic theorist Julia Kristeva. The semiotic is Kristeva's

[16]"To Gilbert Imlay, [Paris] September 22 [1794]," in *Collected Letters*, 263.
[17]"To Gilbert Imlay, [Paris] September 22 [1794]," in *Collected Letters*, 263.
[18]"To Gilbert Imlay, [Le Havre] August 17 [1794]," in *Collected Letters*, 258–59.

own move from the Name of the Father to the Mother; as Mary Jacobus argues, Kristeva substitutes the pre-Oedipal mother for the Oedipal father in terms of their relation to the origins of discourse.[19] In *Desire in Language*, Kristeva yokes and opposes the semiotic to the symbolic. Kristeva's symbolic we can understand largely in Lacan's terms; she links it to meaning, signification, representation, the location of sense and of the subject, the entry into language brought about through the agency of the father and the threat of castration. The semiotic is impossibly, but necessarily, outside meaning and subjectivity, calling them into question (it is heterogeneous to signification, operates "through, despite, and in excess of it," and comes before or is outside of "the operating consciousness" of the subject created by the symbolic order[20]). Kristeva gestures to the impossible place of the semiotic by aligning it with (fantasies of) the pre-Oedipal: with immature archaic expression, "uncertain and indeterminate articulation," with the utterances of infants, and particularly with what she calls the maternal chora—the maternal body and its responses to the infant, which embody this antirepresentational, disruptive dimension[21] (a dimension in which the literary critic Dianne Sadoff places that formless and undifferentiated realm that we call "in narrative terminology, the romance"[22]).

---

[19]Mary Jacobus, *Reading Woman: Essays in Feminist Criticism* (1986), 145.

[20]Julia Kristeva, *Desire in Language: A Semiotic Approach to Literature and Art*, ed. Leon S. Roudiez, trans. Thomas Gora, Alice Jardine, and Leon S. Roudiez (1980), 133.

[21]Kristeva, *Desire in Language*, 133. Jane Gallop, in her "The Phallic Mother: Fraudian Analysis" (*The Daughter's Seduction: Feminism and Psychoanalysis* [1982], 113–31), may be right in implying that the pre-Oedipal position is not just a fantasy for Kristeva but always *risks* becoming a developmental fact that seems to offer the mother as a solution to gender problems, as it does in the object-relations psychology on which Kristeva sometimes relies. For a discussion of the political effects of this and other elements in Kristeva's thought, see Jennifer Stone, "The Horrors of Power: A Critique of 'Kristeva,'" in *The Politics of Theory: Proceedings of the 1982 Essex Conference*, ed. Frances Barker, Peter Hulme, Margaret Iversen, Diana Loxley (1983), 38–48; Ann Rosalind Jones, "Julia Kristeva on Femininity: The Limits of a Semiotic Politics," *Feminist Review* 18 (November 1984): 56–73; Domna C. Stanton, "Difference on Trial: A Critique of the Maternal Metaphor in Cixous, Irigaray, and Kristeva," in *The Poetics of Gender*, ed. Nancy K. Miller (1986), 157–82; and Jacqueline Rose, "Julia Kristeva—Take Two," in her *Sexuality in the Field of Vision* (1986), 141–64. Rose argues that the semiotic is actually the least useful of Kristeva's categories; its problem is that it lends itself so easily to the kind of essentialism that this chapter explores, seeming to collapse woman/mother/body.

[22]Dianne F. Sadoff, *Monsters of Affection: Dickens, Eliot and Brontë on Fatherhood* (1982), 124.

Jane Gallop does a canny, perverse, and, I think, sometimes incorrect reading of the problems of Kristeva's semiotic, the dangers of collapsing it with the maternal, of believing the mother controls it.[23] Richard Klein, on the other hand, suggests—and I agree with him—that Kristeva actually constructs the maternal precisely around the very splitting, the doubleness of identity that Gallop argues it totalizes.[24] Perhaps this doubleness will become clearer in a moment if I examine the semiotic in Wollstonecraft's writing as just one aspect of the mother, who is at the same time opposed to that character of herself.

Motherhood is associated with semiotic forces in *The Wrongs of Woman* from the start of the book, which opens with Maria confined within the madhouse. Her confinement there figures that other confinement, childbirth: Maria's imprisonment in the madhouse is the direct result of the birth of her daughter, heir to the fortune her husband wishes to possess. Similarly, another inmate, and fellow female artist, the "lovely warbler" whose songs Maria admires, underscores this interrelation of meanings: she has gone mad "during her first lying-in" (*WW*.2.88), as Wollstonecraft's own sister may have done. The madhouse figures the non-sense of the maternal chora, quite literally in the babble of the mad, "the burden of . . . incessant ravings" (2.84) that is the constant background to Maria's story. The narrator likens Maria's situation to being "in a strange land, where the human voice conveys no information to the eager ear" (2.86), and Maria's ordering of her life in her autobiography is in reaction to, but called into question by, the linguistic chaos surrounding her. When the novel directly associates the breakdown of language and shattering of meaning with the maternal, its effects remain disruptive of order but can be rapturous as well as threatening: Maria's fervent observations on maternity "interrupt" her narrative (10.154), and those observations are so fervent because her pleasure in being a mother is "unutterable" (10.154).

Moreover, the mother is marked within Wollstonecraft's fiction not just through her presence but also through her absence. For although Wollstonecraft gestures to the mother more than is usual

[23]Gallop, *The Daughter's Seduction*, 124.
[24]Richard Klein, "In the Body of the Mother," *Enclitic* 7 (Spring 1983): 70.

in fiction, the maternal space remains curiously vacant too. In describing Mary's mother, the narrator refers to her as a "mere nothing," one of the female "noughts" (*M*.1.2), and that is the position mothers occupy throughout Wollstonecraft's work: Maria's mother becomes important when she dies, and Maria's own motherhood is posited but never realized in her novel—her daughter almost immediately disappears and their time together is only a blank in the text. The mother is shadowy, not completely represented, because her place is outside the signifying order, unrepresentable.

Interruption, partial representation, becomes a narrative principle in the novel; *The Wrongs of Woman* is itself nonsensical, interrupted by violence as well as rapture, especially at its end, which is particularly fragmented, almost meaningless. In place of closure, Wollstonecraft presents competing and contradictory stories, most of which revolve around Maria's response to a new pregnancy (Wollstonecraft was herself pregnant again at the time and died shortly after giving birth). Such semiotic forces would indeed represent for a male critic a romantic "defect" in the woman writer, and in two senses: *de*fect's sense of lack—the lack of sense in her writing, the nonsense of its language (Godwin particularly criticized Wollstonecraft's lack of control over language, her problems with grammar), playing on what a man would see as Wollstonecraft's own essential lack as a woman writer—and also de*fect's* sense of desertion—the woman writer leaving the rank and file of the male (symbolic) order. In her preface to *The Wrongs of Woman*, Wollstonecraft emphasizes that the situation of maternity is the vehicle for such writing: she contrasts her book to ones in which maternity is bypassed altogether—male writing, books (perhaps by Richardson and Rousseau, from whom she distinguishes herself in the advertisement to *Mary*) that treat their heroines as if they had "just come forth highly finished Minervas from the head of Jove" (*WW*.73). Wollstonecraft's novel, on the other hand, is the product of a woman, and one that she suggests is fully formed in the rather formless state we receive it—she warns her readers against dismissing it as a mere sketch, as "the abortion of a distempered fancy" (73).

In Wollstonecraft's writing, then, the mother is double. She is both outside and inside romance: in command of language even to speaking new terms for her own self-definition, to breaking with the ignorance and immaturity of romance, and at the same time subverting the order and meaning of language, partaking of the romance of the infantile and unutterable.

At the beginning of this chapter, I questioned whether it made any difference for the woman writer to write under the Name of the Father or the Mother, to relocate the romantic with the maternal. The terms of my question, I think, provide for its answer, for *difference* is what is crucial, the mother's difference from herself; her connection with romance exposes that the mother in Wollstonecraft is both experienced and an inhabitant of a realm in which experience is meaningless. She is both the one who knows—the one Gallop calls the phallic mother—and the one outside of and undercutting knowledge—the maternal chora.

This self-division extends and dissolves the very category of Name: of language, and of writing. By moving from the father to the mother, we emphasize that naming, language, is not just the function of the transcendental signifier, the phallus, but also of the undertones and side-effects of signification—its babble and noise—that won't leave it alone, that call it into question. And the category of the mother, alternatively fixed and undercutting itself, is created by and reflects this very movement. The mother actually is what Monk Lewis fears—she is half man, partially constituted as a subject, within mastery and language. Maria's desire "to be a father, as well as a mother" (*WW*.13.180) to her daughter suggests Wollstonecraft's recognition of her double role. Locating the woman writer with motherhood, difference, and division allows her to make sense—and nonsense—within the paternal order, to work within it without completely accepting its rule. And that, I think, makes all the difference.

Directing my argument about the mother is what has become a standard critical move: the maternal is that which threatens a system of power—patriarchy or representation—and is cast out accordingly. Her absence shores up the system. And yet that system can never dispatch her because she is part of it. Or rather, I've made that system part of the maternal, relocating this play of difference within the mother—she is what is subverted as well as what subverts. But I want to push my argument a little further by asking, why the mother? What might be involved in using her as an emblem of difference, and what might be the problems of doing so? One objection might be that locating difference within the mother is a regressive fantasy of plenitude that actually collapses difference: she becomes the Mother who is—and therefore has—everything, a new appearance of an old friend, the Phallic Mother, and once again gets aligned with sameness, with the phallus. I'm intrigued by the collapse of difference implied in conjuring it, and would like to follow it, to get to the same place along a different route, by raising another objection we could make to the use of the maternal.

For isn't examining a text in terms of the category of the mother also a regression to a dangerous essentialism that feminist critics have been trying hard to avoid? Doesn't recourse to the mother simply collapse the woman with the body in the worst way—reduce her to the reproductive function that has always entrapped her? And isn't that especially risky when discussing women writers, since traditionally maternity has been the only type of experience they have been thought able to depict? I might respond to that objection by saying that my use of the term "motherhood" means something more than just experience. But one answer to whether the category of the mother sheers off into essentialism would have to be yes. And yet, why? And does that pose a problem?

I want to examine this collapse into the body and biology by turning again to Mary Wollstonecraft's writing. Writing about the body is particularly attractive to Wollstonecraft: Godwin quotes an introduction of hers to an early conduct book, in which she wishes that her audience were ready for stories about "the organs of generation."[25] Wollstonecraft's display of the body within her writing seems to be the offense for which her most vehement critic, the

---

[25]William Godwin, *Memoirs of Mary Wollstonecraft*, ed. W. Clark Durant (1927), p. 200. Godwin is quoting here from Wollstonecraft's "Introductory Address to Parents," in her *Elements of Morality*. The passage he quotes reads: "I would willingly have said something of chastity and impurity; for impurity is now spread so far, that even children are infected; and by it the seeds of every virtue, as well as the germ of their posterity, which the Creator has implanted in them for wise purposes, are weakened or destroyed. I am thoroughly persuaded that the most efficacious method to root out this dreadful evil, which poisons the source of human happiness, would be to speak to children of the organs of generation as freely as we speak of the other parts of the body, and explain to them the noble use which they were designed for, and how they may be injured. . . . [But] many people would have been shocked at tales, which might early in life have accustomed their children to see the dreadful consequences of incontinence; I have therefore been induced to leave them out" (200–201).

Reverend Richard Polwhele, attacked her. In a note to his poem *The Unsex'd Females* (1797), he objects to that very conduct book piece: "Miss Wollstonecraft does not blush to say . . . that 'in order to lay the axe at the root of corruption . . . it would be right to speak of the organs of generation.' "[26] Polwhele, however, only seems to be objecting to Wollstonecraft's attention to the body; what actually bothers him is how much she ignores it, how much she bucks the essentialism in which he grounds his attack. What is horrifying to him about what he calls Wollstonecraft's "new philosophical system" is that it "confounds the distinction of the sexes"[27]—and Wollstonecraft does, in fact, write in *A Vindication* that "the sexual distinction which men have so warmly insisted upon, is arbitrary" (13.318). For Polwhele, the difference between men's and women's bodies determines the difference between their minds: woman's weaker physique ensures what he calls her "comparative imbecility"[28] and "inferiority . . . in the scale of intelligence."[29] For Polwhele, Wollstonecraft's "philosophy" is what unsexes her—makes it impossible to tell that she is female. Moreover, the implications of Wollstonecraft's system unsexes men as well: Polwhele misquotes Wollstonecraft, for according to Godwin's version of the text, she writes only that she is trying to "root out this dreadful evil" not that she wishes to "lay the axe at the root of corruption." Polwhele's misquotation shows that what bothers him about Wollstonecraft's system is the threat of castration. Rather than displaying the organs of generation in a way that shows clearly who's who, Wollstonecraft wants to mix up the boys and the girls. Polwhele goes on to write:

> I shudder at the new unpictur'd scene,
> Where unsex'd woman vaunts the imperious mien;
> Where girls, affecting to dismiss the heart,
> Invoke the Proteus of petrific Art.[30]

Representation and essentialism go hand in hand: to depict something is to place it within sexual difference. What horrifies Pol-

[26]Richard Polwhele, *The Unsex'd Females* (1797), 11n.
[27]Polwhele, *Unsex'd Females*, 27n.
[28]Polwhele, *Unsex'd Females*, 20n.
[29]Polwhele, *Unsex'd Females*, 19n.
[30]Polwhele, *Unsex'd Females*, 19n. Polwhele calls such "unsex'd females" "the female Quixotes of the new philosophy" (7n).

whele is that Wollstonecraft refuses to do this; she aligns herself instead with the "unpictur'd" and "protean" rather than the "petrific."

Critics like Laura Mulvey and Mary Jacobus have continued the argument that any representation inscribes essentialist distinctions.[31] Given this argument, the maternal as sign—even as sign for the unsignifiable—is only the extension of the logic of representation. For this very reason, French feminists collapse woman with her body, her maternity; by flaunting the maternal body, they expose the built-in essentialism of any structure of knowledge, disrupting its smooth and secret workings.

But another approach is to refuse such essentialist constructions of the maternal, to argue that representation—even the representation of the body—is just that: figurative, not literal. What distinguishes Mary Wollstonecraft's treatment of the body is that it is not about the body at all; it points, through Polwhele's reaction to it, to how the body becomes just another figure, a metaphor, in Polwhele's case an impossible fantasy of some clear-cut ground of reference—a fantasy that Wollstonecraft refuses. The body is a metaphor for something else for Wollstonecraft, as the shift from the literal to the figurative (in her advertisement to *Mary*) illustrates: "In an artless tale, without episodes, the mind of a woman, who has thinking powers is displayed. The female organs have been thought too weak for this arduous employment. . . . Without arguing physically about *possibilities*—in a fiction, such a being may be allowed to exist; whose grandeur is . . . drawn by the individual from the original source" (xxxi). In *Mary*, Wollstonecraft finally provides a tale of organs—female organs. But the mother, the "original source," of which they're an extension, is not the womb but the mind, and these organs produce thought—and stories—rather than children. The body becomes a metaphor for writing; the physical leads to the fictional. The oscillation between the literal and figurative—just as between the novel and romance, men and women, or the two aspects of the maternal—presents another pair of differences that can't quite be kept apart, that keep collapsing into each other. My first conclusion about the importance of the maternal for women's writing emphasized difference. I

---

[31]Laura Mulvey, "Visual Pleasure and the Narrative Cinema," *Screen* 16 (1975): 6–18, and Jacobus, *Reading Woman*, 110–36.

want now to propose a different conclusion that emphasizes sameness. A move to the maternal is also a move to the same, a move
that undercuts the distinctions between mother and father, literature and life, other and self. And Monk Lewis's and Polwhele's
need for difference, their horror when it breaks down, are instructive: as readers and critics, we become no different from them if we
don't recognize our similarity to them. Our own insistence on
difference is, like theirs, to stave off a threat, the threat of the
indeterminable, which undoes genre, gender, even identity,
which, at least on one level, implicates us in categories from which
we wish to distinguish ourselves. The category of women's writing, for example, although a useful fiction, in its reliance on supposedly clear-cut gender distinctions must be recognized *as* a fiction, a difference we impose for our own purposes. So, I would
also say that the move from the paternal to the maternal actually
makes no difference, if we keep in mind the ways they inhabit each
other. But, in saying that, I'm not disagreeing with my earlier
conclusion: I'm just saying the same thing.

II

But let me begin again. For this logic of repetition, this oscillation
between sameness and difference, organized around women's
writing, the mother, and the woman's body, takes another form as
well: in a familiar logic, motherhood takes its meaning only
through comparison and contrast with its supposed opposite. The
oscillation between sameness and difference defining woman, giving meaning to her by giving meaning to her body, is also the
oscillation between madonna and whore, another of those divisions that keep collapsing and re-forming.[32] The figure of the pros-

[32]One difference between the madonna and whore rests in whether or not they
(re)produce—the madonna is that virgin mother whose intact body yields a surprising production, while the body of the prostitute, repeatedly violated, yields nothing but more such exchanges. But the recognition of the empty exchanges the
prostitute is made to represent does not necessarily uncover the supposed economic, historical, and material realities underlying women's cultural definition.
Foucault's critique of the repressive hypothesis suggests a dynamic in which traditional culture actually itself emphasizes rather than ignores the prostitute; women's
cultural construction seems even to *depend* on such divisions as those between
madonna and whore. The preservation of these divisions acts to purge the category
of maternity from what phallogocentric ideology perceives as contamination or

titute, as much as the figure of the mother, seems to reduce woman to her body, to insist on the body as woman's essence, her material reality. And, as critics' responses to the split between the mother and the prostitute in Wollstonecraft's writing show, this particular division has been considered important because it introduces a material element of woman's construction that might otherwise be ignored: such critics emphasize the body—the prostitute's body—because they argue that insisting on it might uncover an important hidden essence, the necessity of material and economic factors to the construction of reality. Focusing on the prostitute, they imply, would reveal the ideology behind conventional forms, an ideology that makes writing romantic rather than realistic because it masks economic relations with erotic relations.

One approach to Wollstonecraft's writing might be to argue that her emphasis in it on the maternal body is a strategy meant to deflect or deny woman's identity as prostitute, and hence to deny her own implication as woman in what she called the system of "commerce." Her private letters to Imlay and her *Letters Written during a Short Residence in Sweden, Norway, and Denmark* show that she found such a system dangerously depersonalizing, and some feminist critics interested in a materialist critique argue that Wollstonecraft does attempt to ignore or occlude what the prostitute represents.[33] By ultimately ignoring the economic exigencies

---

threat, to make it part and upholder of that order, while the collapse of madonna and whore ensures that such categories need vigilant policing, hence making it seem as if it is woman, not the order itself, that is divided and threatened. Such cultural strategies also manage the supposed economic realities that an emphasis on prostitution is meant to uncover, for making it an economic question at all can play into a moral ideology that necessarily scapegoats the economic; think of the stereotypical logic (in Richardson in the contrast between Clarissa and the prostitutes with whom Lovelace houses her, in Dickens in Fagin's gang from whom Nancy must distinguish herself, and—still with us today—in the story of the Mayflower Madame) which emphasizes the fallen woman's supposed autonomy and responsibility, her *choice* of the (supposedly lucrative) career of prostitution over, say, honest death.

[33]She worries throughout this text that her reader "may think me too severe on commerce" (Mary Wollstonecraft, *Letters Written during a Short Residence in Sweden, Norway, and Denmark,* ed. Carol H. Poston [1976], letter 13, p. 119. See also letter 23, pp. 187–90, and letter 24, pp. 192–93). The "baleful effect of extensive speculations on the moral character" (letter 23, p. 190) she feels is such that businessmen must necessarily become like Maria's husband, imbruted by greed and display "till they term all virtue, of an heroic cast, romantic attempts at something above our nature" (letter 23, p. 187).

pointed to by the very story of the prostitution of the woman's body, they argue, Wollstonecraft winds up back in old patriarchal traps, telling the same old story about women that the male order tells.

Yet Wollstonecraft's treatment of the prostitute—she discusses that figure in her reviews, in *A Vindication*, and most obviously in her fiction, in the story of Jemima[34]—remains as complex and divided as her treatment of the mother; it points to the tensions within the construction of woman, available to us through divisions within the romantic forms connected to them. One way to consider how the figure of the prostitute gives form to such tensions in Wollstonecraft's writing is by considering it as a figure, a form, a body. Rather than simply accepting the materiality of this figure, however, as critics we might question why it is so often the symbol for the material. What does such use of the prostitute tell us about women's writing—not just about women's fiction, but about feminist criticism as well?

I want to return once more to the nineteenth century's reflections on the eighteenth, to the endurance of attitudes about the woman's body that attend different local representations of prostitution in those different centuries. "Novels with Purpose," an influential review written by Justin McCarthy in 1864 for the *Westminster Review*, responds to what it sees as a spate of novels about women's sexual corruption in terms familiar from Wollstonecraft's writing. McCarthy writes: "The best justification for the adoption of such topics . . . assuredly is that women may perhaps be thus redeemed from the possibility of remaining in that imbecile and ignorant condition which the romancist commonly regards as innocence, and which woman is so generally encouraged to cherish as her special virtue, even by those who are so earnest in describing it as the principal cause of her ruin."[35] Charlotte Brontë is one of the few women writers McCarthy cites as seeing through such specious innocence. Indeed, about fifteen years earlier, in *Shirley*, Brontë had

[34]For Wollstonecraft's short discussion of prostitution in her reviews, see her Review of *The Evils of Adultery and Prostitution, Analytical Review* 14 (September 1792): 100–102.

[35][Justin McCarthy], "Novels with a Purpose," *Westminster Review*, n.s. 26 (July and October 1864): 45.

complained about women's ignorance in terms that McCarthy's also echo: "Fathers! cannot you alter these things? . . . You would wish to be proud of your daughters and not to blush for them—then seek for them an interest and an occupation which shall raise them above the flirt, the manoeuvrer, the mischief-making tale-bearer. Keep your girls' minds narrow and fettered—they will still be a plague and a care, sometimes a disgrace to you."[36] McCarthy and Brontë are similar in blaming a false innocence that is really ignorance for women's corruption, but they cast that blame differently. Brontë puts it onto patriarchal society, making it the fathers' burden. Mc-Carthy, sympathetic to Brontë's work and the problems it confronts, revises it nonetheless to make women's victimization their own charge.[37]

McCarthy does, however, recognize that the forces prompting women to fall are strong. Like Brontë, he sees that the very idea of woman is plotted, if not plotted against. Like hers, his reading points out the implicit narrative of ruin built into women's cultural construction. It is not surprising, both suggest even as they deplore it, to read so many stories of women who fall, since the

[36]Charlotte Brontë, *Shirley*, ed. Andrew and Judith Hook (1974), ch. 22, pp. 378–79.

[37]McCarthy shifts the blame through recourse to conventional assumptions about the woman's body. He specifically commends Brontë's informed and experienced depiction of her heroines not because it shows women's strength and shrewdness but because it shows "women and girls endowed with human passion" (McCarthy, "Novels with a Purpose," 49). And such "endowments," not surprisingly, refer to the body. McCarthy ends his essay by describing Brontë's attempts to present the passions as a literal stripping away of false dress: "A Parisian critic lately, when noticing some objections urged against the numerous undraped Graces, and Bacchantes, and Nymphs, and Ledas in the season's Exhibition, drily remarked that so long as vast skirts and hoops and spoon-bonnets endured, it was a relief to get a glimpse of the true outlines of womanhood under any circumstances. We own to something of a kindred feeling in regard to our English fiction" (49). In arguing this, McCarthy isolates one of the paradoxes undermining women's writing—how her attempt to write "true" womanhood (perhaps by attempting to disentangle her construction from the erotic, certainly part of Brontë's struggle, as it was of Wollstonecraft's) is seen nonetheless, even by a sympathetic male critic, in terms of the eroticized body. Defining woman in terms of her body keeps the woman responsible for her ruin, even as she tries to script plots that go beyond it: such a constraint maintains the logic of blaming the victim and follows in the tradition of "the woman tempted me." Just as Arabella's rationality inflames Glanville, who by such a response maintains her within the sexuality that rationality might otherwise threaten, so Brontë's depiction of women's boredom, misery, and ambition is perceived as just another story of seduction.

category of woman is already necessarily degraded, her mind fettered by an ignorance that propriety dangerously confuses with innocence—an imbecility that delivers her over to the sexual designs of others. McCarthy and Brontë are also similar because Brontë too remains trapped within the destructive cultural logic McCarthy so easily accepts: that such results cannot be wholly innocent. She too ultimately winds up blaming woman for her fall, blaming the woman who tells tales, the woman writer. Like McCarthy, Brontë too implies that there remains a disturbing connection between the woman disgraced and that "mischief-making talebearer," the romancist—as if such writers do not merely describe but somehow create these dangerous fabrications.

Such narrative outlines are familiar. They are not the coinage of the nineteenth century alone but its inheritance from its literary predecessors, those eighteenth-century fathers (and mothers) of the novel. The heroine's plot in the eighteenth century describes this trajectory into ruin; the plots of such novels as Richardson's, for example, self-reflexively arise from the plots and subterfuges of those characters within them, the Lovelaces and Mr. B——s, who attempt to ensnare innocence by playing on ignorance.[38] Wollstonecraft's critique in *A Vindication* of the collapse of innocence and ignorance as strategic—a way to keep women preyed upon and powerless as they are exchanged among men—specifically lays the blame for the cultural construction of woman at the feet of the tale-bearers: she especially indicts sentimental romances as providing nothing but such plots, catering to ignorance, inflaming imagination at the expense of reason, and materially contributing to woman's degradation.

Yet Wollstonecraft, like Brontë, is a tale-bearer herself (and Brontë's phrase suggests the double bind for women writers, implying the way that even women's relation to storytelling seems defined in terms of the body—the "bearing" of tales echoing the bearing of children). The questions I posed earlier in the chapter

---

[38]It is the very play between ignorance and innocence—Clarissa's or Pamela's extraordinary blindness to the evil intentions of others places them in situations where their principled refusal to submit is their only defense—that constitutes the dramatic tension of their stories. And it's interesting that, for McCarthy (quoting Heine), Pamela's innocence is only an "anatomical chastity"—he locates this tension in terms of and on the site of the body (McCarthy, "Novels with a Purpose," 46).

remain: as Mary Poovey has phrased it, how can a woman writer be a proper lady? The cultural construction of woman seems to foreclose any alternative to the one in which experience equals ruin; such, at least, are the assumptions not only of McCarthy but also of Wollstonecraft's critics (especially the outspoken Polwhele), who effectively censured her according to the logic that, if she had made a reputation as a writer, she had lost it as a woman.

It is precisely such logic that Catherine Gallagher has recently interrogated by turning again to the body of the woman, and its relation to (women's) writing. She opposes to the model of paternity and inheritance traditionally associated with authorship another model: the metaphor of author as whore. This association (not simply a product of the eighteenth or nineteenth century, she argues, but part of the Western tradition, going back to classic times) helps account for women's anxiety of authorship, for "when women entered the career of authorship, they did not enter an inappropriately male territory, but a degradingly female one."[39] According to Gallagher, unlike the father's "procreative Word," the prostitute's generative acts simply proliferate, but do not (re)produce: "The gender distinction in literary theory is . . . between the natural production of new things in the world and the 'unnatural' reproduction of mere signs. According to the father metaphor, the author generates real things in the world through language; according to the whore metaphor, language proliferates itself in a process of exchange through the author."[40] In this male economy of things and signs, a woman writer, unable to claim paternity, can occupy only a marginal, inherently alienated and disenfranchised position. She becomes a whore, a sterile purveyor of used (and useless) goods. For Gallagher, the metaphor of writer as whore is a metaphor of exchange alienated from productivity, writing from materiality. The differences she describes between it and the metaphor of writing as paternity—which takes *its* authority from its a supposedly firm grounding in, and creation out of, the solid facts of life—describe epistemological differences underlying what have

---

[39]Catherine Gallagher, "George Eliot and *Daniel Deronda*: The Prostitute and the Jewish Question," in *Sex, Politics, and Science in the Nineteenth-Century Novel*, Selected Papers from the English Institute, 1983–84, n.s. 10, ed. Ruth Bernard Yeazell (1986), 40.

[40]Gallagher, "George Eliot," 40, 41.

often been seen in current critical debate as competing strategies of *reading*. This debate—about whether interpretations should emphasize "mere" signs or material conditions—is particularly important in feminist criticism: our different definitions of feminist politics seem to come down to whether we see woman more as construction or as material object, sign or body.

In implicitly arguing for the material grounding of (women's) writing, Gallagher's association of the prostitute with proliferating and ungrounded uncertainty seems to depart diametrically from the traditional construction of the prostitute, which aligns her directly through the supposed materiality of her body with material conditions and historical fact. I shall return at the end of this chapter to the differences within the construction of this figure—especially to Gallagher's revision of the traditional meaning of that figure, to discuss whether it is actually a revision at all. But I need to look first at the way the prostitute has, in practice, generally stood for the material, and to do so I turn now to Karl Marx, that emphasizer of material conditions.

The early writing of Marx contains examples in which the prostitute represents what he calls in another context "the world of things."[41] In *The Economic and Philosophic Manuscripts of 1844*, Marx critiques naive (i.e., untheorized) communism as a regressive stage, which remains tied to private property, although it makes the possession of such property universal. Marx underwrites his argument through recourse to the figure of the prostitute; such universal private property, he writes:

> finds expression in the brutish form of counterposing to *marriage* (certainly a *form of exclusive private property*) the *community of women*, in which a woman becomes a piece of *communal* and *common* property. It may be said that this idea of the *community of women gives away the secret* of this as yet completely crude and thoughtless communism. Just as the woman passes from marriage to general prostitution, so the entire world of wealth (that is, of man's objective substance) passes from the relationship of ex-

[41]Karl Marx, *The Economic and Philosophic Manuscripts of 1844*, trans. Martin Milligan and Dirk J. Struik, in *Marx and Engels: 1843–44*, vol. 3 of Karl Marx and Frederick Engels, *Collected Works*, 50 vols. projected (1975–), p. 272.

clusive marriage with the owner of private property to a state of universal prostitution with the community.[42]

The prostitute is a symbol for property, the thing possessed. At the same time, for Marx, prostitution is also the symbol for the workers' alienation from their labor—the people's "original sin," in which they had "nothing to sell except their own skins"[43]—which represents for him the way that "labour itself becomes an object."[44] The brilliance of Marx as an analyst of the material is precisely his emphasis on the way supposed abstractions, such as labor, become literal, become objects to be exchanged, entities producing effects.

---

[42]Marx, *Economic and Philosophic Manuscripts*, 294–95.

[43]Karl Marx, *Capital: A Critique of Political Economy*, ed. Frederick Engels (1906), 785.

[44]Marx, *Economic and Philosophic Manuscripts*, 272. Marx continues the metaphor in which the prostitute represents the world of things and is herself an object by suggesting: "money is the *procurer* between man's need and the object, between his life and his means of life" (*Economic and Philosophic Manuscripts*, 323). That is, money provides the perverting access to the material world that changes man's relation to the material (to woman, for example; see his discussion of how man's [sexual] relation to woman figures his relation to the material world in a way that is "*sensuously manifested*, reduced to an observable *fact*" [*Economic and Philosophic Manuscripts*, 296]), and changes that relation from a natural to an economic one, makes woman into prostitute (although later Marx collapses the distinction between pimp and whore, calling money "the common whore, the common procurer of people and nations" [*Economic and Philosophic Manuscripts*, 324]). The way the prostitute figures both the material and the corruption of true relations with the material suggests the complexity of this figure in Marx's writing; her relation to money suggests the way she might also stand for the ungrounded exchanges of capitalism. Irigaray has examined the way the prostitute comes to symbolize the split for Marx and Engels between use and exchange value, suggesting an abstract quality in excess of her materiality—suggesting exchange itself. See Luce Irigaray, "Women on the Market" and "Commodities among Themselves," in her *This Sex Which Is Not One*, trans. Catherine Porter, with Carolyn Burke (1985), 170–91, 192–97. See also Luce Irigaray, *Speculum of the Other Woman*, trans. Gillian C. Gill (1985), 119–23. Yet, as my chapter argues, the prostitute becomes a symbol for such abstractions in order to try to ground them, to lend them her supposed materiality. This tendency to literalize without comment in Marx's thought (which infuses even his figurative language) seems to me to comment on the kind of complaint expressed by Foucault: that "while there are some very interesting things about the body in Marx's writings, Marxism considered as an historical reality has had a terrible tendency to occlude the question of the body, in favor of consciousness and ideology" ("Body/Power," *Power/Knowledge: Selected Interviews and Other Writing, 1972–77*, trans. Colin Gordon, Leo Marshall, John Mepham, Kate Soper, ed. Colin Gordon [1980], 58–59).

Prostitution becomes for him *the* symbol of such literalness, of man's reification, his fall into the painful materialism of capitalism.

In literary analyses, the prostitute is so conventionally the shorthand for objective reality within history that reference to her inevitably introduces reference to historical evidence (even by those critics who seem least likely to read that way).[45] It is just such attention to class and history, Cora Kaplan argues, that makes feminist analyses effective, that keeps them from simply being more re-plottings of the daughter's seduction. In an essay specifically critiquing a failure of feminism within Mary Wollstonecraft's work, Kaplan writes that feminist "appropriation[s] of modern critical theory—semiotic with an emphasis on the psychoanalytic— . . . must engage fully with the effects of other systems of difference than the sexual [systems such as class or race], or they too will produce no more than an anti-humanist avant-garde version of romance."[46] They will

> unintentionally reproduce the ideological values of mass-market romance . . . [in which] the other structuring relations of society fade and disappear, leaving us with the naked drama of sexual difference as the only scenario that matters. Mass-market romance tends to represent sexual difference as natural and fixed— a constant, transhistorical femininity in libidinized struggle with an equally "given" universal masculine.[47]

[45]In the preface of *Reading for the Plot*, for instance, Peter Brooks sets up the plot of that study as a dialogue between formalism and psychoanalysis, yet the chapter in which he focuses on the figure of the prostitute, entitled "The Mark of the Beast," discusses in detail the historical and material determinants of the serial novel as a literary mode of production. See Peter Brooks, *Reading for the Plot: Design and Intention in Narrative* (1984); see xiii–xvi for his discussion of formalism, 143–70 for "The Mark of the Beast." Similarly, Jane Gallop, who has come almost to represent ahistoricism to critics impatient with such reading (such as Andrew Ross), ends her book, *The Daughter's Seduction*, with an uncharacteristic discussion of class, economic commerce, and history, within the context of a discussion of the governess. In its structure (its references to women's exchange and Lévi-Strauss, for example) this discussion repeats some of the standard arguments about prostitution—displacing, perhaps, such conventional consideration of material conditions from her earlier analysis of the Sadian whore, an analysis readers like Ross find shocking in its ignorance of these conditions. See Jane Gallop, "Keys to Dora," *The Daughter's Seduction*, 132–50; for her discussion of the Sadian whore, see 89–91. See also Andrew Ross, "Viennese Waltzes," *Enclitic* 8 (Spring/Fall 1984): 71–82.

[46]Cora Kaplan, *Sea Changes: Essays on Culture and Feminism* (1986), 148–49.

[47]Kaplan, *Sea Changes*, 148.

By forcing the reader to confront the realities of class and history, Kaplan implies, the prostitute, that site where the economic and erotic must converge, dispels the delusions of romance, the blind desires that obscure the other plots in which women are entrapped.

It is precisely for her refusal to confront the example of the prostitute that Kaplan criticizes Wollstonecraft. Despite all her feminist impulses, Wollstonecraft remains for Kaplan entrenched in liberal bourgeois notions of gender and subjectivity that attempt to maintain the autonomy of the middle-class feminine individual by differentiating her from that specular other, the whore. In order to preserve the romance of the individual, Wollstonecraft falsely insists on "true" womanhood's difference from, rather than identification with, the de-individualized prostitute: for Wollstonecraft, as representative of *her* class, " 'true womanhood' had to be protected from. . . the debased subjectivity and dangerous sexuality of the lower-class prostitute," Kaplan writes. "In *A Vindication*, working-class women are quite unselfconsciously constructed as prostitutes and dirty-minded servants corrupting bourgeois innocence."[48]

Similarly interested in material history and class, Mary Poovey agrees that an ignorance of such categories leads feminism—and Wollstonecraft—into dangerous romance, into a repetition of the traps for women that feminism and the woman writer hope to escape.[49] Turning from *A Vindication* to Wollstonecraft's novel, *The Wrongs of Woman*, Poovey points out, however, that Wollstonecraft does not simply ignore or revile the prostitute. The story of the prostitute Jemima offers "a radical, indeed feminist, story"—a "decidedly *un*sentimental" story that "has the potential to call into question both the organizational principles of bourgeois society and the sentimentalism that perpetuates romantic idealism" especially within the sentimental romance.[50] Poovey argues that

[48]Kaplan, *Sea Changes*, 168, 169. For another discussion of the significance of prostitution within Wollstonecraft's political ideology which questions in passing our impulse to find twentieth-century political approaches more radical and advanced than Enlightenment positions, see Frances Ferguson, "Wollstonecraft Our Contemporary," in *Gender and Theory: Dialogues on Feminist Criticism*, ed. Linda Kaufman (1989), 51–62. This essay is a reply to Timothy J. Reiss, "Revolution in Bounds: Wollstonecraft, Women, and Reason," in Kaufman, *Gender and Theory*, 11–50.

[49]Poovey, *The Proper Lady*, 109.

[50]Poovey, *The Proper Lady*, 104, 103, 104.

Wollstonecraft, because of her own individual position, is simply unable to develop such "revolutionary implications" of the demystification of romantic love and individual effort, the foregrounding of the way "the individual's situation—his or her position within class, gender, economics, and history—really delimits freedom and virtually defines the self.'"[51] Wollstonecraft's reluctance to "relinquish the individualistic values tied up with the sentimental structure itself," to give up the romance of womanhood that promises her satisfaction and fulfillment especially in romantic love, Poovey argues, makes her break off Jemima's story and turn from the unmediated horrors of woman's material life that she begins to sketch there.[52]

Material feminists such as Kaplan and Poovey provide an important perspective from which to read Wollstonecraft's work and the figure of the prostitute in cultural discourse. Prostitution is important to such readings because they see it not simply as metaphor but as referring to an important condition of women's reality. Sexuality separated from the mystifications of love or reproduction, relocated in terms of brute materialism and economics—the violence done to the body of the prostitute, the money paid her—also becomes in such readings a crucial metaphor for the treatment of women in general. Prostitution seems an effective focus for the reading Kaplan and Poovey advocate because it represents *the* condition in which romance (defined as sexual love) is shown to be a question of economics. To these critics, however, Wollstonecraft's treatment of the prostitute chooses romance over economics; to them, Wollstonecraft sacrifices that figure in order to make the prostitute's sexual commerce seem extraordinary and abnormal, rather than the type of the relations between the sexes.

Such denials, they argue, also determine the very structure of her writing; Mary Poovey suggests that the style of Wollstonecraft's language, especially its abstract diction, grows out of these ideological assumptions, out of her desire to "dematerialize" feminine desire—to avoid the bodily realities of sex and the physical consequences of class.[53] Although I might question whether concrete diction is any more concrete—closer to its referent?—than other

[51]Poovey, *The Proper Lady,* 109.
[52]Poovey, *The Proper Lady,* 108.
[53]Poovey, *The Proper Lady,* 78.

word choice, I want to continue along the direction these critics have charted to ask another question: what difficulties might there be for our feminist analyses in taking the prostitute as a symbol for the material? It seems to me that Wollstonecraft uses this figure not so much to emphasize the material herself but to confront just those problems of representation involved in such an emphasis.

An attention to those problems seems to me to give Wollstonecraft's writing its very shape. Just as the prostitute stands for the breakdown of the distinction between the public and the private (exposing supposedly intimate erotic encounters as simply another exchange within economic institutions), Wollstonecraft encodes that breakdown into her writing. Her insistence on the private might be not just wishful regression but also what Wollstonecraft claims it is, political strategy. *A Vindication* revises sentimental stereotypes precisely by insisting on them, repeating them with a difference. It is a political tract that quite deliberately takes the form of a conduct book, locating women's struggle in "a REVOLUTION in female manners" (*VRW*.13.317). The inseparable and radical equation of private and public is part of Wollstonecraft's political message—she writes insistently throughout *A Vindication* that public virtues "must ever grow out of the private character" (12.279). Kaplan and Poovey importantly demonstrate how Wollstonecraft's insistence on private character may grow out of an unconscious desire for individual autonomy, but just as important are the moments in Wollstonecraft's work that show that her insistence also grows out of something else too: the quite explicit recognition that private character is itself an institution, a form of representation.

In *The Wrongs of Woman*, as in *A Vindication*, Wollstonecraft may be unable to imagine an alternative free of the representational constraints of the existing order, but she still recognizes that, within that order, all women are prostituted.[54] Jemima's story es-

[54]In the letter appended to the "Author's Introduction" of *The Wrongs of Woman*, Wollstonecraft writes that her aim in the novel is "to show the wrongs of different classes of women, equally oppressive, though, from the differences of education, necessarily various" (Author's Introduction.74). Within the cultural structure she considers, all women are defined in terms of prostitution, and class differences register that similar characterization differently. Wollstonecraft suggests, for example, that the supposedly chaste women who inexorably assign guilt to lower-class prostitutes actually "assume, in some degree, the same character themselves" (*VRW*.8.249). The very ritual of a fashionable girl's coming out, for instance, is

pecially makes clear the way romantic love is the mystification of economic transactions, played out on the body of the woman, and this lesson is not actually broken off; the rest of *The Wrongs of Woman* to some degree repeats it. Maria's husband marries her, has sex with her, even barters her, according to his need for money. *The Wrongs of Woman* is the fictional continuation of *A Vindication* especially in its emphasis that bourgeois women, like Maria, and women of other classes, like Jemima, are connected through their status as bodies.

Yet Wollstonecraft's response to such a dynamic may be different from the ones materialist critics supply not because she cannot follow through on the critique she sketches, but because she recognizes problems within it. Even though in the author's introduction to *A Vindication*, Wollstonecraft insists that she "shall be employed about things, not words!" (Introduction.82), the story of Jemima reveals how just such an emphasis on the material, when symbolized by the body of a woman, might continue rather than undo the violence done to women. Using the prostitute as a metaphor for material analysis, for a way to "materialize" writing, may be one more repetition of this figure's exploitation. On the one hand, Wollstonecraft's writing about the prostitute may insist that the reader pay attention to the body of the woman in order to learn some material lessons. On the other, however, her writing suggests that perhaps all that readers ever do is pay attention to the woman's body and that they need to confront some of the problems that arise from doing so.

Jemima's story shows that when prostitution is aligned with writing through the metaphor of the body, it can also be at the

---

another way "to bring [a woman] to market" (*VRW*.12.289), and it is just such insensibility produced by commercial speculation that Wollstonecraft finds obscene. In *The Wrongs of Woman,* she characterizes a marriage based on economics rather than passion as "a mere affair of barter . . . [involving] secrets of the trade" (10.153). The privileging of passion here may indeed be unironized and reveal Wollstonecraft's adherence to regressive, class-bound categories, her wish that some relations were outside economics, although, as Kaplan insists, the intricate interrelations between sexual drive and social organization make impossible any simple causality (i.e., assuming that class determines our representations of sexuality, or vice versa). Wollstonecraft's work makes available, however, some of the complexities of those interrelations, especially by insisting on them as questions of representation—that different (class) contexts make readers see things differently and make things different.

expense of the category of woman. Jemima's body, to which she becomes reduced, is, throughout her story, an instrument to be written on by the characters within the story (a practice we cannot avoid continuing as critics when we use her as a metaphor for whatever purpose).[55] Wollstonecraft, in fact, identifies different forms of marking on the woman as similarly exploitative. The violent blows with which Jemima's father "did not fail to leave the marks of his resentment on [her] body" (*WW*.5.104), and the ways she is later "branded with shame" (5.118) by her reputation as prostitute and thief, are similar to the real letters literally marked on her, when, during her apprenticeship, she "was sent to the neighbouring shops with Glutton, Liar, or Thief, written on [her] forehead" (5.106). Such decidedly unsentimental writing suggests the dangers to women of making metaphors literal, of insisting on some "real" category of woman as the vehicle for meaning, of making her the literal bearer of the tale.

Wollstonecraft's fiction provides some access to the danger to women involved in emphasizing the material in such a way. Early in *Mary*, Wollstonecraft presents a startling vignette which suggests that writing on the body of the woman necessarily does violence to it. Mary herself is figuratively impressed with an indelible image that both determines the course of her own story and is also the emblem for it: the image of a woman's mangled body.

> A little girl who attended in the nursery fell sick. Mary paid her great attention; contrary to her wish, she was sent out of the house to her mother, a poor woman, whom necessity obliged to leave her sick child while she earned her daily bread. The poor wretch, in a fit of delirium stabbed herself, and Mary saw her dead body, and heard the dismal account; and so strongly did it impress her imagination, that every night of her life the bleeding corpse presented itself to her when she first began to slumber. . . . The impression that this accident made was indelible. (*M*.2.6)

This short, stark vignette is in part a tale of economic distress (the mother forced to earn her daily bread), in direct contrast to Mary's—

---

[55]For another discussion of the relation between criticism and the figure of the prostitute as a marked body, see Nancy K. Miller, "Reading as a Woman: The Body in Practice," in *The Female Body in Western Culture: Contemporary Perspectives*, ed. Susan Rubin Suleiman (1986), 354–62.

and Wollstonecraft's—romances. Such tragedies of labor and priva-
tion could be seen as the true story of womanhood, the antitheses of
the frivolous romances that Mary's mother reads and Mary enacts.
Yet this tale also might itself be a romance as well: it follows almost
directly after the narrative tells us that Mary has such "a fondness
for reading tales of woe . . . [that] made her almost realize the
fictitious distress" (M.2.6), a juxtaposition that reasserts this vignette's own fictionality, the way that this too is a tale of woe
introduced by Wollstonecraft into her own story. It calls attention to
Mary's sympathetic (if not sentimental) response to it, suggesting
that she might be trying, in her attitude, to make her experience
conform to the expectations romance sets up. The chapter ends
shortly thereafter by indicting Mary as "too much the creature of
impulse" (M.2.7), and her reaction to this vignette might be considered romantically impulsive and excessive—the novel's inclusion of
it itself using the body of a woman to produce this effect, as part of
its own romantic detailing of Mary's exquisite moral sensibility.
Being too easily impressed has conventionally been considered
romantic; Poovey tells us that Maria, for example, is romantic precisely because she is (overly) responsive to her uncle's stories:
"Because Maria has not personally experienced her uncle's disillusionment, she responds as contemporary moralists feared women
'naturally' respond to sentimental novels; she is 'imprinted' with
sentiments as she projects herself, a heroine, into his text."[56] Yet
Wollstonecraft herself also uses the metaphor of an indelible mark to
critique this very attitude; Mary's silly mother is similarly struck by
reading romances; their stories of love force on her too a "fatal
image!" of a romantic life that makes her dissatisfied with her own
(M.1.2), an excessive romanticism Wollstonecraft criticizes.
Wollstonecraft goes on to lament in the letter appended to her
preface to The Wrongs of Woman that inferior literary productions, full
of such stage-effects, "may more forcibly impress the mind of common readers" (74) than more realistic stories. The doubleness of
Wollstonecraft's attitude toward romance (her stories continue to
make use of it even as they criticize it) means that despite her
critique of the indelible image of women's sacrificed body as a

[56]Poovey, The Proper Lady, 98–99.

danger of romance, that image underlies Wollstonecraft's own sup-posedly realistic writing as well.

The Wrongs of Woman has its own such fatal image, "her infant's image . . . continually floating on Maria's sight" (1.75).[57] The image of her daughter (murdered, she fears, to allow her husband to inherit her legacy), thus impressed on her, figures the pervasive sacrifice of women's bodies—Jemima's, Maria's, Maria's daughter's—to men's material gains. These fatal images pervade women's stories—both romantic tales and realistic tales of economic distress. Wollstonecraft's heroines are imprinted with this lesson, so that the woman's body, seen as a blank on which to inscribe, inscribes again and again in Wollstonecraft's fiction the dangers of doing so.

The repetition of such dismal accounts structures Wollstonecraft's fiction; her heroines, who helplessly repeat them, seem drawn to such scripts. The supposedly romantic and realistic characters are similar in this: like Mary in her fondness for tales of woe, Jemima notes that she " 'had often, in [her] childhood, followed a ballad-singer, to hear the sequel of a dismal story, though sure of being severely punished for delaying to return' " (WW.5.111). Jemima herself enacts a compulsive sequel, forcing her suitor to expel the servant he had made pregnant, just as she herself was originally expelled by her master (prompted by his wife) after he had ruined her. This servant, however, rather than choosing prostitution, com-mits suicide, and of all the misery in her story, Jemima seems most impressed by the fatal image of her corpse: " 'Let me not recal the horrid moment!—I recognized her pale visage" (5.116). This ser-vant's story makes manifest the way women's choices are reduced to their bodies: they may either barter or destroy them.

---

[57]Maria is also "haunted by Mr. Venables' image, who seemed to assume terrific or hateful forms to torment me, wherever I turned.—Sometimes a wild cat, a roaring bull, or hideous assassin, whom I vainly attempted to fly; at others he was a demon, hurrying me to the brink of a precipice, plunging me into dark waves, or horrid gulphs" (WW.13.179). Interesting to my argument here is the way Venables's image emphatically refuses his bodily form, metamorphosing into almost anything but that. This may imply a revision of Wollstonecraft's earlier novel, in which the fatal image that floats on women's sight is most often that of their male lovers (M.5.13; 16.37; 18.40; 19.43; 25.57; 27.63). In her novels, Wollstonecraft seems to be working through the problem of how the representations of men and women relate to the representation of the body and to the essentializing tendency implicit in conjuring up the figure of the body.

That Jemima forces a repetition of her own story is not surprising, for that story too is already itself a repetition, a replay of her mother's. Her corruption is attributed to her mother's fall—"I was born a strumpet; it ran in my blood" (5.108)—and her mother's story, with which Jemima begins her own, inspires further tale bearing throughout. Jemima's stepmother, for instance, spins out of it the malicious tale she tells Jemima's father; her stepmother's " 'principal discourse [Jemima tells us] was to recount my faults, and attribute them to the wicked disposition which I had brought into the world with me, inherited from my mother' " (5.104). That a mother's tale is the only real inheritance she can pass on to her daughter is evident from Maria's story; Jemima's story goes on to emphasize that the only way women can gain interest and influence is by bearing such tales (Jemima's wicked master, for instance, gives her grudging assistance when he realizes the scandal that could be caused by her telling everyone that he has made her pregnant). Stories of violence enacted on women's bodies connect mothers and daughters who may share no other connection. Although Jemima blames her life of prostitution on her lack of a mother, for instance (just as the mother's absence leads to the nursery girl's death—a death self-imposed, suggesting the extent to which women bear within themselves the roles they are given), she is able to read her own life by reference to her mother's story, to give it meaning by fitting it into a tradition that gives her some connection with that mother.

Such a tradition is different from the male tradition; such stories differ from men's stories about women, not in how they find a way to refuse the body but in how they directly reveal that that body is the vehicle for and the currency of those stories, what makes meaning legible in them. As Wollstonecraft notes in *A Vindication*, the woman's body is the payment woman must make to man for her maintenance, no matter how miserable, within the status quo (4.164–65). Such stories reveal clearly how man grants woman meaning only in terms of that body. The tale of woe Maria passes on to other women is what experience teaches her: that men pay attention not to such tales but only to her body—the attorney wishes to help her, not because he is persuaded by her sad narrative but because "my eloquence was in my complexion, the blush of seventeen" (WW.7.134). Similarly, Darnford originally comes to her rescue, defending her against Venables's slanders, because he observes, with "manly interest" that "my countenance told a very different story" (13.175).

Darnford's heroics are more for his own sake than Maria's; in criticizing her for investing him with romantic qualities he does not possess, the novel exposes that she is attractive to him because she allows him to pose as a hero.[58] Darnford's abandonment of Maria at her adultery trial shows that men allow women to embody the loss of reputation in order to maintain or magnify their own. Early in their own courtship, Wollstonecraft chides Godwin for grounding poetic creations in her, creating poetry by enumerating her "perfections": "Do not make me a desk 'to write upon,' I humbly pray."[59] Wollstonecraft may object to Godwin's use of her as a foundation for his writing because in such transactions the woman conventionally disappears altogether. What was supposedly passion for her gets revealed as passion for something else, for what she critiques elsewhere as the desire to fill "a niche in the temple of fame," to rise above "the black rolling steam of time, that silently sweeps all before it into the shapeless void called—eternity" (VRW.9.261).[60] The Wrongs of Woman especially exposes how men attempt to secure their reputations, their good names, by depriving women of theirs, by making use of their bodies. It is only when Maria's husband's "character in the commercial world was gone. He was considered . . . on 'Change as a swindler" (WW.11.160) that he attempts to retrieve his good name by selling hers, selling her into prostitution by bartering her to an influential business associate, making use of Maria's body when all the rest of his goods are gone (11.162).

The contrast between (writerly) reputation and "the shapeless void called—eternity" comes back to the problems involved in

[58]When Maria begins to muse on Darnford's perfections, even before she has seen or knows very much about him, she herself realizes the way she is setting him up as a hero, and realizes "how difficult it was for women to avoid growing romantic, who have no active duties or pursuits" (WW.2.87).

[59]"To William Godwin, July 1, 1796," in Collected Letters, 331.

[60]That such relations between men and women are transactions of power is suggested by the description in A Vindication of power in similar language: "Power, in fact, is ever true to its vital principle, for in every shape it would reign without control of inquiry. Its throne is built across a dark abyss, which no eye must dare to explore, lest the baseless fabric should totter under investigation" (10.264).

using the prostitute as the site for material and historical criticism. Because the prostitute is so insistently a body, that figure may be used to attempt to connect and stabilize what Mary Jacobus calls the "chaotic, formless, and multitudinous" facts of history, wishfully to give a body to history itself.[61] Yet history as form remains constructed, and constructed according to the same assumptions that plot our fictions—an identification made clear by *The Infernal Quixote*, a novel (published in 1801) that joined in the censure of Wollstonecraft's writing by having its heroine err not through reading sentimental romances but through reading *A Vindication* and Godwin's *Memoirs* of Wollstonecraft's life—that is, through reading the history of women's oppression and the story of a woman with a history. Even Catherine Gallagher's analysis, which seems to relate the figure of the prostitute directly to such uncertainty and chaos, by aligning such uncertainty with that figure which has come to stand for brute materiality, may be said to allay the anxiety generated by uncertainty, to stabilize it through the very figure she chooses to represent the problem of representation. The prostitute stubbornly remains a metaphor for the body precisely because a focus on her body seems to do away with metaphor. By seeing the body as the site of discourse, the bearer of meaning, as all of us as critics increasingly do in this post-Foucauldian age, and by choosing the body of the prostitute, traditionally the bearer of disease as well as meaning, to represent our new historicism, we may be attempting to cure the ideological contagion that has plagued the writing of even the most committed feminist by quarantining it, marking the body of the woman as we used to mark the doorposts of sick houses, as the site of that exchange.

[61]Mary Jacobus, "The Law of/and Gender: Genre Theory and *The Prelude*," *Diacritics* 14 (1984): 52. Jacobus is discussing the way political revolution is in particular frequently embodied in the figure of a woman, given a woman's face, to make it readable. Her implication is that such figurations (attempt to) stabilize a subversion that nevertheless continues to undermine the structures of representation—both in literary texts and political institutions. I might argue instead that using the figure of the woman to embody *subversion* rather than stability (as certain critical approaches attempt to do) still uses this body as a figure and, hence, may not be all that different a strategy.

4

Streetwalkers and Homebodies: Dickens's Romantic Women

Lennox's and Wollstonecraft's novels, on one level, seem to maintain romance as a consoling realm: their novels seem to set it up as a (woman's) form within which women writers and their heroines can escape or elude constricting power relations. Yet their treatment of romance also reveals the way such power relations trap us all in wishful structures. Such treatment does not only provide a way to attempt to circumvent power; it also allows a way to analyze power, and Lennox's and Wollstonecraft's portrayals of this system emphasize how woman is deployed as a category within and enabling it.

Charles Dickens's novels continue to use women and romance to seem to deny and console. Dickens's work appears to manifest its wishfulness differently from that of the women writers I have analyzed so far; rather than gesturing to some autonomous female realm in his work, the figure of woman and the form of romance become scapegoats whose implication in power suggests autonomy for men and novels. Yet, although such differences seem to point to the difference between male and female writers, their different stakes in constructing women and romance, Dickens's work also breaks down such categories of gender and genre. What his work defines as the feminine and romantic also inhabits it, and reveals its own inheritance within a system of power.

I

Dickens's stories take place, critics have long recognized, within the painful and indifferent network of forces in which his characters find themselves and which his novels not only depict but reflect. The interminable and meandering power of Chancery is just one instance of the dim ineluctable oppression that suffuses Dickens's fiction—an oppression needing not so much simply to be revealed (for it is apparent on every page and critics have been accounting for it in psychoanalytic, or economic, or even formal terms for generations) but to be analyzed for the way it operates in and the effect it has on Dickens's work.[1]

D. A. Miller, in a translation of Dickens's world view into a Foucault-inspired rhetoric of power, argues that one tactic of this system of control acted out in Dickens's fiction is that it deliberately presents itself *as* oppression. Such a presentation strategically implies that this system exists only in its localizable, painful ·effects: investing one sphere as the site of constraint and control implies that there is a place outside it, a realm of freedom. Yet power, as Foucault has repeatedly defined it, is as much part of what we as its subjects call resistance to oppression (or whatever else that we might perceive as positive and liberating) as it is of oppression itself. The endless and nebulous bureaucratic workings of Chancery trouble the illusion of escape in Dickens's work, such an argument suggests, by revealing that the mechanisms of control are not simply those of clear-cut dominance and force. They are not even locatable because they are part of everything, including the most banal and familiar.

Moreover, the illusoriness of a place outside power is also part of Dickens's story. That prisons are actually inescapable—and that we as subjects carry them with us always (and even gladly)—might stand in as the readily available moral to such novels as *Tale of Two Cities, Great Expectations,* and *Little Dorrit.* Dickens's novels analyze, even as they operate within, this system, just as current criticism does, and as readers we inherit much of our contemporary sense of

[1]For the best recent analysis of this indifferent network, see D. A. Miller, *The Novel and the Police* (1988), 58–106. Dominick LaCapra accuses Miller of thinking the text just uncritically relays such networks without granting them the same access to critique that Miller's own essay implicitly claims for itself; see LaCapra, "Ideology and Critique in Dickens's *Bleak House," Representations* 6 (Spring 1984): 116–23.

the individual's lack of autonomy within the system that creates and disposes of it from depictions of it such as those in Dickens.[2]

That Dickens's work must also perform the very operations of power it describes is a truism in a system where not to do so is unthinkable. But that Dickens's work thematizes its own entrapment changes significantly our sense of those operations and how we chart them, if only to make us see the desperation with which his work reacts to such knowledge, the subtlety with which it attempts to manage its predicament, or accommodate itself to it. For all of Dickens's characters do, in one sense or another, struggle (if only to come to terms) with the encompassing network that defines and controls them, no matter how conditional such struggle may be, no matter how necessarily it may backfire. The degree of their ability to evade what their texts set up as inevitable might be one index to what critics have also long recognized as another inherent element of Dickens's novels—the quality of romance within them.

Setting up romance in opposition to power makes romance more than simple idealization or wish. In this chapter I consider how romance becomes for the novel the imaginary locus of dissatisfaction, rebelliousness; it becomes the traditional epitome of that which challenges or escapes restraint, namely, desire itself. The identification of romance with desire—that unsatisfiable "want of something" which Dickens felt propelled *him* through life—sug-

---

[2]Despite all Foucault's attention to the positive effects of power (the generative power of life that he discusses at the end of the first volume of *The History of Sexuality*, for example; see Michel Foucault, *The History of Sexuality: An Introduction*, vol. 1, trans. Robert Hurley [1980], 135–59), the most effective model of normative power relations remains for him the prison. As he makes the case in *Discipline and Punish*, the prison occupies a "central position" in the working of power; it provides (what I can hardly escape calling) the governing metaphor for his depiction of our implication as subjects in that power (Michel Foucault, *Discipline and Punish: The Birth of the Prison*, trans. Alan Sheridan [1979], 308). The centrality of the image of the prison to his own argument suggests that Foucault's analytics of power must inevitably continue to see power on some level as domination (if only by implication through such metaphors) because it cannot magically divest itself of the attitudes and rhetoric it examines. Foucault is aware of this, although critics have argued that that awareness does not make enough of a difference in his practice; see Nancy Fraser, "Foucault's Body-Language: A Post-Humanist Political Rhetoric?" *Salmagundi* 61 (Fall 1983): 55–70. Although a useful discussion of the way Foucault repeats the gestures he is critiquing, Fraser's essay may oversimplify Foucault's rationale for doing so: it rewrites him in terms of a political pragmatics that winds up, as Fraser admits, looking quite conservative.

gests too the way romance inhabits whatever attempts to reject and disclaim it.[3] By constructing transgressive desires as romance—what it is not—the novel makes them other, attempts to disown them. This strategy of displacement and denial provides one way to regulate impossible desires, allowing at the same time a way to indulge them; in being disowned they become safe enough to be allowed to operate.

Such a deployment of romance is similar to the treatment of imprisonment within Dickens's novels, which, even as it localizes that threat, nonetheless recognizes the impossibility of escape. Dickens's attention to form in one of his novels often (conventionally) considered romantic, *The Old Curiosity Shop*, shows how romance becomes a structural principle in his works, one that rebels against a system set up in terms of constriction and imprisonment by ignoring, deferring, or attempting to unsettle the kind of narrative closure Dickens especially associated with a well-ordered novel. Romance is constructed by the novel as a way to disown the novel's own problems of form, especially those that point to problems of ideology, of being contained within a controlling system of assumptions, representations, and behaviors.

[3]Edgar Johnson, vol. 2 of *Charles Dickens: His Tragedy and Triumph* 2 vols. (1952), p. 625. I want to emphasize that, in embodying desire, woman is only a scapegoat. The desire associated with her is not essentially hers but patriarchy's projection onto its idea of woman. Woman is simply the traditional—and the most convenient and satisfying—other, but marginal male characters certainly embody this impulse in Dickens too. In *The Old Curiosity Shop*, the character with the sexiest name, Dick Swiveller, also moves "after a sinuous and corkscrew fashion" (Charles Dickens, *The Old Curiosity Shop*, ed. Angus Easson [1972], ch. 23, p. 236; all future references [hereafter abbreviated *OCS*] will appear in the text), and Dick too leads the plot astray: his romance with the Marchioness is a detour from the novel's main story, one so attractive it threatens to split the book in half (Thackeray, for instance, said, "[I have] never read the *Nelly* part of *The Old Curiosity Shop* more than once; whereas I have Dick Swiveller and the Marchioness by heart," [from "Jerome Paturot," quoted in *Dickens: The Critical Heritage*, ed. Philip Collins (1971), 91]). Quilp, that (conventionally romantic) grotesque who embodies the impulse to transgress limits, especially through his sexual power, fittingly succumbs to waywardness gone out of control; the posse that has come to seize Quilp gets lost, and aimlessly circles while he drowns (*OCS*.67.620). Dickens's other books make sense in these terms as well: Pickwick's book is episodic because Pickwick too embodies desire, if only because he is continually on the run from sexuality. It is the men Dickens offers as typical—exemplars of patriarchy—who do not wander. And just as men can stand for desire, they can also represent (and often do) the conservative power of the home.

In Dickens's work, romance appears as transgression especially through its association with woman, herself like romance displaced and other. Woman is Dickens's emblem for the restlessness of romance, its persistent, uneasy attempts to escape; her wayward roving enacts the narrative disquiet of romance. One persistent motif in Dickens is what Ellen Moers, in another context, has called his "agitating women": those restless, errant women, such as Nell, Nancy, or Lady Dedlock, who roam through his works.[4] By constructing women as carried away by transgressive desires, Dickens's novels place men on the side of order; his novels construct as male the very englobing system of power that these errant women attempt to unsettle or escape. Rather than denying their own implication within power, then, Dickens's novels displace their own resistance to it in such a way that they (and the male order they represent) can claim control over, or at least associate themselves with, that power.

Yet the very act of managing their own impossible desires by rewriting them through the agency of women and romance exposes what it attempts to conceal: that men and novels don't inscribe others within power but are inscribed within it themselves. The ending of *The Old Curiosity Shop*, for example, betrays the indifference of the world in which the male order attempts to gain privilege and control, and the price that order must pay even for the illusion of doing so. The accession to power is simply another form of imprisonment, which keeps that group called men orderly and docile within the very system of discipline they attempt to use.

In order to counter or revise such a perception, parallel to the romance of wandering in Dickens's work is that other romance, the romance of the home. Women are not only scapegoated in Dickens's novels for their attempts to escape prison, but women are, paradoxically but accordingly, those inmates most completely imprisoned. The home, women's proper place, is as much as Chancery an emblem of the intrusive permeations of domination and management. And although the home as romance seems opposed to that other romance, wandering—the home representing the very en-

---

[4]Ellen Moers, "*Bleak House:* The Agitating Women," *The Dickensian* 69 (January 1973): 13–24. I am indebted to her for her brief thoughts on women's walking, both in this essay and in her book *Literary Women* (1976; 1985), 130.

closure that wandering seeks to escape—these two romances are actually also similar because their function is the same: the romantic home also consoles the male order, suggesting that women are imprisoned inside it by men. The streetwalker and the homebody turn out not to be all that different.

At the heart of my argument is the contention that, for all their wishful scapegoating of others, Dickens's novels also acknowledge that neither the novel nor the male order can escape the submission and compliance it projects on women and romance. It is perhaps a part of this failure to sustain such a consolation that romance in Dickens's work continues to exercise "an awkward interest (awkward because romantic)," as he calls it in *The Mystery of Edwin Drood*.[5] The interest of romance endures, in fact, *because* of its awkwardness: it does not simply provide Dickens's fiction with a way to manage its desires or identify with the controlling system in which it operates; it also (and awkwardly for that system perhaps, ultimately disrupting its smooth operations, forcing its ever necessary vigilance and constant permutations) repeatedly exposes Dickens's fiction as existing within that system.

The importance of woman in Dickens's work is that she is, like romance, symptomatic: her vicissitudes demonstrate the forces at play in that work. As well as scapegoating her, Dickens's fiction also identifies with her, aligning her romantic character with writing itself. In Dickens's novels, woman becomes an emblem of the way writing, too, is imprisoned within and provides a field for the operations of supervision and control. Yet the treatment of women within Dickens's fiction should also warn that such identification can be only another ploy of dominance. The current struggle for authority within the institution of academic literary criticism, for instance, makes use of such a ploy in its relation to feminism. In this chapter I consider the utility of women in Dickens's works— especially in *The Old Curiosity Shop, Bleak House,* and *Great Expectations*—as well as in current debate. But in unraveling the collapse of different figurations of romance and of woman, I demonstrate that such utility is also always tenuous.

[5]Charles Dickens, *The Mystery of Edwin Drood*, ed. Arthur J. Cox (1974), ch. 3, p. 53.

II

Dickens's contemporaries and early critics unhesitatingly labeled his work as "romance,"[6] relying, more or less roughly, on the distinction between romance and the novel formulated long before by Clara Reeve and repeated by Sir Walter Scott in the *Encyclopedia Brittanica*: a distinction between "the ordinary train of human events," on the one hand, and "wild adventures" and "the marvellous," on the other.[7] Dickens's work, although taking adventures and marvels in part for its content, also seemed romantic to his critics because of what they agreed on as its major flaw: "The thing which Dickens has yet to do, is to write a good story."[8] This association of romance with deviations of plot, a link implicit in Scott's contrast of romance with the novel's smooth train of events, influenced Dickens's critics, who saw romance as an error of form in his novels, a quality that disturbed them and needed to be controlled. The trouble with his stories lay in their structure— "The plot is invariably his great difficulty"—because they seemed to lack direction, go easily astray.[9]

In faulting those novels, for example, a reviewer of *Oliver Twist*, confounded by its (lack of) "plot, if it be not an abuse of terms to use such an expression," grounded that novel's structural problems in its romance: "The whole tale rivals in improbabilities those stories in which the hero at his birth is cursed by a wicked fairy and protected by a good one."[10] A reviewer of *Our Mutual Friend* (who titled his review "Mr. Dickens's Romance of a Dust-heap") agreed:

---

[6] A reviewer of *Sketches by Boz*, for example, proclaimed that from the start Dickens's subject was "the romance, as it were, of real life" (from the *Spectator*, quoted by Robert Newsom, *Dickens on the Romantic Side of Familiar Things: 'Bleak House' and the Novel Tradition* [1977], 1). A reviewer of *Bleak House* found in Lady Dedlock's story "a romance of to-day" (from *Blackwood's Edinburgh Magazine*, excerpted in *Dickens's "Bleak House": A Casebook*, ed. A. E. Dyson [1970], 90).

[7] Clara Reeve, vol. 1 of *The Progress of Romance through Times, Countries, and Manners*, 2 vols. (1785; 1970), p. 111; and Sir Walter Scott, "An Essay on Romance," in *Chivalry, Romance, the Drama*, vol. 6 of his *The Miscellaneous Prose Works*, 6 vols. (1827), pp. 154–55.

[8] From *Putnam's Magazine*, excerpted in Dyson, *Dickens's Bleak House*, 75.

[9] Unsigned Review of *Bleak House*, in the *Illustrated London News*, in Collins, *Dickens: The Critical Heritage*, 281.

[10] [Richard Ford], *Quarterly Review*, in Collins, *Dickens: The Critical Heritage*, 84.

Dickens is not happy in plot because "he has sometimes and often devised most unnatural positions and situations"; the reviewer found as much romance in that book as in the "half grotesque and half horrible episodical thread of Miss Haversham" [sic] in *Great Expectations*.[11] In such critiques, romance slips over from a problem of content to one of structure.

Such early critics are not alone in tracing a connection between romance and discursive, episodic plot; modern theorists of romance trace this connection too. Northrop Frye has suggested that romance is the form that comes closest to pure story, a vagrant "and-then" form, carried along by its own momentum from one discontinuous event to another.[12] Patricia Parker also characterizes romance as "a sequential and processional form," but to Parker the sequential remains "within a frame in which presence, or fulfillment, is always in some sense placed at a distance."[13] According to Parker, this distant end is what gives meaning to the divagations of romance, what makes them *err*. But this dynamic of the text which romance lays bare is, Roland Barthes suggests, one element of narrative encoded within every text:" "whereas the sentences quicken the story's 'unfolding' and cannot help but move the story along, the hermeneutic code performs an opposite action: it must set up *delays* (obstacles, stoppages, deviations) in the flow of the discourse. . . . [It] interrupts the sentence, suspends it, turns it aside."[14] For Parker, when this principle becomes marked and takes over, when the delays intensify and the end becomes more open, a text is romantic. Although she differs from Frye in emphasizing an endpoint from which romance's story veers, her focus, like his, is on the process: it is the veering away, the pausing and backtracking, that is romantic.[15]

[11]Unsigned Review, in the *Eclectic and Congregational Review*, in Collins, *Dickens: The Critical Heritage*, 459.

[12]Northrop Frye, *The Secular Scripture: A Study of the Structure of Romance* (1976), 47. This spinning out of a tale, according to Frye, is "the romantic element" in works like *Little Dorrit* and *Our Mutual Friend*, and such "a sprawling octopus of a plot . . . which we can hardly follow at the time and cannot remember afterwards, seems to be almost an anti-narrative" (40).

[13]Patricia Parker, *Inescapable Romance: Studies in the Poetics of a Mode* (1979), 13.

[14]Roland Barthes, *S/Z*, trans. Richard Miller (1974), 75.

[15]For a thorough discussion of the way narrative forces are in *excess* of closure and the way resistance to closure generates narrative, however, see D. A. Miller's first book, *Narrative and Its Discontents: Problems of Closure in the Traditional Novel* (1981).

In his fiction, Dickens himself implicitly defines romance as a deviating and-then form. One of his Christmas stories, "Mugby Junction," under the running head "A Lesson in Romance" contains the following instruction in the principles of romance: young Polly

> commenced a long romance, of which every relishing clause began with the words: "So this," or "And so this." As, "So this boy," or, "So this fairy;" or, "And so this pie was four yards round, and two yards and a quarter deep." The interest of the romance was derived from the intervention of this fairy to punish this boy for having a greedy appetite. To achieve which purpose, this fairy made this pie, and this boy ate and ate and ate, and his cheeks swelled and swelled and swelled. There were many tributary circumstances, but the forcible interest culminated in the total consumption of this pie, and the bursting of this boy.[16]

By the relishing clauses that characterize romance, Dickens primarily means embellishments, but the word "relish" in its root form carries the sense of "to release or relax." The form of romance, its connecting clauses, relaxes the forcible interest of the plot. Tributary circumstances swallow up the culmination, and with relish, just as the boy swallows up the pie. That the romance here transforms and yet is part of a didactic tale—the bursting boy a comic lesson to all greedy children that burlesques the didactic form while engaging in it, much as Dickens's own novels do— suggests the consolatory function of romance: the explosive anti-closure of romance can be placed in service of and made to enforce a particular agenda.

Miller's more recent work on the novel reconsiders the deconstructive and psychoanalytic tendency of this earlier work.

[16]Charles Dickens, "Mugby Junction," in *Christmas Stories*, vol. 32 of *The Gadshill Edition of the Works of Charles Dickens*, ed. Andrew Lang, 33 vols. (1897–99), p. 164; this edition hereafter abbreviated *The Works*. For the linking of women and romance through pie in Dickens, see "Nurse's Stories," in *The Uncommercial Traveler*, vol. 29 of *The Works*, pp. 176–80; and "The Holly-Tree," in *Christmas Stories*, vol. 31 of *The Works*, pp. 123–24. Dickens gives us different versions of a sinister romance of a pie that he heard as a baby from his nurse. Her narration of romances links women with the form but so does the content of this particular romance: in "Nurse's Stories," Captain Murderer, after his various wedding nights, bakes his brides into pies and happily eats them.

The formal release and dissipation of romance carry with them sexual associations, and, following Barthes, Parker ties this structural understanding of romance to an erotics of the text:

> The suspensions which for Barthes become part of an erotics of the text recall not only the constant divagations of romance and its resistance to the demands of closure, but also the frustration . . . of what Barthes calls the teleological form of vulgar readerly pleasure—the desire to penetrate the veil of meaning or to hasten the narrative's gradual striptease—by a continual postponement of revelation which leaves the reader suspended, or even erotically "hung up."[17]

Such an erotics is often grounded in the figure of a woman, a seductress teasing toward yet delaying consummation, endlessly desirable because unavailable, and who, like the boy, is ultimately often sacrificed too, extinguished by what are constructed as her own desires.

The *Arabian Nights Entertainment*, or *The Thousand and One Nights*, is the premier example of romance as an endless drifting story manifested in a woman's devious leading on. A labyrinth of digression, this story slides on and on—a thousand and *one* nights. The teasing provocativeness of the *Arabian Nights* is figured in Scheherazade, who stands in for the text itself, is the emblem of its romance: Thackeray's collusion of the two, for example—he hopes all "have found *their* romancer—their charming Scheherazade"— is typical.[18] Scheherazade too is threatened with extinction, which she must put off, and her romance connects the coyness of women and of plot: the popular (mis)conception of Scheherazade's story, owing partly to bowdlerized translations and partly to an inevitable logic, is that she puts off sexual as well as narrative climax from night to night. And the *Arabian Nights* was one of Dickens's favorite romances. As he revealed to John Forster in his autobiographical

---

[17]Parker, *Inescapable Romance*, 220–21.

[18]William Makepeace Thackeray, "De Juventute," in *Roundabout Papers*, vol. 22 of *The Charterhouse Edition of the Works of William Makepeace Thackeray*, 26 vols. (1901), p. 79. Quoted by Margaret Annan, "The *Arabian Nights* in Victorian Literature" (Ph.D. diss., Northwestern University, 1945), 54.

sketch (later included in *David Copperfield*) it was one of the books of his childhood that formed his imagination.[19]

In Dickens's most extended frame-tale, *The Old Curiosity Shop*, the formal waywardness of romance and its connection through women to desire become most clear. This work too is a tale prompted and prolonged by desire—Quilp's for little Nell, Dickens's for Mary Hogarth. George Gissing called Nell "a child of romance,"[20] and that her death is necessary for the novel to end shows not just that she stands in for its romance (by ending her rambles the novel short-circuits the detours of romance) but also that she exposes the purpose that romance serves: Nell's sacrifice to the closure of the novel suggest the way it needs to project out, to pursue and kill off, what are really its own dissatisfactions with closure and all that closure implies. The male order projects its own dissatisfactions with order onto a woman so that it can indulge these feelings at a distance, converting its own discomfort and even disturbing rebelliousness into a form that is displaced and manageable. By ultimately killing the woman off, that order seems to get rid of its dissatisfactions. In *The Old Curiosity Shop*, such romantic impulses are managed and controlled at a still further remove: contained within a frame that is governed by the appropriately named Master Humphrey. Such structural complexity suggests the elaborate lengths to which the narrative seems pushed in its endless compromises. It suggests too the overkill with which it meets the threat represented by women's desires.

The Old Curiosity Shop grew out of Dickens's weekly periodical, *Master Humphrey's Clock*. The governing conceit of *Master Humphrey's Clock* was a club, whose members met to read tales to each other. This governing story provided the periodical with a frame, a narrative device of lasting interest for Dickens, as his Christmas stories illustrate. The frame intrigued him because, as

---

[19]John Forster, vol. 1 of *The Life of Charles Dickens*, 3 vols. (1872), p. 9. George Gissing also found it the most important romantic influence on Dickens's writing; see George Gissing, *Charles Dickens: A Critical Study*, vol. 20 of *The Standard Edition of the Works of Charles Dickens*, 22 vols. (n. d.), pp. 29–30. See also Annan, "The Arabian Nights," 201–2.

[20]Quoted by Loralee MacPike, " 'The Old Cupiosity Shape': Changing Views of Little Nell, Part I," *Dickens Studies Newsletter* 12 (June 1981): 37.

he said of *Master Humphrey's Clock*, it supplied an "almost inexhaustible field" for him to mine, linking together wildly discontinuous events without the novel's demand for unity, and, in his early plans for the periodical, Dickens drew his ideas of its form directly from that framed tale, the *Arabian Nights*.[21] Yet although Dickens designed *Master Humphrey's Clock* precisely for its discontinuity, that very quality seemed to worry him. Would the work have any point or interest? He considered heading it with a quotation from the *Spectator*, promising "to give it over, as soon as I grow dull,"[22] and as early as the first installment, he was bothered by what some of his critics characterized as "the article's slow pace and lack of incident."[23] According to Forster, Dickens's concerns were justified; his audience was bothered by the disunity of the work: "with the discovery that there was no continuous tale the orders at once diminished."[24]

The Old Curiosity Shop was introduced in order to bring *Master Humphrey's Clock* into line. In search of a narrative to contrast with the frame, Dickens inserted what was at first meant to be a short tale and, immediately after including "the little child-story,"[25] as he called it, wrote to his publishers that he had begun "to give [*Master Humphrey*] a less discursive appearance."[26] *The Old Curiosity Shop* was designed to oppose the "discursive," which in its root sense means "to run to and fro." In the preface to the completed novel, Dickens's relief in its unity and directedness is apparent: "The first chapter of this tale appeared in the fourth number of MASTER HUMPHREY'S CLOCK, when I had already been made uneasy by the desultory character of that work. . . . The commencement of a story was a great satisfaction to me" (*OCS*.Preface.41). Dickens's assumption is that the nature of *The Old Curiosity Shop* as story—as a "child-story" that grows up to be a novel—necessarily gives it focus and closure. Perhaps it is because this novel was originally

[21]For the "inexhaustible field," see "To John Forster [14 July 1839]," in vol. 1 of *The Letters of Charles Dickens*, ed. Madeline House, Graham Storey, and Kathleen Tillotson, 6 vols. (1965–), p. 564. For mention of *The Arabian Nights*, see "To John Forster, [14 July 1839]," in *Letters*, 1: 564.

[22]"To John Forster, 13 September 1840," in *Letters*, 2: 127 n3.

[23]"To W.C. Macready, [29 January 1840]," in *Letters*, 2: 13 n3.

[24]Forster, *Life of Charles Dickens*, 1: 179.

[25]"To John Forster, [?8 March 1840]," in *Letters*, 2: 40.

[26]"To Messrs. Chapman & Hall, [9 March 1840]," in *Letters*, 2: 41.

conceived to give aimlessness a focus that it becomes such an end-obsessed story; the end of Nell's story must be the definitive end, death, to overemphasize its function as well as overcompensate for its failure to fulfill that function.

For fail it does; the romantic episodic quality of *Master Humphrey's Clock* also infects this novel; it too rambles and digresses. Contemporary critics immediately questioned its unity and closure. One thought that the novel was "without much elaborateness of plot, or apparently fixedness of purpose in the mind of the author."[27] Dickens answered, "I never had the design and purpose of a story so distinctly marked in my mind, from its commencement." But he admitted, "I know a great many people are of [your mind]."[28] Forster, too, thought the novel involved "less direct consciousness of design on [Dickens's] own part than I can remember in any other instance of all his career,"[29] and this judgment survives to this day, echoed by critics such as Edmund Wilson, who find it "an impromptu yarn, spun out."[30]

Yet Dickens's disclaimers against romantic restlessness screen its attraction for him. Modern critics also note the animating importance of romance in Dickens's work. John Kucich argues that "what Dickens meant by Romance . . . would seem to be, quite simply, energy"; Elaine Showalter suggests that for Dickens, "this ceaseless activity and motion, for all he paints it dark, is the source of life and human values."[31] Although readers may question the humanist idealization implied in the triumph of "life" that such upbeat formulations express, romance remains a necessary—and necessarily denied—element permitting the operation of Dickens's delicately balanced fictional system.

The Old Curiosity Shop announces its own romantic discursiveness by opening with a "ramble" (1.44). Master Humphrey, on one of his idle nightwalks, runs into Nell, who has lost her way, and he returns her to it by the most devious and intricate route

[27]"To Thomas Latimer, 13 March 1841," in *Letters*, 2: 233 n4.
[28]"To Thomas Latimer, 13 March 1841," in *Letters*, 2: 233.
[29]Forster, *Life of Charles Dickens*, 1: 178.
[30]Edmund Wilson, "The Two Scrooges," in *The Wound and the Bow: Seven Studies in Literature* (1947), 18.
[31]John Kucich, *Excess and Restraint in the Novels of Charles Dickens* (1981), 193; Elaine Showalter, "Guilt, Authority, and the Shadows of *Little Dorrit*," *Nineteenth-Century Fiction* 34 (1979): 27.

(1.46). Such a proliferation of indirection calls attention to itself, setting the stage for the rambling of the rest of the novel. With Master Humphrey's disappearance from the novel—perhaps he can disappear precisely because of this—Nell inherits his aimless, peripatetic motion. When she meets Master Humphrey at the very beginning of the story, she is lost, implying that she has a direction; yet, after his exit, when she flees London with her grandfather, she too becomes an aimless wanderer. This emphasis on random walking renders literal the romantic "discursive" character of the book. Moreover, this master's immediate obsession with and assumption of authority over Nell set up woman's attraction and usefulness for the patriarch(y): he loses Nell within mazes that he himself supposedly controls—both the deliberately confusing path he guides her through and the story he tells about her. She takes over his random motion, making it a woman's problem, set up in such a way that he has power and control over her and over it.

This romantic impulse is an important element in the book because it strings out even as it leads up to satisfying the demands of closure. Romance catches up the plot in its own movement and makes it heedless of its goal, just as, during Kit's journey to find Nell, despite his hope and anxiety for what lies at journey's end, he finds himself as he hurtles toward that end hypnotized by the twistings and turnings of the "road itself" so that everything collapses into that road: "a wall, a ruin, a sturdy gable-end, would rise up in the road; and when they were plunging headlong at it, would be the road itself" (70.640). *The Old Curiosity Shop* continues the digressions and wanderings of *Master Humphrey's Clock*, prolonging the very resolution it was meant to create; Dickens admits: "I am breaking my heart over this story, and cannot bear to finish it."[32] To justify drawing out Nell's death, he tells Forster: "I only began yesterday, and this part of the story is not to be galloped over, I can tell you. . . . I tremble to approach the place a great deal more than Kit."[33] He takes care to suggest that *The Old Curiosity Shop* never really does end. The book continues after its conclusion as a tale of little Nell that Kit repeats again and again to his children, just as

32"To George Cattermole, [?22 December 1840]," in *Letters*, 2: 172.
33"To John Forster, [?8 January 1841]," in *Letters*, 2: 181.

Master Humphrey is telling us that tale now.[34] Dickens neatly sums up the tension between romantic perpetuation and novelistic resolution in his metaphor for the writing of *Master Humphrey*, the winding of Master Humphrey's clock. "Wind, wind, wind, always winding am I," he writes; "and day and night the alarum is in my ears, warning me that it must not run down."[35] The notion of winding catches the doubleness between the novel and romance in Dickens's writing—"to wind up" means to finish as well as to keep going, and Dickens's fiction works because it can swing back and forth between the two.

The swing of this pendulum is especially effective because of the figure caught below it. *The Old Curiosity Shop* is Nell's story; her "image sanctifies the game" (31.306), and, modern prejudice aside, Dickens meant readers of the book to be like the inquisitive landlady in the story, "who had a great curiosity to be made acquainted with every particular of Nell's life and history" (46.433).[36] Her story is one of romantic deferral, the deferral of her death; her wanderings through the countryside draw out that death and emblematize the structural principle that the novel claims to suppress while indulging it. Such deferrals diffuse the blame for that death—for Nell ultimately does die, of course, and despite the (self-interested)

---

[34]The bachelor's letters to Mr. Garland are also installments of the novel in miniature: "he had dwelt upon them from first to last, and had told there such a tale of their wanderings, and mutual love, that few could read it without being moved to tears" (*OCS*.68.628–29).

[35]"To Walter Savage Landor, 26 July 1840," in *Letters*, 2: 106.

[36]The landlady's curiosity, in a text entitled *The Old Curiosity Shop*, might be seen as an example of how a pernicious surveillance sets up the realm of the ordinary. Significantly, the responsibility for such monitoring is deliberately shifted to a woman (and to the domestic—she is a landlady, a professional homebody—a category about which I will have something to say later in this chapter): the landlady herself admits "curiosity you know is the curse of our sex, and that's the fact" (*OCS*.46.433). The landlord's response to her statement ("The landlord scratched his head, as if he thought the curse sometimes involved the other sex likewise" [*OCS*.46.433]), in its ambiguity, catches the doubleness of Dickens's attitude: on the one hand, perhaps, his response seems to imply that the consolation of scapegoating doesn't quite work—men *do* remain curious, however much they blame women for it—at the same time it implies that it does work—men *aren't* curious; women's curiosity is to blame for getting men in trouble, "involving" them in something of which they are innocent.

denials of the literary fraternity of Dickens's time, Nell's name, at least, implies that her death is built into her very characterization from the beginning—and, by diffusing it, allow reader and narrator to enjoy it without feeling too complicitous in it.

That the male order may be culpable for her death is actually important to its claims, since such control over her might attest to male power. Such power over romantic women is carefully figured, directed away from aggression and violence, and supported instead by that well-worn bedrock, men's sexual power over the inferior sex. Nell's supposed leading on toward a desired consummation, and yet her teasing away from it, suggest the way such anxious desires get localized as sexuality. It's no accident, for example, that Master Humphrey's eyes light right away on Nell's bed in the old curiosity shop; similarly, an early illustration of Nell has her lying in it, and her death ultimately fixes her there for good. Quilp's pursuit of Nell, which drives her there, highlights one aspect of this sexuality. It recalls the biographical story of Dickens's own enduring longing for his sister-in-law, who died in his arms. The biographical debate about Mary Hogarth largely agrees on her relation to *The Old Curiosity Shop;* in that novel, Dickens's guilty desire for his wife's sister—guilty both because illicit and because he felt it caused her death—are figured by Quilp's pursuit of Nell, which also ends in her death(bed).[37] But whatever feelings of remorse such stories imply are equally matched by their celebration of male sexual power. Quilp's own death may be a punishment for his desire, but it also figures its power (a power emblematized by Quilp's burning red cigar [4.82–83]), for Nell dies after him, as if his desire has given her life, kept her going. She is the ground on which that desire plays.

At the same time, however, the book suggests that Nell must, according to idiomatic logic, be lying in a bed that she herself has

[37]For a discussion of the critical debate about Mary Hogarth's influence, see MacPike, "'The Old Cupiosity Shape,'" and also Michael Steig, "The Central Action of 'The Old Curiosity Shop,' or Little Nell Revisited Again," *Literature and Psychology* 15 (Summer 1965): 163–70. Steig's statement that when Nell's death finally comes, it is a relief, for "like the rape of Clarissa, it's good to have it over" (167), not only illustrates that that death is sexualized but betrays the function of such sexualizing for its (male) audience: it provides (or ought to) an easy sacrifice of woman to design, a way of stopping dead the trouble she causes. Such readers want to cry: "The deed is done; the novel lives!"

made. Nell is more than "pure as the newly-fallen snow" (72.658), more than a blank white ground on which male appetite can be projected. Certainly Nell seems the best example in Dickens, if not in English literature, of the absolute denial of any active female sexuality. Yet Dickens's attempts to deny Nell even gender, his harping on her status as child rather than young woman—or even the fourteen-year-old girl he says she is—also seem excessive, overdetermined denials.

We can see the connection of Nell's wandering and her sexuality at that epitome of morally dubious motion, the racetrack, in her first attempt at begging:

> There was but one lady who seemed to understand the child, and she was one who sat alone in a handsome carriage, while two young men in dashing clothes, who had just dismounted from it, talked and laughed loudly at a little distance, appearing to forget her, quite. There were many ladies all around, but they turned their backs, or looked another way, or at the two young men (not unfavourably at *them*), and left her to herself. She motioned away a gypsy-woman urgent to tell her fortune, saying that it was told already and had been for some years, but called the child towards her, and taking her flowers put money into her trembling hand, and bade her go home and keep at home for God's sake. (OCS.19.213–14)

The erring woman, alone in her carriage, emphasizes the inherently sexual nature that Dickens's work accords to woman's independent motion, but the distinctive suggestion of this tableau is this woman's responsibility for her fortune. She has not been acted on so much as she herself has acted, as the other ladies, ignoring her but gazing approvingly at the young men, suggest; their desire for the men highlights and repeats what they profess to condemn, what once must have been the fallen woman's own favorable glances, her active desire. Nell, as passive and innocent mirror of male desire, is not the only model for female sexuality in the book. Moreover, Nell's innocence is in question: that this strayed woman is the only one who understands Nell, and that her plea to her is so desperate, suggest a greater identification than that she was once penniless too; there is more of a similarity between them as fellow travelers. Nell's very agitation (she trembles), given its context, heightens the identification. It is a gesture drawn from the Victorian stock of conventional sexual markers—trembling can signal desirability and desire.

Nell's death demonstrates that the male order needs a category of female sexuality because it needs to project and drive out its own ultimately unsatisfied (because unsatisfiable) desires. Quilp's death marks the violent extinction of just such desires. Projecting sexuality onto Nell, and then killing her, is a way of leaving men with only diffused and negotiated desires, purged of all the insurgent force this text characterizes as monstrous—Quilp-like—and, hence, needing to be conquered. The erotic recompense of Nell's death scene (and critics have long pointed to its sexual charge) is denied to the malcontent, Quilp, but is, telling, given to a boy and a group of old men, as if a reward for their very powerlessness. They are reanimated by it, but not threateningly, just as are the group of living dead who gather at Nell's graveside (72.657–58).

The single gentleman's unmasking at the end of the book seems to emphasize that Nell's sacrifice is meant to profit the world of men, for her deathbed gathering brings about the reunion of the younger and elder brothers. But that reunion is an empty one; the reader is told the grandfather never does actually acknowledge his brother (72.660). Similarly, it is hard to accept that that brother is also Master Humphrey, an identification that is not so much a failed overelaboration of the story as it is a reiteration of the impossibility of the very identifications—bonds—Dickens's story tries to foster. The conventional climactic recognition scene never comes off, disturbing the closure of the novel, and upsetting both the identification of the male order with such regulating novelistic desires and its identification of such devices with power. Overturning closure or putting it into question does not provide a realm of freedom in The Old Curiosity Shop; the only realm Dickens can imagine for that is death, a pyrrhic victory indeed, for he fails to imbue Nell's death with any transcendent meaning, as he was the first to admit.[38] The saving and life-giving relations (between men) that the male order imagines for itself remain unrealized within the novel, only a fantasy of "consol[ation]" (71.651) that the younger brother seeks for the vio-

[38]Dickens writes: "I can't preach to myself the schoolmaster's consolation [that death has meaning because 'good deeds' come from 'dusty graves'], though I try"; "To John Forster, [?8 January 1841]," in Letters, 2: 181–82.

lence and indifference of his world. That Dickens figures this younger brother as Master Humphrey, a weak and misshapen cripple, suggests just how ironic and muted is his novel's sense of men's mastery in this world.

Closure is complicated within Dickens's work because it recognizes closure not just as completion and unity but also as (what is implied in its root meaning) enclosure, barring, imprisonment. Kit's imprisonment, one among many in Dickens's fiction, offers a clear example of the sense of enclosure and constriction that suffuses the world of that fiction. While in prison, Kit dreams "always of being at liberty, and roving about, now with one person and now with another; but ever with a vague dread of being recalled to prison; not that prison, but one which was in itself a dim idea, not of a place, but of a care and sorrow; of something oppressive and always present, and yet impossible to define" (61.556–57). Similarly, Pip, in a novel overshadowed by the bulk of Newgate prison, characterizes his education in the law of his fathers as the heavy obligation of what he calls to "walk in the same all the days of my life."[39] It is as a "thick curtain . . . [falling] on all interest and romance" and "never," he reports, "has that curtain dropped so heavy and blank, as when my way in life lay stretched out straight before me" (GE.14.135). This vision that the very passage through life is a prison itself accounts for the melancholy of *Great Expectations*, its resigned acceptance that we must convert our great expectations into common unhappiness.[40] Pip learns that the romance of his life is illusory, and the bleak path leading from the forge is the best and only way.

The common unhappiness that pervades Dickens's fiction becomes just another of his conservative ideals expressly because it is not shared in common; it is denied, or at least made bearable, at the expense of others. The heavy obligations of conscience that pain Pip when he strays from the path of virtue remind him of another rigidity: "Conscience is a dreadful thing when it accuses man or boy; but when, in the case of a boy, that secret burden co-operates with another secret burden down the leg of his trousers, it is (as I can

[39]Charles Dickens, *Great Expectations*, ed. Angus Calder (1965), ch. 7, p. 73; all future references to this book (hereafter abbreviated *GE*) will appear in the text.
[40]As suggested by Freud, "The Psychotherapy of Hysteria," in vol. 2 of *The Standard Edition of the Complete Psychological Works of Sigmund Freud*, trans. James Strachey, 24 vols. (1953–74), p. 305; this edition hereafter abbreviated *SE*.

testify) a great punishment" (GE.2.44). Literally that burden is the piece of bread Pip has secreted for Magwitch, but the double—sexual and legal—senses of "testify" point to a crucial link between Pip and the convict, who is also a "man with a load on *his* leg" (2.45). Magwitch's awakening of Pip to his own guilt and complicity within the structures of power and imprisonment is inherently associated with sexuality. Dickens's novels reduce the system of power relations to the romantic vagaries of sexual relations because sexual relations can be hierarchized. The reduction wishfully aligns authority once more with men. Moreover, those subjects in the supposedly privileged male position don't simply feel that the loads upon their legs are burdens. As Freud notes in "Medusa's Head," rigidity that looks like a punishment can also be felt as apotropaic, a man's reminder to himself of his own power.[41] That Pip's phallic burden "co-operates" with his conscience, with the self-regulating power that aids in constraining and imprisoning desire, suggests an urge not just to elude and wander from, but to identify with and control, that power.

The opposition between the straightforward march to closure and the deferrals of wandering is constructed and strategic, just as are those set up between men and women, or the novel and romance. The insistent restlessness inhabiting *The Old Curiosity Shop* suggests that such indirection is really no different from any more straightforward path; the first page of the novel shows that such detours, rather than leading to freedom, carry their own sense of oppression. Dickens, in an image that sets the tone for the novel, has Master Humphrey imagine the thoughts of a sick man, cut off from the world but forced to listen to it parade past his window: "that constant pacing to and fro, that never-ending restlessness, that incessant tread of feet" depict "the stream of life that will not stop, pouring on, on, on" (OCS.1.43). The novel emphasizes that such movement is much more a prison to the man forced to listen to it than the quiet grave in which he will ultimately lie. The grave, in fact, seems the only escape possible, and Dickens ironically poses this sphere, with its meaningless autonomy, to the self-perpetuating system from which it delivers us, contrasting "those who lay so

41Freud, "Medusa's Head," SE, 18: 273–74.

still beneath the moss and turf" with the "old restlessness" and "the useless strife in which they had worn away their lives" (17.187). In its grimly insufficient way death remains the culmination of Dickens's novel too, remains the only means of rescue for Nell from her imposed and oppressive wandering.

The agent of that wandering, Nell's grandfather, epitomizes the relation of the novel to her. Claiming to love and consider her in all that he does (and Master Humphrey, as spokesman for the book, insists the reader believe him: he "never doubted that his love for her was real" [1.55]—an insistence that helps demystify the attitudes and behaviors commonly called love, revealing that it too can be a tactic), her grandfather uses Nell as the excuse for his unacceptable desires—specifically his obsession with gambling, an activity that might be a metaphor of the book's logic, a desire that not only feeds on its own exercise but expects reward and privilege simply because it wants them. Nell is supposed to sanctify that game in particular. Not only does Nell's grandfather exploit her in pursuit of it and his own interests, but he expects her to care for him all the while. Although the book condemns his attitude—his question, " 'What would become of me without her?' " (27.273) meets with Mrs. Jarley's sharp rebuke for its selfish reversal of roles—such condemnation serves the purposes of the novel and is of no real aid to Nell. Instead, the novel presents the grandfather's blind and selfish treatment of her as diseased and extraordinary in order to screen its own complicity with it, its own reliance on such treatment as one of the rules of its own game.

Yet even the grandfather, who operates by scapegoating Nell, sometimes seems shocked into recognizing his (mis)use of her: even he pauses in the midst of blaming her for the "close eternal streets" through which they wander, of berating her for keeping him from the gambling that provides the fantasy of an impossible route out of those streets, even he stops to cry " 'Ah! poor, houseless, wandering, motherless child! . . . has all my agony of care brought her to this at last!' " (44.415). Yet the identification of Nell's wandering with her houselessness suggests that such a complaint is also in part as self-interested as the rest of the grandfather's perceptions. It points, in fact, to another kind of romance and another kind of consolation within Dickens's fiction.

Dickens's best-known statements about romance come in "A

Preliminary Word" to his periodical *Household Words* and in the Preface to *Bleak House*. One of the goals of *Household Words* is "to show to all, that in all familiar things, even in those which are repellent on the surface, there is Romance enough, if we will find it out."[42] In the Preface to *Bleak House*, Dickens likewise asserts that, in that novel, he has "purposely dwelt upon the romantic side of familiar things."[43] As the titles *Bleak House* and *Household Words*—and as Dickens's claim that he is "dwelling" on romance—suggest, Dickens's emphasis on the familiar becomes a romance of the home, the domestic circle that his works most closely associate with women. *Household Words* was particularly meant for women—a family magazine, which catered to housewifely interests and education—and *Bleak House* is in large part a celebration of women's home virtues: the prefaces to both announce Dickens's domestication of romance. Domestication, as its etymology suggests, is never very far from dominion; the home (*domus*) always presupposing its master (*dominus*).

That this home is meant to be a sanctuary from wandering, and from the dissatisfactions and longings that wandering entails, the scene at the racecourse, when the fallen woman bids Nell "go home and keep at home for God's sake," already implies. To the street-walkers who travel his novels, Dickens opposes that overtly roman-ticized sentimental stereotype, the tranquil Angel in the House, who is seemingly untroubled by sexual desire. Throughout his work, he deploys the home to coopt romantic movement: Dickens's paean to home midway through *The Old Curiosity Shop* explicitly stops the forward movement of his story (Dickens introduces this praise with "Stay" [38.362] and "let us linger in this place" [38.363]). Similarly, a character in *Pickwick* tells us "there's romance enough at home without going half a mile for it," a statement that might be the moral to *Bleak House*.[44] In that novel, Dickens directly sets the repose of the fireside against outside bustle. Jarndyce points the contrast between home and active life, identifying home life with women

[42]Charles Dickens, "A Preliminary Word," in *Miscellaneous Contributions*, vol. 19 of *The Standard Edition of the Works of Charles Dickens* (n.d.), p. 3; this volume hereafter abbreviated *Misc*.

[43]Charles Dickens, Preface, *Bleak House*, ed. Norman Page (1971), 43. All further references to this work (hereafter abbreviated *BH*) appear in the text.

[44]Charles Dickens, *The Posthumous Papers of the Pickwick Club*, ed. Robert L. Patten (1972), ch. 21, p. 361.

and reserving the active life for men, when he separates Ada and Rick: " 'She remains here, in her home with me. Love her, Rick, in your active life, no less than in her home' " (*BH*.13.232–33).[45] The home is almost the manifestation of formal closure in Dickens even more emphatically than in other novelists, the notoriously sentimental setting up of housekeeping at the end of his stories marking their culminations and resolutions.

The opposition between restless activity and stable home is meant to hide their similarity, to hide that they both serve the same consoling function. But if the home is reassuring in Dickens's work, it is not just because, as D. A. Miller suggests, Dickens uses it to represent the exemplary autonomous sphere outside the network of control. Rather, the home also attests to that network and its oppression. Despite the generous complications of his argument, Miller's conclusions—that the home and family are the banal embodiment of the same indifferent disciplinary system embodied in oppressive public institutions—restate what Dickens's novels, and feminist readers of them, have already said: that the home is a prison. The home is consoling to the *male* order, because it traditionally constructs the home as the woman's sphere, her proper place. Just as it serves the male order to represent the dissatisfactions of its desire as women's problem, and so displace and indulge them, it also reassures that order to transfer its awareness of its own oppression and imprisonment onto women. It achieves such a transfer by emphasizing women's inescapable imprisonment and confinement within the domestic, within the ordinary and insuperable details of daily life.

Bagnet's motto—"Discipline must be maintained" (*BH*.66.930)— then does not so much refer to the family's voluntary policing of all its subjects, as Miller has claimed, as it focuses that attention on the women within the family, whose peculiar servitude is what Bagnet actually demands when he says it, no matter how comically or ironically that demand is presented. *Bleak House* indeed presents Mrs. Bagnet's seeming autonomy, and even authority, as comic grotesquery, benign because clearly understood as comic, a reversal

---

[45]Yet, in keeping with the subversion in Dickens's writing of its own explicit ulterior romanticism, this distinction is an imposed one that the novel breaks down: Esther, for example, despite her praise of home duties, actually travels quite a bit (I am indebted to Margaret Berg for this observation).

of (what the novel believes ought to be) women's actual domestic subjection. Part of and attesting to the force of that subjection is that women do not necessarily accept it voluntarily and do not find it so benign. They are not as happy in it, for example, as is Nell's bird in its cage: the contrast of that lively caged bird with Nell's still body on her deathbed seems more than the conventional allegory of *vanitas;* it also emphasizes the options open to women and points the moral to those who, however innocently, stray. The happy inmate, embodied by that impossible character Esther Summerson (and she is perhaps so insipid and unbelievable because of this), is a romantic projection conveying a familiar mixed message. She is romantic in the sense of being other: *her* imprisonment ensures male freedom according to the logic the book sets up when the housekeeper, Mrs. Rouncewell, argues that Lady Dedlock's disclosure of her guilty domestic secret will free the housekeeper's favorite son from prison.[46] And she is also romantic in the sense of being ideal: her characterization keeps the dim sense of oppression neatly masked and sentimentalized in the "obligations of home" (6.113) that she willingly embraces.[47] Esther is the heart of this novel's romance: its first critics recognized her story as "sadly romantic enough," tacitly acknowledging that the very purpose of romance is to displace sorrow on women.[48] With her basket of keys, she is also the embodiment of home in *Bleak House,* a warder who actually locks herself up: she monitors most closely her own emotions so that she can remain happily incarcerated within Bleak House (and that name is also her euphemism for her pending marriage with Jarndyce).

Jarndyce's relation to Esther especially posits a male order that is in control of women's subjection, and, if not free from the prison

[46]A woman's guilt does ultimately free George, who then willingly chooses to stay with his mother in Chesney Wold, bringing an end to all his wanderings. George's freedom from prison may be the blind that permits this self-incarceration within the home. The book depicts George restraining himself within a realm foreign to him out of deference to his mother, whose domain it really is—an excess of filial piety that is part of the humor of his character. But the comedy hides a wish—that men aren't really part of the domestic—to cover over a suspicion—that men too are entrapped within the kind of structures the home represents.

[47]The plots of many of Dickens's novels, in fact—consider Estella in *Great Expectations,* or Bella in *Our Mutual Friend*—train women for this role, or, as these novels present it, raise them to this ideal.

[48]Review of *Bleak House,* in the *Athenaeum,* excerpted in Dyson, Dickens's *"Bleak House,"* 50.

itself, then at least able to subject others. Jarndyce's response to his own implication in the Chancery suit has been to organize and administer Bleak House(s), converting the desolation caused by Chancery into what seems a private asylum, recovering Bleak House from its initial (and seemingly essential) similarity to Tom's-All-Alone (8.146–47). Yet that transformation is maintained only by employing Esther, as housekeeper, to keep it up vigilantly. Esther, as willing servant, custodian of all Bleak House represents, ensures that Jarndyce will be its "generous master" (6.117). Her honorific for him, Guardian, suggests that he needs especially to appear a *benignant* master over her, one divorced from the kind of brutal exploitation on which mastery depends, one who somehow exerts no oppression. But Jarndyce's guardianship makes Esther's relation to him little different from that of the cottager wives to those they explicitly acknowledge as their masters. " 'I'm a-watching for my master,' [Liz tells Esther]. 'If he was to catch me away from home, he'd pretty near murder me.' 'Do you mean your husband?' [Esther asks]. 'Yes, miss, my master' " (8.161–62). Jarndyce is like these masters if only because he wishes, against what would be Esther's will (if she had one), to keep her mistress of Bleak House and become her husband. Jarndyce's mastery, and Esther's pliancy, cannot be better represented than in the way he hands her over to Woodcourt, making clear her identity as chattel—a transaction that serves not just to point his power and beneficence but to propagate the institutions, the Bleak Houses, over which he is master.

Women's enclosure within the home circle also draws off the more general and pervasive constrictions of closure—not just, as Nell demonstrates, because women are sacrificed to closure but, as Esther shows, because they also willingly create it. Esther is "intent upon the perfect working of the whole little orderly system of which [she is] the centre" (37.587). Esther seems to keep in order more than just the home; unlike Nell, whose rambles dissipate and protract the plot of her novel, Esther's steady, homely virtues seem to keep her book tidy. Critics have long recognized that Esther is the focus of both narratives in the book, the peg that holds them together.[49]

Yet Esther's relation to closure is illusory, although to recognize it

---

[49]See, for example, A. E. Dyson, *"Bleak House:* Esther Better Not Born?" in Dyson, *Dickens's "Bleak House,"* 271.

as such holds no promise for her of an escape from constraint. The stylistic hallmark of Esther's narration is circumlocution. Esther's confusion and deferrals extend even to the conclusion of her story, which, rather than closing the novel, never fully ends but stops on the threshold of another and-then: "—even supposing—" (67.935). Her voice converts onto a personal and domestic level the nebulousness and aimlessness of the engulfing system of power in which she operates. The endlessness of Esther's narrative echoes the way women are characteristically sacrificed to the perpetual enslavement of the everyday: the monotonous and self-perpetuating drudgery performed by slaves of the home like Guster or the Marchioness also reflects the dynamic by which such an overly elaborate and interminable system extends and prolongs itself.

Desultoriness and circumvention are, once again, restatements of the very logic they seek to elude. Esther's double, Lady Dedlock, for example, seems antithetical both to Esther and to the home she represents. Unlike Bleak House, her home, Chesney Wold, is no home at all—"Fairy-land to visit, but a desert to live in" (2.58). But although—or because—Lady Dedlock's transgression with Hawdon has precluded the possibility of any home life (she confesses to Esther, " 'I have no home left' " [55.816]), she is introduced gazing longingly at a domestic scene; her transgression is converted into a renewed appreciation of the domestic, a reassertion of its claims.

Lady Dedlock's sexual transgression is figured in terms of wandering; it has placed her on a "dark road": " 'From day to day, sometimes from hour to hour, I do not see the way before my guilty feet' " (36.565–66). The disclosure of her secret literally takes her out on the street, precipitating the reckless tramp through the countryside that ends in her death. Yet, although Lady Dedlock is compared to that great lady of unquiet pacing, Lady Macbeth (48.706), her reckless tramp only seems to threaten what it actually reasserts, the home and the governing order. Not only has home life been made particularly precious to Esther because of her mother's disregard of it, but Lady Dedlock's return to Hawdon at the end of the book brings together parents and child in the graveyard, reuniting them in an accession to the family so powerful in its symbolic expiation of sexual guilt that it cleanses Esther of the taint of illegitimacy and permits her to enter the family circle; after this reunion, the objections of Mrs. Woodcourt or even Guppy to Esther's right to a home magically dissolve.

Lady Dedlock's transgression not only establishes Esther even more firmly within the home circle, it also seems to grant men power over that circle. Her sacrifice to the sanctity of home life identifies the home with power, conflating both in a single, never-ending, and indifferent succession to which women, not men, are sacrificed. Tulkinghorn, for example, employs such logic to trap Lady Dedlock: "'As to sparing the girl, of what importance or value is she? Spare! Lady Dedlock, here is a family name compromised. One might have supposed that the course was straight on—over everything, neither to the right nor to the left, regardless of all considerations in the way, sparing nothing, treading everything underfoot'" (48.716). Keeping woman in her proper place—underfoot—guards patriarchy, shoring up lineal descent and saving the family name; by persistently thrusting women beneath this juggernaut's wheel, the novel also allows patriarchy to identify itself with the headlong course of power, which deflects and coopts even what seems the most random or reactionary motion. Nor is such an attitude merely the sophistry of villains: Bucket, too, claims control of women's supposed errancy when he tells Esther he is keeping her wandering mother "in train" (57.828).

Tulkinghorn's death (like Sir Leicester's incapacitation) suggests not only the tenuousness of the men's claim to such power but also their tenacity in asserting that claim, even to the sacrifice of instrumental members. The novel makes a point of mentioning that Tulkinghorn's death actually ensures Lady Dedlock's own (55.815–16). The male order regroups around a figure who dramatizes (the wish) that the member *is* instrumental: Mr. Bucket, who solves the case and reasserts closure by aid of his hypnotizing forefinger. He does so not just at the expense of women but with their help—not only the help of invaluable Mrs. Bucket (enthralled, the text suggests, as much by that forefinger as Mrs. Quilp is by Quilp's burning cigar) but also of that exemplar of order, Esther (whose narration may be Dickens's fullest representation of the inside of a woman's mind because it shows one so brainwashed by and intent on maintaining the male order).

The need to beat wayward women into line may explain Dickens's own obsession with the murder of Nancy, his insistence on ending his public readings with an enactment of that scene.[50] One consoling myth of the Dickens canon, if not of culture, is that beaten women become docile and disciplined subjects, more ready to follow the lead of their men. As Bucket tells us, "any fool knows that a poor creetur like her, beaten and kicked and scarred and bruised from head to foot, will stand by the husband that ill uses her, through thick and thin" (52.836). But Nancy, who exemplifies the principle of standing by her man, also dispels its consolation. Nancy doesn't quite fit the bill. Although she tries to remain constant to him by omitting his name from her indictment of others, he takes the very mission on which she does this as an attempted escape from his lockup (fittingly, she goes to walk on London Bridge with Rose and Mr. Brownlow).

Upon learning of her supposed inconstancy, Bill will not spare the girl. He goes to murder Nancy, taking the straightforward route Tulkinghorn identifies as the path to domination: "Without one pause, or moment's consideration; without once turning his head to the right or left, or raising his eyes to the sky, or lowering them to the ground, but looking straight before him with savage resolution . . . the robber held on his headlong course."[51] Yet his path is not so straightforward; its goal, Nancy's death, fails to conclude Sykes's journey. After Bill murders her, he is immediately possessed by her ghost. His ability to control the movement to which he has sacrificed her vanishes, and he becomes a victim of it himself: "Soon he was up again, and away,—not far into the country, but back towards London by the high-road—then back again—then over another part of the same ground as he already traversed—then wandering up and down in fields, and lying on ditches' brinks to rest, and starting up to make for some other spot, and do the same, and ramble on again" (OT.48.424). Bill's restlessness is, like that of Dickens's wandering women, a response to power, the only difference being that in his case the agency of that power is more distinctly localized: he is chased by the king's officers, and in his frenzy he conveniently hangs himself, sparing them the trouble. Bill's sacrifice is as necessary as Nancy's for the safe home set up for

[50]Johnson, *Charles Dickens*, 2: 1102–14.

[51]Charles Dickens, *Oliver Twist*, ed. Peter Fairclough (1966), ch. 47, p. 421; all future references (hereafter abbreviated *OT*) will appear in the text.

Oliver and Rose at the end of the novel, and although the novel partly accounts for this male sacrifice in terms of class (Bill's violent end substitutes for the better-born Monk's more subdued death), Dickens's treatment of gender shows that class provides another displacement of what is a threat to all men.

Dickens expresses his recognition that men are not free of the power relations they attempt to elude in part through his identification with Nancy, his assumption of her victimization. His obsessive murdering of her was also self-murder: he enacted the scene against the advice of doctors and friends, who told him the excitement on top of his ill health was suicide, as indeed it was. Dickens's figuring of romantic restlessness in terms of walking is particularly revealing not only of his own identification with victimization but also of his desire to elude it. Robert Newsom points to a short piece of Dickens's, "Night Walks," in which Dickens literally becomes a streetwalker (as, in life, he actually was: every reader of Dickens's life recognizes his wayward twenty-mile tramps through London as its hallmark). Streetwalking was, in fact, the impulse at the very heart of Dickens's work: he acknowledged quite explicitly that it was vital to this creative powers.[52]

Dickens's identification with woman shows that he recognizes her portrayal as symptomatic. His representation of woman lays bare the way power inscribes itself; it points ultimately, through the repeated failure of the male strategy to control or differentiate itself from her representation, to the way men, like women, are also inscribed in power. And that identification also exposes the inscription of Dickens's texts within power. Ellen Moers, examining the perceived threat of women's activity to male power in *Bleak House*, suggests that such fears in the novel have their source in anxiety about writing, in the male uneasiness about the growing power of female writers.[53] This uneasiness, however much it might owe to social fact, also expresses a recognition that the construction of woman functions just as writing itself works; like the construction of woman, writing cannot offer an escape from the

[52]See Newsom, *Dickens on the Romantic Side of Familiar Things*, 107–13; Fred Kaplan, *Dickens and Mesmerism: The Hidden Springs of Fiction* (1975), 76; and Johnson, *Charles Dickens*, 1: 518, where Dickens blames his inability to write in Italy on missing his London night walks.

[53]Moers, "*Bleak House:* The Agitating Women," 22–24.

contingencies and restrictions of that unrecognizable set of forces that have come to be called power. Inscribed within those forces, writing necessarily provides one more field in which power operates. (And because that field of forces determined by social and historical facts also determines them—it always inhabits, at any rate, the endeavor to perceive and organize facts, determining the logic of representation by which history becomes available—the question of causality remains moot.)

Yet Dickens's identification with woman also betrays the reassuring power of identification itself and points to the versatility of the dynamic of the other, the way it seems to allow identification while preserving distance. Dickens's own collusion of romance and women exposes the doubleness of the male position, which can concurrently imagine itself as inside and outside of power. In Dickens's most self-revelatory novel, *David Copperfield*, which chronicles Dickens's own growth as a writer, young David enters into storytelling by putting himself in a *woman*'s place—David's love for Steerforth prompts him to become his Scheherazade. The identification with women and romance, it seems, is meant to further the connections between men. But even such identification is itself consolatory; Scheherazade, although under a threat, is ultimately spared, which may explain why the *Arabian Nights* was Dickens's favorite romance. The purpose of romance remains: to provide a way to lessen the very constraints it also reveals.

III

The interplay between the streetwalker and the homebody is restaged in the recent critical debate between deconstruction, on the one hand, with its emphasis on errancy and transgression, and the analytics of power, on the other, with its focus on the totality of control. Within this debate, woman—and her discourse, feminism—are crucial, if often unrecognized, terms. Both schools make use of constructions of women to further their claims and provide romantic consolations for their contradictions, inconsistencies, gaps, or self-indictments. Both schools have also profited from feminist inquiry: deconstruction's concern with the marginal, for example, learns from as well as lends itself to feminist discussions of women's impossible position within an order that cannot recognize them; similarly, investigations of the private as the micro-sphere of supposed public domination owes much to feminism's refusal to allow a schism between the public and private.

Recent attention to the wandering of the text (such as by Barthes and Parker) is predominantly deconstructive. Alice Jardine, for example, traces to Derrida's work—to *Dissemination* and *Margins of Philosophy*—an emphasis on "the adventures of a certain wandering, without telos or finality, without domination or mastery. In order to pry apart the metaphysical oppositions that have chained us, we must begin to follow the movements of difference-in-motion (*physis*) before it is chained by truth, syntax, and sign."[54] Derrida's followers have seemed to point to this model of wandering as the means to transgress order and domination, and Derrida's rhetoric has specifically seemed to open up the possibility of such transgression for women—or rather to suggest that the position of woman is by definition transgressive. Although Derrida may claim that there is "no *name*" for this wandering difference, he also asserts as feminine the unrepresentable, the transgressive and erring, the involuted hymenal boundaries, the maze of invaginations, which prompts him to wish to write "as (a) woman."[55]

Yet the pervasive idea that deconstruction promises a realm outside the metaphysical assumptions it assails (and that it claims that realm for its own operations) is inaccurate and misleading. As Derrida himself has suggested throughout his work, transgression relies on and calls forth, in an endless cycle, the very law it subverts.[56] What is problematic to feminism about deconstruction is not that the old order persists (as it must) within deconstruction's own play. What is problematic is *where* it persists, precisely where readers of deconstruction might least expect to find it, given the

---

[54]Alice A. Jardine, *Gynesis: Configurations of Woman and Modernity* (1985), 130.

[55]Derrida's claim that there is "no name" comes from Jacques Derrida, "Différance," in his *Margins of Philosophy*, trans. Alan Bass (1982), 26. The other claims may be found in Derrida, "La Question du style," *Nietzsche aujourd'hui?* (1973), 1: 229; quoted by Stephen Heath in "Male Feminism," *Men in Feminism*, ed. Alice Jardine and Paul Smith (1987), 4.

[56]See, for example, his claim that "it is not a question of junking these concepts [the sign, with its logo- and ethnocentric assuredness], nor do we have the means to do so. . . . Breaks are always, and fatally, reinscribed in an old cloth that must continually, interminably be undone" (Jacques Derrida, *Positions*, trans. Alan Bass [1981], 24).

critique of phallogocentrism basic to deconstruction: woman becomes one site on which that approach consistently repeats the
gesture of mastery.

Derrida's recourse to woman as metaphor for the unrepresentable and inconsistent still relies on an old essentializing logic, on
which the complications of the play of language and its refusal of
reference still depend and which they cannot completely subvert
(but even partially serve). By relying on the familiar construction of
woman as herself inconsistent and incomplete, biologically and
sexually lacking, this logic also repeats that construction. Derrida's
critique of the supposed need of feminism for some simplistic referential category of woman has led to his skepticism of, if not antagonism to, feminism.[57] But feminism also must be skeptical and can
never simply make assumptions about its relation to deconstruction, even as it borrows from its methods.

At the same time, the current reaction against deconstruction
can also make use of women in the consolatory way that Dickens's
novels do. Identification with the symptomatic woman acts out the
inevitable collapse with the other. That collapse, however, can also
be a further strategy to claim power: Lady Dedlock as the wandering mother reveals the maneuver by which that woman of symptoms—the hysteric—allows the text to continue to try to inscribe
power as well as be inscribed within it. Dickens brings together his
two avatars of romance, recast as wandering hysterics and hearth-
tending mothers, in a strategy of collapse that betrays how collapse
itself is useful.

Madwomen and mothers. When stated baldly this might seem
an odd coupling indeed, yet their pairing has been useful for different approaches of feminist literary theory as a way to expose gender ideology. Although such feminisms have attended to women's
particularity—the differences between madwomen and mothers—
they have also found connections and similarities between them.
Perhaps the most familiar example of the association of hysterics
and mothers appears in feminist responses to Freud's treatment of

[57]See Jacques Derrida and Christie V. McDonald, "Choreographies," *Diacritics* 12
(1982): 66–76, especially 70–76; and James Creech, Peggy Kamuf, and Jane Todd,
"Deconstruction in America: An Interview with Jacques Derrida," *Critical Exchange*
17 (Winter 1985): 1–33.

Dora. Dora refuses his treatment, some feminists claim, precisely because Freud will not follow up the insight granted him by Dora's first dream—that "the mystery," as he tells her, "turns upon your mother"—because he refuses to understand Dora's unhappy recognition, that (despite the self-interested lies of the men in her world to their mistresses and patients) the only role for women is her effaced and ignored mother's.[58]

Dickens's portrayal of a figure like Lady Dedlock also pairs hysterics and mothers; she is driven by her repressed nature into mad frenzy that ultimately becomes flight—maddened, in fact, because she *is* a mother. Connections between these two figures are apparent in the terms popularly applied to them as well: "the mother" is the archaic synonym for hysteria; hysterics and mothers are also both "confined," and this confinement has made them especially useful figures for some feminisms, providing a focus through which to examine "women's sequestration or invisibility in patriarchal and phallocentric systems" as the ground and prop of those systems.[59] One common form of the connection between the madwoman and the mother is typified by some French feminist readings—the hysteric's insistent bodily presence stands for, refers back to, and is given sense by the horizon of the unrepresentable mother.

Yet these invaluable anatomies of patriarchy may not take their questioning and interpretation far enough; by connecting the hysteric and mother, however implicitly, they also act out the logic of the systems they expose. A more current rephrasing of the association of the hysteric and mother might see in the hysteric's tortured body not subversion but the symptom of her cultural incarceration, might associate the unrepresentability of the matrix generating her

[58]Freud, "Fragment of an Analysis of a Case of Hysteria," *SE*, 7: 70. For readings of *Dora* that foreground the connection between hysterics and mothers, see, for example, Jerre Collins, et al., "Questioning the Unconscious: The Dora Archive," *Diacritics* 13 (Spring 1983): 37–42, and Sharon Willis, "A Symptomatic Narrative," *Diacritics* 13 (Spring 1983): 46–60.

[59]Mary Jacobus, *Reading Woman: Essays in Feminist Criticism* (1986), 286. Jacobus engages particularly with the strategies of French feminists such as Luce Irigaray or Julia Kristeva. For a similar argument that also draws from Anglo-American object-relations psychology, see Margaret Homans, *Bearing the Word: Language and Female Experience in Nineteenth-Century Women's Writing* (1986); and for one that works from Marx, Foucault, and the new historicism, see Eve Kosofsky Sedgwick, *Between Men: English Literature and Male Homosocial Desire* (1985).

not so much with an invisibility eluding control as with the om-
nipresence of a vast system of control that is ineluctable.

But is the hysteric's relation to the mother in even this last,
Foucauldian, paradigm of power relations I just paraphrased actually all that different? Foucault too, in *The History of Sexuality*, cou-
ples hysterics and mothers in his critiques of the prevailing sexual
system: the mother, he writes, is "the most visible form of . . .
hysterization."[60] Connecting the mother and the hysteric in this
way may allow us to see them as constructions, to see sexuality as
simply a strategy through which power deploys itself. But such a
connection may also continue a long history in which a proper
mastery of these figures has been crucial: Foucault's collapse of the
hysteric and mother, for example, supports an argument directed
at refuting Freud (and Lacan), in the same way that Freud had
redefined the hysteric in his refutation of Charcot. To keep our
feminist investigations from unwittingly replaying and supporting
such (male) moves for power, we might wish to question the logic
we often just assume.

What would happen if we separated these two figures, mothers
and hysterics—if only to forestall their inevitable collapse? By
doing so, we might be able to determine not just the function of
their equation—the ways it serves phallocentrism—but also why
these two in particular are equated. Feminist scholarship is already
engaged in similar work in many areas; different feminists have
examined the ways that Freud, for instance, seems to have antici-
pated and stymied our attempts to "think back through our mothers" (the project Virginia Woolf sets us); they have shown that
Freud's view that woman's essential neurosis can be explained and
cured only by the maternal is just another way to appropriate
woman to the *paternal*, to reassert her dependence on man, her
inferiority and subordination to him, figured in the equation in
which motherhood equals and satisfies penis envy.[61]

---

[60]Foucault, *History of Sexuality*, 1: 104. I might say that such a coupling points to
the sense of "coupling" that means, according to the *Random House Dictionary*, "the
association of two circuits or systems in such a way that power may be transferred
from one to the other."

[61]For an example of just such an investigation, see Mary Jacobus, "In Parenthesis:
Immaculate Conceptions and Feminine Desire," in *Body/Politics: Women and the Discourses of Science*, ed. Mary Jacobus, Evelyn Fox Keller, and Sally Shuttleworth (1990),
11–28.

I want to conclude my reading of romance in Dickens by examining what the fusion of madwomen and the mother tells us about the role of gender in the analytics of power and about the role of feminism in current critical debate. The fusion of the hysteric with the mother domesticates power relations simply because it is fusion; contemplating an unlocatable, pervasive field of force that absorbs the subject, and locating and specifying that field as the mother, furthers a fantasy of benign identification, of osmosis and harmony with a nurturing source—furthers, in short, that romantic fantasy of the pre-Oedipal that I discussed in the chapter on George Meredith's fiction. Although this fantasy is imagined as being played out between women, I might argue that it is actually phallocentric—that an analysis that reads the hysteric back to the mother is essentially a male fantasy, one that acts out what Alice Jardine calls the logic of "male paranoia." Paranoia, as Freud's reading of Schreber demonstrates, involves not just an identification with women; its desire for the breakdown of boundaries is in service of an imagined merging of the subject with the forces authorizing and subordinating it, a fantasy of union with "that being who has no boundaries" whom Schreber called God but, Jardine notes, has often been called Mother.[62] Paranoia seems to allow a more privileged relation to systems of power than hysteria. The paranoid's privileged position becomes apparent in Freud's tacit—and wishful—hierarchy: (female) hysterics are bodies to be inscribed and analyzed within systems; (male) paranoids are involved in the very production of those systems. Such privileging is not surprising, for in their own dependence on fantasies of totality, whether called God, Mother, or even psychoanalysis, Freud and Schreber (as Freud recognized) share a paranoid logic.[63]

[62]Jardine, *Gynesis*, 98; see her discussion, 98–102.

[63]Freud writes: "It remains for the future to decide whether there is more delusion in my theory than I should like to admit, or whether there is more truth in Schreber's delusion than other people are as yet prepared to believe" ("Psycho-Analytic Notes on an Autobiographical Account of a Case of Paranoia," *SE*, 12: 79). Freud also makes the connection between paranoids and analysts in "Constructions in Analysis." He writes: "The delusions of patients appear to me to be the equivalents of the constructions which we build up in the course of an analytic treatment" (*SE*, 23: 268).

For a reading of women's relation to paranoia and theory which discusses these and other connections, see Naomi Schor, "Female Paranoia: The Case for Feminist Psychoanalytic Criticism," in her *Breaking the Chain: Women, Theory, and French Realist*

It has been suggested recently that paranoia is the subject's most salutary response to our implication within power relations.[64] But paranoia can be consoling as well as salutary, providing a structure that identifies those defined as male subjects with ultimate authority—an identification that at the same time seems to circumvent the oppressive logic that has previously made identifications with power appear as the products of a clear-cut desire to dominate. Foucault-inspired criticism has been particularly useful in pointing out how the supposed exemption of the subject from systems of control actually shores those systems up. But simply recognizing and making explicit that we all—men and women both—are inscribed within power doesn't settle anything and can lead to an embracing rather than a denial of power, an opposite but just as dangerous response. The different histories we construct as feminists tell us that (that group we call) men has always tried to embrace power by exercising it over women and that men's domination of women is one way that men can console themselves for, and seem to deny, their own subordination to authority. One part of the feminist task right now might be to point out that oppression has not disappeared simply because we have ways of rethinking and complicating it—oppression still could be part of the structure of that thought; we might counter the claim that no one owns power with the observation that some wield it nonetheless.

One way to continue questioning oppression might be to question the collapse between the hysteric and the mother—ultimately to question the strategy of collapse itself, especially insofar as it involves an ironing out of all differences—including gender differences, however various critics might locate those. As different feminists have begun to point out, current descriptions of power

Fiction (1985), 149–62. Keep in mind that for Freud hysteria and paranoia could be related in women through the figure of the mother. In "Female Sexuality," he writes that the first attachment to the mother, the pre-Oedipal phase, "is especially intimately related to the aetiology of hysteria, which is not surprising when we reflect that both the phase and the neurosis are characteristically feminine, and further, that in this dependence on the mother we have the germ of later paranoia in women" (SE, 21: 227).

[64]By D. A. Miller, The Novel and the Police, 70. See also his reply to Dominick LaCapra's response to that argument: Miller, "Under Capricorn," Representations 6 (Spring 1984): 129. See too Dana Polan, Power and Paranoia: History, Narrative, and the American Cinema: 1940–50 (1986).

relations seem to break down the gender distinctions feminism relies on, replacing patriarchy, phallogocentrism, or the symbolic order with an undifferentiated system—one not explained by gender, but explaining and dispensing with it, as merely one tactic of control among many.[65] I might question whether this is prescription as well as description, itself just one more restatement of what we represent as male logic, and one that in supposedly eliminating gender actually only effectively eliminates woman, installing instead the very homosocial male grid it analyzes, authorizing the male position even as it recounts the control and violence it sees exercised on those occupying it. I shall investigate the problems of this current critical paradigm of power relations for recent feminism—examine the way feminism has been if not appropriated then reinflected, as Nancy Miller or, following her lead, some feminist respondents in the anthology *Men in Feminism* might call it. The differences between recent feminist literary criticism and other critical discourses are difficult, if not impossible, to hold apart because they lie in nuances of tone and style: whether or not those differences are ultimately outside anyone's range, and whether or not anyone can isolate them, my attempt to do so might at least help note the way that current attempts to de-emphasize gender distinctions can mean an emphasis added that reasserts the male register.[66]

In the nineteenth-century novel, two restless and hysterical figures especially capture the imagination, providing, as blank enigmas that continue to prompt interpretation, the very screens on which we as critics project our understandings of hysteria. We could, in fact, argue that one figure is the interpretation of the other, for Dickens's Miss Havisham followed close upon Collins's own woman in white, the appearance of Anne Catherick in Collins's

[65]See, for example, Naomi Schor, "Dreaming Dissymmetry: Barthes, Foucault, and Sexual Difference," in *Men in Feminism*, 98–110.

[66]For her discussion of these important inflections, see Nancy K. Miller, "Emphasis Added: Plots and Plausibilities in Women's Fiction," *PMLA* 96 (January 1981): 36–48. The question of enunciation and tone is implicit in many of the essays in *Men in Feminism*; for representative selections, see Alice Jardine on "syntax or intonation" (56) in "Men in Feminism: Odor di Uomo or Compagnons de Route?" in *Men in Feminism*, 54–61, and Meaghan Morris on innuendo and punning in "in any event . . . ," in *Men in Feminism*, 173–81.

novel embodying for Dickens one of the most memorable scenes in literature and immediately prompting his reworking of it.[67] Anne Catherick of *The Woman in White* and Miss Havisham of *Great Expectations* stand out as romantic figures; as I have shown, Dickens's early critics found Miss Havisham especially romantic, and Count Fosco himself, in *The Woman in White*, recommends the plot he has built up around Anne to "the rising romance writers of England."[68] And Anne Catherick and Miss Havisham embody too Breuer's definition of hysteria as "suffer[ing] mainly from reminiscences"[69]—for their bodily agitation (Anne's "nervous, uncertain lips" [*WIW*.48] and Miss Havisham's "impatient fingers" [*GE*.12.126]) stems from their apparently unspeakable memories. Unlike Freud's and Breuer's hysterics, however, their cases seem distinguished not by how much they are forced to forget but by just how much they remember: Anne, although slow to gain an impression, is tenacious in recalling it (*WIW*.121), a relation to memory perfected in Miss Havisham, whose whole existence enshrines reminiscences of ill treatment she cannot eradicate. The transparent relationship of symptom to memory seems obviously to call into question what Foucault terms "the repressive hypothesis" of psychoanalysis.[70] Yet in order to maintain that hypothesis and the privileges it allows, these books seem merely to beckon readers elsewhere for our archeologies, mapping out on the body of the *text* a depth psychology that points to a textual unconscious, takes readers behind the stories of the hysterics to an external origin—the story of the mother, which gives sense to the text as a whole.

That these are women in white already suggests as much.[71] Their inappropriate white dress—others in Anne's novel find her

67Martin Meisel, "Miss Havisham Brought to Book," *PMLA* 81 (June 1966): 281.

68Wilkie Collins, *The Woman in White*, ed. Julian Symons (1985), 48. All future references to this book (hereafter abbreviated *WIW*) will appear in the text.

69Josef Breuer and Sigmund Freud, "On the Psychical Mechanism of Hysterical Phenomena: Preliminary Communication," *SE*, 2: 7; Anne's identity as a hysteric is emphasized by the original of her story, the hapless Madame de Douhault, who was immured in the Salpêtrière, which was later to become the most famous site of hysterics; see Clyde K. Hyder, "Wilkie Collins and *The Woman in White*," *PMLA* 54 (1939): 299.

70Foucault, *History of Sexuality*, 1: 10.

71For an extended discussion of literary figurations suggested by women in white, see Sandra M. Gilbert and Susan Gubar, *The Madwoman in the Attic: The Woman Writer and the Nineteenth-Century Literary Imagination* (1979), 613–21.

white clothes "particular" (*WIW*.117), as clearly Miss Havisham's bridal dress also is—itself marks their insufficiency and gestures to something beyond them; Miss Havisham's story relies on the reader's assumption that what one critic emphasizes as "faded virgin white" is unnatural, that she has become hysterically immobilized in what would have been the proper development from bride to mother.[72] Miss Havisham's unnatural mothering of Estella (Dickens's revision of Collins makes his figure more economically both hysteric *and* mother, emphasizing the strategic collapse between them) only reinforces her inadequate progression into maternity and sends the reader, like Pip, looking elsewhere. The mystery of *Great Expectations* turns out to be not this mysterious woman's: Herbert recounts her history quite easily halfway through the book. Instead, Pip follows Miss Havisham's story back through Magwitch and Estella to arrive ultimately at Estella's real mother, Molly, who connects all the threads of the novel. Likewise, Walter Hartright makes no headway in restoring Laura's identity and fortune, and the plot of his novel remains tangled, as long as he suspects that "the way to the Secret lay through the mystery, hitherto impenetrable to all of us, of the woman in white" (*WIW*.475). Only when he realizes that Anne knows nothing, that it is her mother, Mrs. Catherick, who alone is "in possession of the Secret" (*WIW*.492), can his search and the novel begin to wind up.

The mother too is inherently associated with romance in these works. Nell must be sacrificed, for instance, not just because she is wandering, but because she is houseless and motherless: she lacks the guidance of that pattern of control who would take her within this other circle of romance and keep her in order. Similarly, when the character in *Pickwick* notes that "there is romance enough at home" (foreshadowing that exemplary instance of the woman imprisoned by the home, which ought to be *enough* for her, Miss Havisham in Satis House), his particular romance tells the story of a suffering mother.

That the mother, in a sense, controls and shapes these novels is in keeping with cultural and linguistic constructions of her. The connections of the mother with creation go without saying, of

---

[72]Meisel, "Miss Havisham"; the phrase I quote appears on 279, but see his further discussion, 282–85.

course, but they can be easily reworked in such a way as to connect them with current theories of totalizing power, of the structures of discipline creating the very subjects that make them up. Feminist exponents of matriarchy might argue, for instance, that the mother's confinement during delivery is meant to deny what they see as a sign of her predominant creative and controlling power: her power quite literally to give birth, to produce subjects. Such views are also similar to those of Karen Horney and Melanie Klein in their debate with Freud about the construction of femininity. They not only insist on a dread that prompts men to disparage women in order to allay their own envy and fears, but they locate that dread as dread of the mother.[73] Recent feminist object-relations psychology works from this view, namely that the mother has been reviled and occluded because of the power she possesses as well as the subject's difficulty in separating from her; they argue specifically that the mother's role as caregiver equates her with the structures of discipline that define the subject, which therefore rebels against them. The power they accord her position is so all-encompassing that writers such as Dorothy Dinnerstein argue that its problems can lead to total annihilation, to nuclear apocalypse.[74]

(Let me digress a moment to say that I am neither suggesting that these assumptions represent fact—their pretension to fact, to an essential identify of the mother as well as of gender, actually risks collapsing them with the very phallocentric positions they are attempting to refute—nor suggesting that we should adopt them. Rather, I review them only to suggest some of the ways in which the mother gets linked to fantasies of power and to consolations within those fantasies—a dynamic these views of the mother expose but also act out too unself-consciously themselves. Whether [what we call] male subjects or female theorists make the equation, the mother comes to stand for a total and totalizing system. But even if they don't take their observations far enough, I think these theorists useful in indicating the way such a connection serves the male order—feminist object relations, for example, implies that

[73]See Karen Horney, "The Dread of Woman," *International Journal of Psychoanalysis* 13 (1932): 348–60; and Melanie Klein, "Early Stages of the Oedipal Conflict," *International Journal of Psychoanalysis* 9 (1928): 167–80.

[74]Dorothy Dinnerstein, *The Mermaid and the Minotaur: Sexual Arrangements and Human Malaise* (1976).

women are made primary caretakers to provide patriarchy with a convenient scapegoat for its ills.)

The construction of the mother who governs *Great Expectations* appears to present both the mother's totalizing power and the subject's difficulty in separating from her: Pip (in a binding oscillation of incorporation and "repulsion" that seems to allow him no comfortable position) tells us that the "government" (*GE.7.79*) of even his foster mother, Mrs. Joe, is all-embracing, monitoring his (hopes of self-) creation and preventing his deliverance, or delivery, as an autonomous subject—"I had no hope of deliverance through my all-powerful sister, who repulsed me at every turn" (*GE.2.46*). In a more extreme example that is simply the logical extension of Pip's case, Jaggers shows off the great strength of Molly, who is believed by everyone to have destroyed her child; she embodies the total control of the subject, its creation *and* destruction. Every mother in this book is, if not so obviously omnipotent, similarly bad (those I haven't already mentioned include Herbert's and Startop's mothers, who seem to figure in the book just to make this point), and Dickens's criticism of them all turns to some degree on their abuse of power, the ways they ignore (Mrs. Pocket) or overdo (Mrs. Startop) their duty. Dickens's criticism implies, however, a tacit standard of motherhood, one closer to the mother that spoils than the mother that neglects—an implied ideal of an all-giving mother who devotes perfect care to the subject she produces, not—as in Startop's case— spoiling him by identifying him with herself, but by giving up all claim to self and to power, existing only as a reflection of his glory.[75] In *The Woman in White,* Walter (whom Mr. Gilmore notes takes "the romantic view" of things [*WIW.142*]) approvingly calls this quality of self-abnegation "that sublime self-forgetfulness of women, which yields so much and asks so little, turn[ing] all her thoughts from herself to me" (*WIW.565*). And it is important to remember that Pip's real mother—"Also Georgiana"—in dying may not so much have abandoned him as left him free, or that Molly too has actually given up all control of Estella and become herself a kind of slave, immured by Jaggers. "Natural" mothers, then, seem to underwrite this standard, forgetting themselves so much that they all but disappear. The

---

[75]Remember that Startop, the mama's boy, looks exactly like his mother, whom he adores (*GE.25.226*).

continued specter of these mothers (one of the first questions Mag-witch asks Pip is, " 'Where's your mother?' " [GE.1.37], implying how determinant of "the identity of things" [GE.1.35] and of Pip her very absence is, just as Molly remains the crucial, though shadowy, key to the plot) suggests, however, that the novel worries that the threat they represent within it persists beyond its wishful construc-tion of their self-abnegation.

The standard of self-effacing motherhood may be impossible, available only in death, but that doesn't forestall the punishment of those who fail to achieve it. The most obvious and sobering case is the smash-up of Mrs. Joe. Foster mothers in fact seem scapegoats who abuse their power precisely in order to be humbled for it (and, at the same time, deflect that attack from what may be the taboo—because total—power represented by the "real" mother). Pip's dou-ble Orlick—who calls Mrs. Joe "Mother Gargery" (GE.15.142)—crushes her precisely for her attempt to govern *him*. His brutal overpowering of her reverses with a vengeance the power relations previously existing between Mrs. Joe and Pip. As Dickens makes quite clear, Pip's observation that, after her attack, his sister "showed every possible desire to conciliate [Orlick], and there was an air of humble propitiation in all she did, such as I have seen pervade the bearing of a child towards a hard master" (GE.16.151) puts her in the place of the child Pip once was, and makes him master.

Just as the foster mother is a ploy that denies while preserving the relation between the subject and the mother, the collapse of the hysteric with the mother also seems to promise the hero's freedom, in a way that doesn't compromise him, doesn't make him appear openly resistant to power. By pointing to the mother, confined hysterics such as Anne Catherick and Miss Havisham imply the way subjects are contained within a controlling system. Figuring that system as the mother, however, makes it tolerable, and more tolerable for the hero than the hysteric. Anne Catherick tells Wal-ter, " 'I don't get on well with [my mother]. We are a trouble and a fear to each other' " (WIW.123). Yet Walter gets on with Mrs. Catherick very well: just as Walter is his own mother's favored son, he becomes a favorite with Mrs. Catherick too. Ultimately, she offers him the story she never gives Anne and suggests she would offer him herself, if he would have her (WIW.548).

Moreover, the hysteric supplies the hero with an acceptable route back to the mother, because her collapse with the mother allows an identification that preserves the possibility of differentiation. What distinguishes the hysteric is her refusal actually to become the mother, her insistence on separating herself from the very horizon that gives her meaning. Hysterical pregnancies, such as Anna O's, are important because they are false; that falseness defines them as hysterical. Freud, however, does not use such a subtle distinction to separate the hysteric and the mother. Rather, it is held up as the very benchmark of the hysteric's illness; although Freud largely ignores Dora's mother, he repeatedly tasks Dora with what he sees as her neurotic refusal to assume her mother's role, to allay her penis envy, to satisfy with Herr K. or the young engineer her natural but repressed desire to provide the father with a child. Yet the very distance that is neurotic for the hysteric is not so for the hero. The destiny of his anatomy supposedly makes such differentiation normal for him; he is not meant to *become* the mother. Paranoid rather than hysteric, when merging with the mother (perhaps) he can protect his boundaries by dissolving hers—or so this fantasy runs.

The utility of these hysterics, particularly as women in white, is that the heroes need not simply identify with them, need not risk *becoming* them by taking over their place; instead, they can assume control of them, make use of them, inscribe their own (wishful) stories on the white blanks offered by these women. The very construction of the hysteric, like that of the mother, effaces itself, makes what it represents seem natural and true, rather than an arbitrary or self-interested fantasy. Dora's description of Frau K's "adorable white body" locates this whiteness anatomically, collapsing sexuality and textuality, and suggests the way in which the hysteric's construction in terms of her bodily symptoms permits the illusion of insight, seems to demand the supposedly natural male response to women, the desire to "penetrate" them—Walter's term, as I quoted previously. What men write on the blank tablet of the hysteric comes to seem the hidden truth revealed, brought to light by analysis. And as Dickens makes clear in *Great Expectations*, this wishful "truth" is meant to be the hero/analyst's preference and promotion by, even his control over, power. Recorded on this blank is the male subject's humble propitiation by the matrices of power: a broken Miss Havisham, on her knees to Pip, begs him to inscribe on her "yellow set of ivory tablets" his forgiveness of her (GE.49.409–10), and, in the end, her hysteria is reduced to her mechanical repetitions of that plea and her self-accusation of bad mothering.[76]

In his excellent analysis of The Woman in White, D. A. Miller reveals the ploys of this false monolith of sexual construction, which assumes that men only desire to penetrate and desire to penetrate only women. In doing so, he outlines the connection in that book, although without explicitly unraveling it, between hysteria and paranoia. In his discussion of the way the hysteric provides "the conduit of power transactions between men" he turns to Lady Audley's Secret, considering it as a coda to Collins's novel, a more explicit dramatization of the way hysteria is a function of social power.[77] Miller subtly argues here what feminists such as Catherine Clément have already suggested: that the hysteric does not figure women's subversive resistance to her role but actually emblematizes that role itself and legitimates woman's confinement.[78] What is important to Miller's argument is the way the confined woman is the type for all subjects within power relations—a subject and an agent of power as well. Moreover, Miller suggests that confining the woman, whether in the lunatic asylum or the asylum of family and home, facilitates a process of self-discipline aimed ultimately not at the control of women but at defining the power relations between men. Yet, no matter how subtle, the analysis of women as tokens in a privileged relation between men risks merely repeating that structure, unless we make explicit the different inflections—those of culture, text, and critic—that are involved. To point out what this structure tells us about the subject's attitude to power, rather than just his inscription in it, I turn to another wildly popular sensation novel, Mrs.

[76]Her plea for forgiveness once again reverses old power relations and puts Pip in the place of the mother and, even more, of ultimate authority, for Miss Havisham begs him "with her folded hands raised to me in the manner in which, when her poor heart was young and fresh and whole, they must often have been raised to heaven from her mother's side" (GE.49.410).

[77]D. A. Miller, The Novel and the Police, 169–72 (this chapter is entitled "Cage aux folles: Sensation and Gender in Wilkie Collins's The Woman in White"); the phrase I quote appears on 171.

[78]Hélène Cixous and Catherine Clément, The Newly Born Woman, trans. Betsy Wing (1986), 155.

Henry Wood's *East Lynne*. For *East Lynne* explicitly refers the hysteric, as it refers all else, back to the mother, exposing in the process the fantasies of power involved in that collapse.

East Lynne is the tale of a fallen mother, the beautiful Lady Isabel, who, through the pressure of sensational circumstances and misunderstandings (the novel acknowledges repeatedly that its events seem romantic), runs off from her husband and children, only to repent (too late) and secretly return, disguised, to watch over them.[79] Abandoned to debt and dependence on the death of her profligate father, the young Isabel meets her uneasy situation by falling first into hysteria: her precipitous marriage to Mr. Carlyle, a man she only admires, her later tortured and irrational jealousy of Barbara, whom she believes to be a rival for his affections, are just some of the effects of an ill-fated nervous susceptibility, accompanied always by hysterical tears.[80] Yet this novel makes clear that Isabel is not a special case; hysteria is natural to women (the other women in the novel also cry hysterically throughout it)—natural, it seems, because it is a direct function of woman's most natural role, her maternity: in this novel, women's nervous afflictions appear to come from their motherhood. Isabel has inherited her nervous oversensitivity from her own mother (whose similar impassioned nervousness prompted her to elope with Isabel's father and then waste away repenting the deed); another important mother in this book, Mrs. Hare, has become an hysterical invalid explicitly because she is a mother, separated from her only son.

The frustration of maternity is not what prompts hysteria in this book, however; the very insistence on the collapse between hysteria and maternity itself is the cause. The text does seem at times to try to normalize and naturalize the mother, to locate an unproblematic development into motherhood as what might resolve hysteria and determine normality for women. Isabel's separation

---

[79]Mrs. Henry Wood, *East Lynne*, ed. Sally Mitchell (1984); for references to romance, see, for example, pt. 1, ch. 10, p. 80, and ch. 11, p. 90; pt. 3, ch. 6, p. 378, and ch. 10, p. 417. All future references to this book (hereafter abbreviated *EL*) will appear in the text.

[80]The examples of Isabel's hysteria are extensive; for places where the text particularly uses that term, see *East Lynne*, 1.10.78; 1.12.102; 2.12.258; 3.2.337; 3.4.362; and 3.13.437.

from her children becomes the site, if not the source, of her illness: "But now, about the state of her mind? I do not know how to describe the vain yearnings, the inward fever, the restless longing for what might not be. Longing for what? For her children. Let a mother . . . be separated for a while from her little children: let *her* answer how she yearns for them" (*EL*.3.1.327).[81] Such separation in Isabel's case appears especially destructive because it is cast as unnatural: "A brute animal deaf and dumb clings to its offspring: but *she* abandoned hers" (3.1.332). Yet the text also carefully shows that Isabel's abandonment of her children doesn't cause her hysterical symptoms, just exacerbates them. Upon returning to her children, Isabel learns that hysteria can also be a function of being too much with them, not just in her own case, but in the case of any mother who devotes herself to them; Barbara (who has, just as Isabel dreaded, taken her place and become Mr. Carlyle's second wife) lectures her that such solicitude will, ultimately, "[jar] on her unstrung nerves" (3.2.341). By suggesting that the collapse between hysteria and maternity is vexed, *East Lynne* goes beyond simply outlining that motherhood determines and explains hysteria; it also analyzes and critiques that collapse.

The very exaggeration of Isabel's construction is what exposes the dangers to women that lie in the assumption of a connection between these two states: as an extreme case, she merely exemplifies the extension of what seems a natural logic. Isabel's anxious maternity—her miserable return after her flight, maimed and disfigured, to become the governess in her own family, to minister unrecognized to the husband and children she has abandoned— not only makes explicit the way a mother is a *servant* in her family, but the exquisite agony of Isabel's servility, as she finds she is forgotten or reviled and watches her husband love another and her children die, makes *East Lynne* the premier example of humble propitiation by the mother, of what Julia Kristeva might call her ultimate abjection.[82] Isabel's deathbed confession, her assumption

81Mrs. Hare's yearning for her lost son—separated from her by his fault, not her own—in the opening pages of the book sets up from the beginning the connection of hysteria and maternity: " 'Oh, my boy! my boy!' she wailed: 'my boy! my unhappy boy! Mr. Hare wonders at my ill-health . . . but there lies the source of all my misery, mental and bodily' " (*EL*.1.3.22).

82Julia Kristeva, *Powers of Horror: An Essay on Abjection*, trans. Leon S. Roudiez (1982).

of blame for all her pain, resolves at novel's end her wild extremes, stops her swing from the mother who neglects to the mother who spoils, and secures her into eternity as the mother who conciliates. That resolution confirms and exposes the assumptions behind the model she has only been thought to violate. For *East Lynne* makes clear that the bad mother, nervously pleading for forgiveness, does not merely gesture toward some ideal standard of motherhood; she *is* that ideal. The complete maternal self-forgetfulness the other novels laud is shown here to be Isabel's masochism.

Isabel's abjection directly preserves the social order: her humble return attests to the rightness of society's constructions of maternity, of the naturalness of maternal sacrifice. Isabel and her rival, Barbara, agree in this: that a mother's sacrifices must lead to her children's training, their indoctrination into the laws and morals of society (3.1.327; 3.2.341). Isabel returns to her children precisely to resume their training, feeling more than ever through her transgression of it the rightness of the social order that punishes her. Yet this novel illustrates, even while repeating it, that the mother is in question because she seems a threat, constructed as a symbol for as well as an agent of this order. All the book's insistence on the mother's selflessness actually screens an apotropaic response to the subject's engulfment by that diffuse and exhaustive system: Barbara brings up how easy it is for a mother literally to smother her children, and how often, her husband has told her, mothers do so on purpose—the incidence of such infanticide is on the rise (3.21.500). Isabel seems to ease, if not undo, the threat of such suffocation for that very husband bothered enough to mention it in the first place: her abasement of herself to him—for he, not the children, is really the reason she returns and humiliates herself[83]— makes him the one who engulfs her attention, keeps him from being engulfed by it.

This sensation novel, submitting to its generic requirements, of necessity offers a moral, which seems to be that "people cannot act with unnatural harshness towards a child, and then discover they have been in the wrong, with impunity" (3.18.469). This statement

---

[83]Barbara agrees with Isabel in this too: "I should never give up my husband for my baby," she tells her (*EL*.3.2.343). Dickens also associates this taking care of the father with romance, for when Caddy begs her (bad) mother to take care of Mr. Jelleby after Caddy's marriage, that mother laughs and calls her a "romantic child" (*BH*.30.480).

refers not to Isabel, however, but to the petty domestic tyrant, Justice Hare, whose banishment of his son has kept him from his mother; upon reunion of mother and child, the father falls into imbecility and powerlessness—he "would never again be the man he had been" (3.18.469)—he literally himself becomes "a little child" (3.22.509). Such justice within the novel may not be the result of the kind of feminist subversiveness Elaine Showalter has argued inheres in sensationalism, for it might be that the father's fate reflects not so much feminist retribution as Oedipal inevitability, and that he is punished for mistreating his son, not his wife.[84] His regression simply reverses Oedipal roles without upsetting Oedipal structure. It allows his son to become "master" (3.22.510) while at the same time shifting himself to the other privileged position, that of the child, one not that much different anyway in the logic of collapse that underwrites this system. At the same time, by purging a tyrant who explicitly appears unreasonable, the novel strategically seems to satisfy a rebellious imperative and hence allows a much more reasonable (and more dangerous?) tyrant to continue to operate—the reasonable Mr. Carlyle, whose expectations of having his most trifling opinion or desire attended to differ only speciously in emphasis and tone from the infantile demands of the Justice before his supposed comeuppance.[85] The moral, then, does ultimately redound on Lady Isabel, who remains in the background organizing Carlyle's story just as Mrs. Hare remains a focus with which the struggle between father and son cannot completely dispense. That women are somehow necessary at all keeps them a threat, so that Isabel's repentance about her treatment of Carlyle is required to console the male subject (and

[84]Elaine Showalter, A Literature of Their Own: British Women Novelists from Brontë to Lessing (1977), 153–81.

[85]Although these differences of emphasis and tone are meant to be important, Wood cannot maintain them; Carlyle is her experiment in constructing the perfect man, pieced together by changing the emphasis on old literary clichés of gender— she makes him authoritative, say, rather than overbearing, domestic without being uxorious. Yet, like similar experiments (Mr. Knightly, for instance, or Rochester, or Adam Bede, or the inevitable Harlequin romance hero), this one fails because, given the logic of collapse in which this novel is entrapped, the nuances between Carlyle and Hare (lover and father) are not ones it can adequately theorize or maintain; its attempts, however, to imagine a man that might somehow be different, even though they fail, still point out the need to do so. The attempt to transform what may be an inevitable patriarchal grammar through new inflections reveals the oppressiveness of its categories even while failing to transform them.

such consolation, this novel suggests, as Dickens's novels do, remains one of "romantic sentiment" [3.4.361]). Her lack of impunity convinces him of his own.

From its opening, centering on Isabel's ailing father, Lord Mount Severn, the novel sets up the impulse that prompts its trajectory, the problem it must isolate if not solve: the possibility of male powerlessness. The dead patriarch's heir, furious that provision for his daughter should have been considered by the earl as "out of his power" (1.11.84), may be indicting existing gender arrangements that allow the neglect of daughters; he is also outraged, however, by any diminishment of patriarchal power. Men retain their precarious power in this novel by taking it away from women, especially the women who represent it, their mothers: as Lord Vane tells Isabel, " 'as to my mother—oh well, she can't expect to be master and mistress too' " (3.7.388); his growing up into an attractive figure is directly a function of his doing "battle with [her]" (3.21.502). The unflattering portraits of mothers who exercise power and therefore must be broken—Lord Vane's evil mother, as well as Carlyle's unreasonable sister, that stock comic type of old maid, his foster mother, Cornelia—reflect the way this novel must necessarily function within the system it also exposes. But the register in which it shouts out its logic forces us to attend to it.

What the exaggeration of this novel makes evident is the consoling strategy underlying the construction of madwomen and mothers. The collapse between these extremes, and between woman's omnipotence and servility, reveals and allows a management of anxiety, a negotiation of power. Our very forms of representation, this novel demonstrates, attempt to order existence in a way that will establish for the male subject a comfortable relation to what controls him. Like Miss Havisham's beseechment of Pip, Isabel's plea for Mr. Carlyle's forgiveness as she lies on her deathbed at the end of the novel attempts to clinch that relation—the system of control, through her as its representative, begs his pardon for its existence. Although he cannot ignore or escape it (Isabel turns up where he least expects her), the system offers him through her this consolation: it directly reflects his desires (she runs away because he loves Barbara) and is always there to minister to his needs.[86]

---

[86]This system continues after Isabel's death, when Barbara finally can completely assume her place. The novel ends with Mr. Carlyle admonishing Barbara "to strive

Such consolations for the hero/analyst involve the critic as well. Miller's article on *The Woman in White*, for example, although it presents itself through its subtitle as gender criticism not feminism, nonetheless owes much to feminist criticism, and Miller explicitly acknowledges the work of Gilbert and Gubar and Eve Sedgwick.[87] Yet the use of feminism by critics who specify themselves as somehow outside it too remains, as the essays throughout *Men in Feminism* suggest, "both gratifying and unsettling."[88] Although I admire Miller's insights about gender, I might also want to question how they apply to essays like his own, which can themselves, through their very use of feminism, continue what he himself recognizes as the dynamic in which woman is a conduit of power between men.

Miller's reading of *The Woman in White*, for example, continues a debate with previous criticism, a tacit critique of one kind of deconstruction—a go-round, which in his exchange with Dominick LaCapra, he has personified as two men dancing; he asks specifically about the problems of difference and mastery between their

always to be doing right, unselfishly, under God" (*EL*.3.24.525). And although that unselfishness seems to mean that Barbara must learn to love and care for Carlyle's children "as if they were [her] own," she tells him reassuringly that she will do so because " 'my earnest wish is to please you' " (*EL*.3.24.525, 524).

[87]The problems of Miller's engagement in a feminist debate point out the trickiness of nuance that makes the relation of "gender" critics to "feminist" critics, "male" critics to "female" critics, those writing under the male signature to those writing under the female signature (and the use of his initials nicely problematizes such signatures in Miller's case anyway, pointing up how these categories are never firmly established) so difficult to read. For isn't having "them" read and cite "us" precisely what feminist critics want, as implied by the lists of suggestions those writing for feminism have repeatedly offered (see, for example, Sandra M. Gilbert's list and discussion of "us" and "them," in "What Do Feminist Critics Want? A Postcard from the Volcano," in *The New Feminist Criticism: Essays on Women, Literature, and Theory*, ed. Elaine Showalter [1985], 30–31. See also Alice Jardine's list in "Men in Feminism," 60–61). The problems of how to discuss the differences and relations between feminism and criticism that designates itself as somehow also other, and how to note differences between them without inflecting them merely as the too simple distinction between "them" and "us" (a strained register we ultimately all close our ears to anyway), are precisely what is at issue in this chapter, precisely what it is impossible for it to achieve.

[88]This phrase appears in the standard essay on this topic, Elaine Showalter's "Critical Cross-Dressing: Male Feminists and the Woman of the Year," in *Men in Feminism*, 117. For an instructive discussion of the homophobic structure that this essay uses but ignores, see Craig Owens, "Outlaws: Gay Men in Feminism," in *Men in Feminism*, 219–32.

kinds of criticism, "if it is ever clear, when two men dance, who leads."[89] The complexity of Miller's prose signals that he is well aware of the misogyny (as well as the homophobia) that could be implicit in the exclusion of women that his figure charts; the role of women's exclusion in the homosocial is, after all, part of the argument of *"Cage aux folles."* His knowing and ironic tone throughout this essay and his other recent work implies that his statement here, in part, ventriloquizes the misogyny and homophobia of traditional positions—held, it implies, by someone like LaCapra—and suggests too not just the exclusion of women but also Miller's own willingness (as opposed to LaCapra's) scandalously to play up an identification with them. Yet this is precisely one of the tonal maneuvers that feminism might question because it allows a duplicity that also preserves misogyny. Such duplicity is inescapable; as Christie McDonald has suggested, "in the economy of a movement of writing that is always elusive, one can never decide properly whether the particular term implies complicity with or a break from existent ideology" (and the inescapability becomes increasingly problematic when we complicate the very notion and possibility of "break").[90] Yet Miller's refusal to unpack his own language, his silence here about the notorious doubleness of irony (which he himself clearly recognizes in others, as when he refers elsewhere to "ironic reservations that only refine the ambiguity"[91]), emphasizes that his language does not simply perform but also shares the attitudes it may simultaneously be critiquing. This playful statement about men dancing, for example, dances around but also relies on the assumption that issues of dominance are less complicated or already settled between men and women—men always lead.

In casting its own delicate tonal maneuvers in terms of the dance, Miller's article joins a long tradition that considers implicitly or explicitly the relation of women and their discourse to current critical debate. Although the metaphor of the dance is interesting for a variety of reasons—in the way it domesticates, perhaps in order to trivialize, women's role, in the way it inserts the category of the body into questions of articulation—for the purposes of this

[89] D. A. Miller, "Under Capricorn," 124.
[90] Derrida and McDonald, "Choreographies," 71.
[91] D. A. Miller, *The Novel and the Police,* 79.

argument I could refer to Dianne Hunter's recent work reading hysteria in terms of dance to suggest how this metaphor already begins to position women in a familiar role.[92] The use of this metaphor itself waltzes around the issue of the collapse of hysteric and mother, uneasily pairing and separating them in an ever shifting pattern.

Christie McDonald's statement cited earlier about the inevitable duplicity of language comes in an article entitled "Choreographies," a debate about feminism with Jacques Derrida, theorist of that school of criticism against which Foucault-inspired work like Miller's seems directed. Yet feminism is a contested site for Derrida too. In this article, as well as in the later "Women in the Beehive," Derrida emphasizes the contradictions within assuming a feminist position that undermine the ground on which to construct it. Expert at delicate maneuvers, Derrida warns against attempting to freeze the dance of his discourse into one position: "I will go so far as to say that it is *to not read* the syntax and punctuation of a given sentence when one arrests the text in a certain position, thus settling on a thesis, meaning or truth."[93] But his treatment of feminism has a drift and tenor, if not a truth: although Derrida recognizes a provisional need for the categories of feminism and the institution of women's studies, he recognizes too that the denial of ground for women, although it "is not anti-feminist, far from it . . . is not feminist either."[94] In his wariness about feminism, Derrida implies an identification between what he calls the "lone dance" of his own ideas and theory and the lone dance he advocates for women, so that they may divorce themselves from the teleology of movements (such as the women's movement); yet for many feminists that very identification and divorce remain wrong notes prompting false steps.[95] Even those feminists most influenced by Derrida can be disturbed

[92]Including, for instance, the recent production of the play, *Dr. Charcot's Hysteria Shows* (April 1988, Trinity College, Hartford, CT).

[93]Derrida and McDonald, "Choreographies," 69.

[94]Derrida and McDonald, "Choreographies," 68.

[95]Derrida and McDonald, "Choreographies," 68. Derrida's identification of deconstruction with women is well known; in these essays, see, for example, his discussion of the resistance to his ideas which he says "seems to be exactly the same resistance—and there's nothing fortuitous in that—exactly the same resistance which is opposed to women's studies" ("Women in the Beehive: A Seminar with Jacques Derrida," in *Men in Feminism*, 196). "Women in the Beehive" might be

by his emphasis; the displacement of women privileged in the endless displacements of deconstruction repeats too familiarly the old stresses in which identification means (her) exclusion.[96]

Derrida's identification with and displacement of woman and her discourse waltzes around a discussion of the mother: to McDonald's troubled question about whether a move, by way of hysteria, to collapse the woman with the womb and mother might not involve "essential loss" of other roles and representations for women (a move perhaps repeated by Derrida's writing), Derrida gestures to (and makes use of) the logic of collapse: "Can [one] dissociate them," he asks. Might they not all ultimately mean the same thing, in a kind of sliding chain in which they wind up serving the same end?[97] Just such a question within criticism that explicitly defines itself as feminist has centered around the metaphor of dancing but has reached a different conclusion, in an attempt to articulate the different roles and representations within feminist discourse, as well as its relation to larger critical debate. The necessity of preserving different voices for feminism, the danger of totalizing and reducing it, is, for Annette Kolodny (and for her critics), the only way to negotiate the battlefield of the critical antagonism toward feminism, the only way of "dancing through the minefield."[98]

Gilbert and Gubar demonstrate that this silencing of women's

---

considered one of the more Foucauldian of Derrida's essays; he emphasizes in it (what is implicit in deconstruction) the impossibility of transgression—"deconstruction cannot be transgression of the Law. Deconstruction *is* the Law. It's an affirmation, and affirmation is on the side of the Law" (197). That he does so in a critique of the way the relation of women's studies to the institution repeats its law, however, suggests the strategic association of women and power that I have been analyzing.

[96]See, for example, Alice Jardine, *Gynesis,* 178–207; and Gayatri Chakravorty Spivak, "Displacement and the Discourse of Woman," in *Displacement: Derrida and After,* ed. Mark Krupnick (1983), 169–95, and "Love Me, Love My Ombre, Elle," *Diacritics* 14 (1984): 19–36.

[97]Derrida and McDonald, "Choreographies," 72.

[98]Annette Kolodny, "Dancing through the Minefield: Some Observations on the Theory, Practice, and Politics of a Feminist Literary Criticism," *Feminist Studies* 6 (Spring 1980): 1–25. See also Annette Kolodny, "Dancing between Left and Right: Feminism and the Academic Minefield in the 1980s," *Feminist Studies* 14 (Fall 1988): 453–66. For responses to Kolodny that stress the need for "diversity" and "dialogism" rather than "pluralism," see Judith Kegan Gardiner, Elly Bulkin, Rena Grasso Patterson, and Annette Kolodny, "An Interchange on Feminist Criticism: On

voices is usually represented through the collapse between the
hysteric and mother, and that it can be deadly. In their reading of
the fairy tale "Little Snow White" (a tale that exemplifies romantic
plots for them), which serves as the introduction to *The Madwoman
in the Attic*, they chart the way the women's roles in that story all
get reduced to one figure, mirroring patriarchy's idea of woman—a
collapse that also effectively makes that idea seem an actuality by
silencing women's writing and suppressing other notions of wom-
en: the end of that story, in which the wicked stepmother is made
to perform a hysterical dance of death in red hot slippers, her
punishment for attempting to be more than the traditional idea of a
mother, for stepping out of place, reflects the way feminist scholarship has been made to perform a precarious kind of hotfooting in
its attempt to negotiate a place for itself.[99] This figure of shoes, the
question of which shoes feminism should strap on (sensible shoes
or elegant pumps?)—a figure, among other things, for which tone
it should adopt in its discourse, which attitude it should take in the
institution—organizes the discussion between Nancy Miller and
Peggy Kamuf about the role of feminism in that institution. This
becomes a debate "on the proper place of Women's Studies"—
should it have a place at all, should it be replaced by gender studies?—a debate ultimately about whether Foucault's ideas can aid us
in finding answers.[100]

The answer to that depends on how those ideas are pitched. One
of the contributors to *Men in Feminism*, Andrew Ross, in an earlier
essay, "Viennese Waltzes," critiques what he sees as Jane Gallop's
precipitous acceleration of "the stately waltz of psychoanalysis."[101]
Ross counters deconstructive and psychoanalytic claims of subversion with a more Foucauldian emphasis on our implication within

'Dancing through the Minefield,'" *Feminist Studies* 8 (1982): 629–75; Nina Baym,
"The Madwoman and Her Languages: Why I Don't Do Feminist Literary Theory,"
in *Feminist Issues in Literary Scholarship*, ed. Shari Benstock (1987), 245–61; and Laurie
Finke, "The Rhetoric of Marginality: Why I Do Feminist Theory," *Tulsa Studies in
Women's Literature* 5 (Fall 1986): 251–72.

[99]Gilbert and Gubar, *Madwoman*, 36–44.

[100]Nancy K. Miller, "The Text's Heroine: A Feminist Critic and Her Fictions," 49;
see also Peggy Kamuf, "Replacing Feminist Criticism," 42–47, both in *Diacritics* 12
(1982).

[101]Andrew Ross, "Viennese Waltzes," *Enclitic* 8 (Spring/Fall 1984): 80. Ross seems
here to be implying that Gallop is caught in the same kind of excess that he criticizes
Cixous for excessively celebrating in hysteria (73).

structures of power: he discusses hysteria (in part through a careful consideration of the effect of tone), to counter the claim for its autonomous expressivity by attending to its utility for a regime, arguing that we shore up power even by dissenting from it. The focus of his indictment of what he calls "a discourse of liberty" that sees itself as exempt is, however, not deconstruction or psychoanalysis but (one kind of) feminism, and part of his point seems to be that "women are not privileged in" oppression.[102] What is at issue is not whether Ross's points are well taken (many of them are) or even that he too strategically displaces a larger institutional debate onto problems of feminism but, rather, a certain immoderation of his own tone in doing so. His critique of feminism, by rather relentlessly indicting it for elitism and bad faith, without at all acknowledging that his own work too must necessarily to some degree "[fall] foul of the same historical and enunciatory obstacles" for which he critiques it, risks making him as an informed reader of feminism just as damaging to it as the "uninformed opponents" that he worries French feminist strategies will unintentionally empower.[103]

Nor is it really feminism—"the degree to which a feminist voice might be imperiled"—that is at issue in all these essays.[104] Feminism becomes the site in them for a debate between men that

[102]Ross, "Viennese Waltzes," 80, 76. Ross's specific readings are carefully nuanced (see, for example, his attentive discriminations about the role of the semiotic in Kristeva's writing, 80). Despite his local understandings of the complexities of different feminist positions, and despite some explicit disclaimers (such as "I have been chiefly concerned with one particular trajectory of the feminist rapprochement with psychoanalysis" [80]), his rhetoric continues to risk totalizing the writers he treats as current "feminism" itself (in formulations, for example, such as "modern feminist theory" [73] or "the feminist version of" [75]). Granted such totalizations are impossible to avoid (my own essay certainly tends to totalize male critics, collapsing their differences into the one particular trajectory I must partially construct in order to examine it; more insidiously, even in the act of explicitly questioning women's relation to totalization, I keep falling into similar shorthand about feminism), but the question is once again the emphasis given to them. It is not surprising that Ross's essays in Men in Feminism partly complicate his position by focusing on the problems of universalizing, although perhaps unfortunate that his discussion of this problem seems explicitly only to indict feminism for it. For a reading of this strategy of projection, see Elizabeth Weed, "A Man's Place," in Men in Feminism, 71–77.

[103]For a discussion of elitism, see Ross, "Viennese Waltzes," 75; of bad faith, 80; the phrases I quote appear on pages 77 and 75.

[104]Ross, "Viennese Waltzes," 78.

ultimately silences that voice (see the essays by Robert Scholes and Denis Donoghue in *Men in Feminism*, which also use feminism to critique deconstruction[105]); feminism is the necessary but excluded third term that connects the competing men even when they are aware of the construction of that triangulation, a triangle, as Mary Jacobus has shown in "Is There a Woman in This Text?" that underlies theoretical positioning as much as it underlies the positions of the Oedipal scenario.[106] Despite his recognition of such structures, Miller enacts them in his essay: his suggestions that the hysteric conserves rather than subverts the status quo come in a debate that is in part a maneuver for institutional power, as do Ross's, and continue the same history in which Freud and Foucault make use of her for their own systems.

Miller ends his discussion of *The Woman in White* not with the hysteric, however, but with the mother, and for him, just as for the heroes in the texts, she reflects his claims. In the sophisticated restatement that Foucauldian criticism allows of the old feminist maxim, "the personal is the political," Miller locates the mother as preserving within the supposedly privatized family the violent homosocial structure it seems to escape, connecting, as different feminists have repeatedly shown they already know she does, the father and son. In addition, the rhetoric her use permits (Miller tells us that "the novel's final tableau" repeats its "prehistory," and "at the end, then, the novel has merely discovered its beginning, in the family matrix"), coming at the end of his own essay, locates her as the symbol not just for the totality of power but also for the totalizing sweep of Miller's own argument and theoretical system.[107]

Such thinking back through the mother—in the sense that she

---

[105]Robert Scholes, "Reading Like a Man," in *Men in Feminism*, 204–18, and Denis Donoghue, "A Criticism of One's Own," in *Men in Feminism*, 146–52.

[106]Jacobus, *Reading Woman*, 83–109.

[107]D. A. Miller, *The Novel and the Police*, 189–90. (See also how Miller's rhetoric implicitly connects the mother and power in his discussion of how the network of power engenders a brutal and monstrous norm that the sensation novel is able, for a moment, to reveal [166].)

Significantly, this chapter ("*Cage aux folles*") does not end here in this totalizing circle but with an autobiographical note, in which the author (casting himself as a hysteric), while relying on the conventional collapse with the mother, at least structurally seems to escape the system described by her too. The consolation of the positioning of (what is by now) the conventional critical afterword, which asserts the critic's own implication in whatever the essay has been critiquing but implicitly becomes the screen that confirms and guarantees the thoughts projected on her—is by no means uncommon in feminism either, and, when it appears in responses to feminism, it often marks critical sympathy or even identification: Miller's description of the mother's construction marks out a position very similar to one an avowed feminist might take. But similarity can itself be invidious, as Stephen Heath's pious reference to his own mother in his essay, "Male Feminism," points up. In avowing his feminism, Heath attempts (as he himself admits) to legitimize his own identification with it; he attempts to bypass the theoretical complications that he recognizes within that identification and clinch it for himself as a special case, by telling us that he has been writing while in the hospital, watching his old and (presumably) dying mother.[108]

The ghoulishness of this particular turn to the mother makes visible the threat to feminism (and the appeal to [male] privilege) that can underlie any identification with it. As feminists, we recognize the implicit desire for mastery within supposedly objective and distanced analyses of women: in *The Woman in White*, Count Fosco's study of the nerves is one of the things that gives him power over women. But we cannot overlook that desire in figures like Laura's uncle, the hysterical Mr. Fairlie, who identify with women's painful inscription within power but who nonetheless, and in fact because of that identification, exercise mastery. Mr. Fairlie's "female" nervousness is the very source of his power over Laura, his excuse to mistreat and neglect her.

And such identification, whether or not explicitly appropriative, shifts the focus of feminism. Not surprisingly, Miller revises and extends Gilbert's and Gubar's discussion of female imprisonment, for example, to restage imprisonment as a male drama. Such a revision relies on the inescapable tautology that, within phallocentrism, all dramas are male, but the way we accept that insight can more or less effect the male order's continuance. Simply to stop

---

undermines that assertion somewhat by making it anterior to the argument of the essay, is certainly not an element of this essay's alone (see, for example, my own afterword) and only reveals one of the compromises we make with the systems in which we operate in order to continue to operate. What's interesting to me here, however, is how the figure of the mother gets invoked to allow or even sanction such compromises.

[108]Stephen Heath, "Male Feminism," 30. See Alice Jardine's reaction to this image, "A Conversation: Alice Jardine and Paul Smith," in *Men in Feminism*, 246–51.

at that insight flattens out important differences of tone and emphasis that distinguish our response as subjects to the dramas of phallocentrism that control us, the different stakes we have in them. The complaint that women alone are not "history's privileged victims," which feminists have begun to hear quite often lately—in this particular articulation from Frank Lentricchia—is a peculiar red herring, a misdirection that continues the logic of oppression these critics wish, as feminists do, to unravel. It is not constructed by them just because they are distressed that the "masculine" may become an "expendable afterthought"—although such distress may be a factor—but perhaps because the impossibilities of articulating our relations to power as subjects make falling back on particular available representations a temporary relief—and the conventional fantasy of the mother has been to make her provide such comfort at the same time that she stands for the very disciplinary tactics that exhaust us. Lentricchia's criticisms appear, for example, just after he has conjured a scene of a young "wave of feminists who are at the verge of open revolt against their mothers," an identification perhaps prefiguring and displacing his own desire for (the lost possibility of) revolt.[109]

Critics such as Edward Said and Paul Bové have cautioned that the recent analyses of power by Foucault and his followers serve actually to institutionalize it further—the logical conclusion of Foucault's reasoning, of course, although it's important to recall that he never pushes it as far as some of his critics, and followers, have—and Said suggests that the only way out of that circle is to break it, to reject Foucault on power.[110] If (rather than forgetting Foucault) we did for a moment want to push him so far and use his

[109]Frank Lentricchia, "Patriarchy against Itself—The Young Manhood of Wallace Stevens," *Critical Inquiry* 13 (1987): 774. For responses to this essay see Donald E. Pease, "Patriarchy, Lentricchia, and Male Feminization," 379–85; Sandra M. Gilbert and Susan Gubar, "The Man on the Dump versus the United Dames of America; or, What Does Frank Lentricchia Want?" 386–406; and Frank Lentricchia's reply, "Andiamo!" 407–13—all in *Critical Inquiry* 14 (1988). See also Melita Schaum, " 'Ariel, Save Us': Big Stick Polemics in Frank Lentricchia's *Ariel and the Police*," *Genders* 4 (March 1989): 122–29.

It's worth emphasizing again that the problem with criticisms of feminism like Lentricchia's is not that they are wrong (although they may be in many places) but that they are so curiously misguided.

[110]Edward Said, "Traveling Theory," *Raritan* 1 (Winter 1982): 41–67. Paul A. Bové discusses how Said's dismissal of Foucault is part of his own ploy for institutional power, in *Intellectuals in Power: A Genealogy of Critical Humanism* (1986), 209–37.

work to trace such circles, it would be because, viewed from a feminist perspective, they describe so well the frustrations feminists all know—the spiral of repetitions and reappropriations that results as we try to resist a system we cannot imagine how to overcome—and to deny that structure could be a wish that also tends to blunt the possibility of any resistance. I don't want to go so far, however, if only because arguing about whether this spiral has a limit somewhere can be one way of ignoring our immediate engagement in power struggles. Our arguments may be more helpful to us as feminists if we make them more local and specific—if we focus, for example, on the way that women's engagement in power struggles hasn't always seemed a given and doesn't yet— on the way women (or their discourse) are still used to facilitate struggles that try to exclude them from any active part.

Biddy Martin observes that pressing Foucault to his logical limits misses the point in a way particularly harmful to feminism, dispensing with both the category of woman and her oppression: "There is the danger that Foucault's challenges to traditional categories, if taken to a 'logical' conclusion, if made into imperatives rather than left as hypotheses and/or methodological provocations, could make the question of women's oppression obsolete."[111] Foucault may be more closely involved in these imperatives than Martin suggests, although Naomi Schor, in her article, "Dreaming Dissymmetry," makes a persuasive case for Foucault's reintroduction of women and of gender as a determining category in the later volumes of The History of Sexuality: nevertheless gender differences do seem problematic, if not elided, in that work.[112] Different feminists have begun to consider the various elisions or appropriations of the category of woman in recent literary criticism; Lynda Boose and Marguerite Waller provide accounts of how the new historicism has finessed difference and preempted feminism in Renaissance scholarship.[113] Such analyses help keep

[111]Biddy Martin, "Feminism, Criticism, and Foucault," in Feminism and Foucault: Reflections on Resistance, ed. Irene Diamond and Lee Quinby (1988), 17. This anthology contains essays on the relations between feminism and Foucault-inspired interpretation in various fields. Such explicitly feminist considerations of Foucault's work itself will aid our different kinds of feminism in examining how his ideas are put into practice, revealing whether or not they are simplified when used.

[112]Schor, "Dreaming Dissymmetry," 106–10.

[113]Lynda E. Boose, "The Family in Shakespeare Studies; or, Studies in the Family of Shakespeareans; or, The Politics of Politics," Renaissance Quarterly 40 (Winter

feminists aware and wary of the effacement of gender within the institution that Foucauldian criticism seems to imply, as it repeats the old call for the replacement of women's studies departments with gender studies. They outline the ways that, although Foucauldian criticism seems best at focusing on local and specific contexts and implicating the critic within power relations, by effacing gender distinctions and ignoring how specific male subjects in specific contexts may profit from feminism (or exploit it for nonfeminist or even antifeminist ends), its curiously unself-reflexive appropriations of feminism do neither. As feminists, many of us have up to now focused on the ways that the collapse of gender can be subversive, but we need to focus too on the conservative power of such strategies, the way the collapse between men and women, as between the hysteric and mother, can be a consoling strategy within power that is at the expense of the very feminism that seeks to expose the workings of that power.

Our feminisms can, of course, profit from an analysis that focuses on the way gender and sexuality are constructs in the service of a dominant discourse; such a project may in fact be said to have a feminist impetus. We need as feminists, however, always to insist on recharting that discourse so that its map takes the battles of gender into account. Pip's position within his novel—an orphan delusively free of the mother, of systems of power—may no longer seem available to critics, as it was never truly available to Pip, and that may even turn out to be a victory, one that feminism can partially claim. But such a change may be too easily reabsorbed within power if critics attempt to take the position of Walter Hartright, a favored son, who, if not exempt from, at least is cozy with, the dominance he ᵣrecognizes. Feminism needs more than ever to insist on the specificities within it, and to foreground the nuances of women's construction that make madwomen and mothers different, rather than to give in to a totalization of gender that makes feminism another blank page on which we write the same old story.

1987): 707–42; Marguerite Waller, "Academic Tootsie: The Denial of Difference and the Difference It Makes," *Diacritics* 17 (1987): 2–20. For other readings of new historicism, see Carolyn Porter, "Are We Being Historical Yet?" *South Atlantic Quarterly* 87 (Fall 1988): 743–86, and Judith Newton, "History As Usual? Feminism and the 'New Historicism,'" *Cultural Critique* 9 (Spring 1988): 87–121.

My reading of the hysteric and mother unfolds my own story too, of course, with its desires and claims for the power of my position. My approach here has remained trapped in the imaginary circuit of rivalry and identification, and I have to a greater or lesser degree simply continued the gesture I have analyzed; despite my attempt to attend to the nuances of these differently inspired critics, I have collapsed them into a single Foucauldian monolith (and not only is Foucault's inspiration registered much differently in the work of Miller and Lentricchia, for example, but other subtleties between them as readers make them respectively much more and much less valuable to feminism). One feminist response to this repetition of what I have just criticized might be to say that to have hysterics and mothers reflect a story that emphasizes the woman's position (the point of view of the woman critic, for example) makes a difference and undoes claims for power, because the tale it tells is about the impossibility of that position. Another response might be that it is actually well and good for a woman to claim a role in what have been male power struggles up to now, to make her way into an (old boy's) network of power. If I wanted to be overly reductive, I could identify these voices as the two poles my argument has been working between—the voice of the hysterical subject, recognizing, and perhaps overplaying her lack of autonomy paradoxically as a way out, and the voice of the controlling mother, perhaps wishfully intent on identifying with the system. Although I am sympathetic to both of these stances—who wouldn't wish to elude or control power?—I don't want to settle for them: what I have tried to suggest instead is the danger of wishful satisfactions, the consolations offered by totalizing systems that such neat images of women represent in miniature and draw us back into. Indeed, such responses seem satisfactory because they can be represented, made to fit familiar images of women. Yet the great strength of feminism, I think, (whatever its relation to power) has been in complicating and refusing familiar images. In doing so, feminism allows another response—an uncomfortable because undefined role (neither hysteric nor mother) that we continue to try to take even as we can't describe it—in which we don't attempt to elude or control power, but recognize our implication in it, and go on.

5

Recycling Patriarchy's Garbage: George Eliot's Pessimism and the Problem of a Site for Feminism

Theorists have long considered the way Western metaphysics has formed around metaphors of sight. Our notions of reality are informed by our understanding of what the visual means, especially by the assumption that the observation of empirical data somehow offers access to universal truth and natural law. So too literature and literary theory have always been intrigued by the relations between the linguistic and the visual. The conventions of literary realism rely on verbal imitations of such supposedly objective observation, proceeding as if a thousand words can actually equal a picture. Recent post-structural literary theory and criticism have investigated in particular this privileging of sight and the way language attempts to lay claim to it. One feminist approach, influenced especially by Lacanian psychoanalysis, foregrounds the importance of gender in its unraveling of the epistemological assumptions implied in questions of representation. By focusing on what critical shorthand terms "the male gaze," these feminists have demonstrated how the scapegoating of women within the specular economy mars its transparency and brings its assumptions to our attention.[1] But more recent—Foucauldian—approaches to the stra-

[1]See, for example, Laura Mulvey, "Visual Pleasure and the Narrative Cinema," *Screen* 16 (1975): 6–18, and her "Afterthoughts on Visual Pleasure and the Narrative Cinema Inspired by 'Duel in the Sun'," *Framework* 15/16 (1981): 12–15. See also E. Ann Kaplan, "Is the Gaze Male?" in *Powers of Desire: The Politics of Sexuality*, ed. Ann Snitow, Christine Stansell, and Sharon Thompson (1983), 309–27. See also such critiques or revisions of the concept of the male gaze as Miriam Hansen, "Pleasure, Ambivalence, Identification: Valentino and Female Spectatorship," *Cinema Journal* 25

tegic use of metaphors of sight have dispensed with the focus on gender, implying that gender divisions into oppressed and oppressor can be simply another attempt to imagine autonomy and escape from a generalized power that locates its supervision in its totalizing field of vision and oversees through its indifferent seeing.[2]

Through an attention to genre, I want to consider in this chapter just how the category of woman might be related to linguistic gestures to the visual. Why, in this debate, is gender division sometimes foregrounded, sometimes ignored? I approach these questions by considering the role of detail in the visual metaphors with which George Eliot distinguishes between realism and romance in her novels. Her works—about the intractability of our social relations, the powerlessness of human will—lead to the same crux that critical theory (especially for those of us working in feminist theory) seems halted at right now: how to think our way out of the very assumptions and constraints determining our thought, how to provide alternatives that aren't just more of the same "narrow, ugly, grovelling existence" that Eliot often paints as the real picture of human life.[3] Eliot's works continually illustrate

---

(Summer 1986): 6–57; Mary Ann Doane, *The Desire to Desire: The Woman's Film of the 1940s* (1987); and Kaja Silverman, *The Acoustic Mirror: The Female Voice in Psycho-analysis and Cinema* (1988).

[2]For discussions of the use of surveillance in literature, which dispense with or critique traditional assumptions about the role of gender division within the specular, see Mark Seltzer, *Henry James and the Art of Power* (1984), 25–58; and D. A. Miller, *The Novel and the Police* (1988), especially 169–72.

[3]George Eliot, *The Mill on the Floss*, ed. A. S. Byatt (1979), bk. 4, ch. 1, p. 362; all future references to this book (hereafter abbreviated *MF*) will appear in the text. This particular phrase comes from a well-known passage in which Eliot directly contrasts romance and realism. She compares the romance of Rhenish castles to the "dismal remnants of commonplace houses . . . the sign of a sordid life" (*MF*.4.1.361) on the Rhone: "Therefore it is that these Rhine castles thrill me with a sense of poetry: they belong to the grand historic life of humanity, and raise up for me the vision of an epoch. But these dead-tinted, hollow-eyed, angular skeletons of villages on the Rhone, oppress me with the feeling that human life—very much of it—is a narrow, ugly, grovelling existence, which even calamity does not elevate, but rather tends to exhibit in all its bare vulgarity of conception; and I have a cruel conviction that the lives these ruins are the traces of were part of a gross sum of obscure vitality, that will be swept into the same oblivion with the generations of ants and beavers" (4.1.362). This passage reveals how the connections between realism and romance are associated with the language of the specular as well as with our inability as subjects to elude the specular, the way the choice between sight/lack of sight remains a paradox: realism, for example, here exhibits only "traces" that tend toward oblivion.

that the alternative—romance, for instance, instead of the realism it counters—is not really different from the original problem. The very structures that teach us to think, theorize, *speculate*, are (by the persistence of visual metaphors that gives us terms like "speculate") constructed so as to control our resistance to them as well. What intrigues Eliot (sometimes, it seems, despite herself)—and intrigues me about her—is the way that gender division operates as the vehicle of such speculation and supposed resistance. Her novels consider the paralysis produced by a recognition of our always coopted contingency (think of all the paralyzed characters in her stories, from Silas Marner to Mr. Tulliver); they consider too how the cause of such paralysis is scapegoated onto women (Hetty, Maggie, even Dorothea, are all cast as Medusae)—and how it devastates them.

Gender is important in a breakdown of the distinction between realism and romance in Eliot's fiction, and its importance turns on the duplicity of detail. Realism directly opposes itself to that alternative mode of presentation, romance, by claiming a special relation to visual data and privileging those data as the real. Realism supposedly presents an objective picture that displays common, everyday details in their proper light; romance sees either too much or too little, charting some illusory realm outside the ordinary. Yet, as Naomi Schor argues, any focus on ordinary or extraordinary detail relies on gender assumptions. "The detail is gendered and doubly gendered as feminine," she writes; it is "bounded on the one side by the *ornamental*, with its traditional connotations of effeminacy and decadence, and on the other, by the *everyday*, whose 'prosiness' is rooted in the domestic sphere of social life presided over by women."[4] This gendering of detail as feminine is so insistent that the association of women and detail persists even in aspects of detail—the decadent, the everyday—that seem contradictory.

In this chapter, I want to elaborate the contradictions implied in the relations between women and detail that Schor's study notes. A focus on detail reveals the double bind constraining the category of woman in literary realism and current critical debate (Schor also notes a "rare prominence" of detail in post-structural theory).[5] It is

[4]Naomi Schor, *Reading in Detail: Aesthetics and the Feminine* (1987), 4.

[5]Schor, *Reading in Detail*, 3. Schor's study isolates the importance of detail within the theories of writers such as Barthes, Derrida, and Foucault: "The ongoing val-

not just that woman cannot escape her association with detail, however paradoxical, but that that association reveals something about her position in the signifying system. Just as she is associated with a doubleness of detail (details so overly elaborate as to force our attention to them, so common as to be almost invisible), she is at the same time doubly related to the specular system (implicated within, if not made the very site for, it, she is also aligned with attempts to escape that system). Such contradictions, though common to all subjects, are scapegoated onto women. The devaluing of women implied in the way she remains always in service to the specular and the impossibility of representing her otherwise provide the theme and the pervasive melancholy of Eliot's work; her awareness of these problems, however, suggests one way feminism might work within the limits of this paradox.

Eliot writes in *Middlemarch* that "it is in these acts called trivialities that the seeds of joy are for ever wasted, until men and women look round with haggard faces at the devastation their own waste has made."[6] The waste of our lives, which, in a typical strategy of power, is made to seem our fault, is even more specifically blamed on woman. An attention to Eliot's work shows how one current approach of feminism, woman's attempt to embrace her association with the detailed refuse of the system representing her—its fragments and frivolities—or (another approach) to embrace her association with ultimate ruin, with nothing at all, with absence, invisibility, blankness—leaves her nonetheless hopelessly trapped. And perhaps we continue to read and revolt against Eliot's fiction because, in the face of that hopelessness, she writes on.

I

Before considering the status of detail, and of women, within that fiction, it might be helpful to outline the feminist context in which my reading proceeds. Just what are the problems recent critical debate has seen in the connections between women and the specular, feminism and the dominant order, that might help to

orization of the detail appears to be an essential aspect of that dismantling of Idealist metaphysics," she writes, "inseparable from the all too familiar story of the demise of classicism and the birth of realism" (3–4).

[6]George Eliot, *Middlemarch*, ed. W. J. Harvey (1965), ch. 42, p. 462; all future references to this book (hereafter abbreviated *MM*) will appear in the text.

unravel similar connections—and problems—in Eliot's work? The invocation of the visual as a means to authority (and dominance) has been of special interest to feminists in their critique of a phallocentric order. In a move that for my purposes equates that order—and order itself—with realism because of their similar claims to objectivity, certainty, truth, feminist theorists such as Luce Irigaray have interrogated the circularity by which the specular is invoked to underwrite theory (*theoria*/speculation), interrogated the way phallocentrism attempts to secure its priority through its valorization of the visual order that supports it. Visual prominence becomes sexual privilege in an economy where the discovery of sexual difference is made (at least by Freud and our culture, if not by the structures of the unconscious) to depend on a sight, in a seamless tautology that then takes as standard what can be seen—that is, the phallic presence that determines the male as the defining category, judged against which the female becomes insufficient or lacking.[7]

Feminist film criticism has followed these suggestions to elaborate the way that the very gaze itself—the world view that determines the world—is male, associated with the male gender position and its claims for mastery, inflicting the hierarchy of gender division through its representation, and positioning and overmastering the woman as its object. In perhaps the best-known statement about the male gaze, Laura Mulvey investigates the phallocentrism of visual representation itself, contending that the very concept of vision is male. Mulvey argues that the structures of the unconscious manifested in patriarchy make the look male, the

---

[7]Freud, for example, "gladly" admitted to Abraham that "the female side of the problem is extraordinarily obscure to me" (quoted in Juliet Mitchell, "On Freud and the Distinction between the Sexes," in her *Women: the Longest Revolution* [1984], 223). For Freud's discussion of the role played by the sight of the penis in establishing the male as the determinative category of sexuality, see Sigmund Freud, "Some Psychical Consequences of the Anatomical Distinction between the Sexes," in vol. 19 of *The Standard Edition of the Complete Psychological Works of Sigmund Freud*, trans. James Strachey, 24 vols. (1953–74), p. 243–58; this edition hereafter abbreviated *SE*. In a critique of the scenario Freud paints in that essay, Mary Jacobus, following Jean Laplanche, points out that, even as Freud sketches it, the moment of decisive seeing meant to establish the penis as standard is actually one of "telling ambiguity"; Freud represses this uncertainty, brings it into line with the expectations of his argument (Mary Jacobus, *Reading Woman: Essays in Feminist Criticism* [1986], 113). For the most familiar and influential critique of male specularity, see Luce Irigaray, *Speculum of the Other Woman*, trans. Gillian C. Gill (1985).

"to-be-looked-at-ness" female.[8] Mulvey goes on to suggest that phallocentrism ultimately depends on the image of the *castrated* woman: "The meaning of woman is sexual difference, the absence of the penis as visually ascertainable."[9] Because what woman reveals is castration, her very visibility both reassures the male order of its possession of the phallus and testifies to woman's exclusion from that order.[10] Mulvey's response to male vision is to advocate that those of us in the position of woman refuse its lures if we cannot refuse to be its object—that we analyze how visual pleasure works to draw us into and hide its gender bias rather than simply succumbing to that pleasure.

Another approach to the specular, rather than refusing its pleasures, advocates an overelaboration of those pleasures, unsettling the specular by an excess of its own logic. This line of argument, making use of a deconstructive attention to the breakdown of categories of inner and outer, central and marginal, advocates an exaggeration of visual detail as a way to expose the phallocentrism of the visual; Jane Gallop, for example, suggests that a hyperattention to details unnoticed or overlooked by the reigning order unsettles its supposedly serene and eternal abstractions. Such attention exposes its own implication in power struggles that it wishes to ignore or to present as settled and done with, since their very existence puts its authority into question. Gallop argues that, as critics, we are driven to gain knowledge of a text when we feel powerless

[8]Mulvey, "Visual Pleasure," 11. For Mulvey, this is the cultural expression of the inequities built into our psychic structure. She writes: "In a world ordered by sexual imbalance, pleasure in looking has been split between active/male and passive/female. The determining male gaze projects its fantasy onto the female figure, which is styled accordingly" (11). Mary Jacobus agrees that the phallocentrism lies within structure—the very structures of representation: "What difference would it make if the viewer was 'she'? None at all; for what other 'way of seeing' has she than to see through his eyes, since his are the terms of representation itself?" (*Reading Woman*, 132).

[9]Mulvey, "Visual Pleasure," 13. In a formulation pertinent to the distinctions often made between the clarity of realism and the opacity of romance, Mulvey also contrasts woman's relation to the law with her obscurity: "Either she must gracefully give way to the word, the Name of the Father and the Law, or else struggle to keep her child down with her in the half-light of the imaginary" (7).

[10]Woman, as image of castration, paradoxically both threatens and allays anxiety. For a further discussion of this double movement, this time linked to that image of woman as the Medusa's head, see Neil Hertz, *The End of the Line: Essays on Psychoanalysis and the Sublime* (1985), 161–93.

in the face of it. Our gesture of knowledge hides within its established certainties our once violent desire to understand and possess an object we are powerless to comprehend fully, to replace uncertainty, anxiety, and confusion with stability and order.[11] Yet the unquestioning assumption of knowledge gains authority only by a ruse: "knowledge that has lost the truth of its roots in desire and aggression is in its very objectivity a lie."[12] Minute attention to detail in our interpretations, Gallop argues, almost of necessity restores those roots, for the attempt "to divine secret and concealed things from unconsidered and unnoticed details, from the rubbish-heap, as it were, of our observations"—a phrase Gallop borrows from Freud—by transforming into significance the very refuse of meaning, unsettles the authority determining knowledge.[13]

Naomi Schor appropriates those subversive qualities of detail specifically for feminism. She writes that the traditional association of detail with the feminine reveals not just what "is perhaps most threatening about the detail: its tendency to subvert" but also the peculiar strength of the feminine position, which is similarly marginal and similarly insubordinate.[14] According to such an approach, an attention to detail attests to and helps maintain the difference that, rather than simply entrapping women in phallogocentrism, might provide the best way for them to negotiate, and perhaps even change, its system of power. Schor writes: "before tearing down the cultural ghetto where the feminine has been confined and demeaned, we need to map its boundaries and excavate its foundations in order to salvage the usable relics and refuse of patriarchy, for to do so is perhaps the only chance we have to construct a post-deconstructionist society which will not simply reduplicate our own."[15] Through an attention to the representative details of gender division, which may be ultimately an attention to "anatomical difference"—and Schor's earlier essay advocating clitoral criticism suggests that she may be thinking of an anatomical

---

[11]Jane Gallop, "Psychoanalytic Criticism: Some Intimate Questions," *Art in America* 72 (November 1984): 11–13.

[12]Gallop, "Psychoanalytic Criticism," 13.

[13]Gallop, "Psychoanalytic Criticism," 13.

[14]Schor, *Reading in Detail*, 20.

[15]Schor, "Dreaming Dissymmetry: Barthes, Foucault, and Sexual Difference," in *Men in Feminism*, ed. Alice Jardine and Paul Smith (1987), 110.

detail traditionally considered trivial according to male stan-
dards— Schor suggests that feminists must hold open the claim to
feminine specificity.[16] As feminists, we must focus on detail, Schor
argues, to insist on sexual *difference* rather than indifferentiation,
even if this means relying on a (revised) essentialism borrowed
from traditional male views of women; such essentialism may be
only provisional, she claims, but it is absolutely necessary in order
to maintain any category of the female unappropriated to the male,
if and when we ever reach the utopia we gesture to in our writing.

Although as feminists we may question how this call to recycle
patriarchy's garbage is any different from what we do now (and we
should remember that Gallop's suggestion to do so is itself already
recycled from Freud), both critics suggest that we must of necessity
try to unsettle from within the system of representation in which
everyone is entrapped.[17] Both identify an attention to detail as the
way we can explicitly play up our implication in the system of
power that produces significance, and in that way perhaps change
its focus, change (but this is the problem), without reduplicating,
that system.

The alternative suggestion, most familiarly associated with
Irigaray, that we refuse such scrutiny (if not the category of sight)
altogether relies on a similar strategy of playing up our implication
within what we wish to reject and suggests that these seemingly
opposed feminist approaches to the specular foundations of metaphysics—to play up or refuse its laws—are not really all that different. Rather than accepting the male visual standard, Irigaray's emphasis on the blind spots and peripheries outside male speculation
is meant to call that standard's illusions into question: in her approach, woman is a dark continent that is "disquieting in its shadow" because she eludes the specular economy which determines
meaning for those in power.[18] The eluding of the specular means

---

[16]Schor refers to "anatomical difference" in "Dreaming Dissymmetry" (110). For
her discussion of clitoral criticism, see Naomi Schor, *Breaking the Chain: Woman,
Theory, and French Realist Fiction* (1985), 149–62.

[17]Gallop claims that this statement represents the side of Freud that is powerless,
an illegitimate impostor, the Freud that feminists may find most attractive (Gallop,
"Psychoanalytic Criticism," 13 and 15). But, even if true, it is important to emphasize that this reveals that Freud, too, is trapped in a system that does violence to him
but does not unsettle that system.

[18]Irigaray, *Speculum*, 135.

especially dispensing with particular details. Gallop, paraphrasing
Irigaray, writes: "All clear statements are trapped in the same economy of values, in which clarity (oculocentrism) and univocity (the
One) reign. Precision must be avoided, if the economy of the One
is to be unsettled."[19] This emphasis on the play of shadows
obstructing or occluding direct perception is as much concerned
with the marginal as one that stresses the almost hallucinatory
clarity of vision that picks out details. And it poses the same question of whether it is possible to transform woman's traditional
association with the marginal by playing it up.

Woman's relation to detail, then, represents a double bind in a
variety of ways: she is caught in an association with details,
whether they represent what is most evident or most impossible to
see. In that way, she points both to the system and to what seems
to deny or escape it. In any case, however, she remains defined by
it. Notwithstanding Schor's celebration of what she sees as a specifically feminine compulsion to duplicity (another recycled banality about women?), this double bind is precisely what has been
used to enable the inequities of gender division, the hierarchy
between men and women. In these responses, the visual remains
(as it seems it must) a central category underlying representation or
epistemology, one with which those of us within representation
(that is, everyone) cannot dispense, against which we continue to
measure ourselves even as we try to imagine changing it or giving
it up.[20] It is because sight has become such a familiar synechdoche
for what makes up our world, the very medium or means of construction with which we confuse that world, that the male order
and its literary expressions attempt to lay claim to and control it.
But is there any way to expose and disown the construction of the
gaze, so that as feminists we can become free from what it represents, from what, after all, those inveterate disciples of phallogocentrism actually find more difficult to claim and control than they
might like to admit?

One recent answer to this question has been no. In a move that,
although useful, is also interesting in its need to deny significance

---

[19]Jane Gallop, The Daughter's Seduction: Feminism and Psychoanalysis (1982), 78.
[20]Irigaray's play of metaphor in Speculum, for example, foregrounds her awareness of such double binds, in its connections of women with fire and light as well as
with darkness and shadow.

to the particulars of gender difference, Foucauldian criticism, building on his discussion of surveillance, has worked from the assumption that the gaze is genderless—or, rather, that gender itself is
another product of the social technologies that uphold an impersonal and regulating reconnaissance. To indict one gender position
for exercising such power, it would follow, is just another instance
in which the illusion of autonomy from power allows power to
continue.[21] This argument is actually similar to the Lacanian interpretation of the status of the gaze, which (when more fully
formulated than the feminist shorthand which sometimes simply
equates the symbolic with male power) argues that the symbolic
order reveals as well as rehearses gender inequities: the symbolic
order is not equivalent to the male province; instead, it exposes
that such a province is imaginary. This Lacanian reading of the
symbolic foregrounds that men and women both are castrated,
constituted within lack, and reveals the motivations and mechanisms by which women are simply made to stand for and draw off
from men the problems of their own lack.[22] Our feminist investigations may have unwittingly furthered the claims of phallocentrism,
then, when they have accorded phallocentrism a power not actually proper to it, equating the male with the very system of dominance which it only desires (to appear) to control. In doing so we
may have sometimes lost sight of the ways that the female, and
feminism, are also in their own ways implicated in such a system,
partaking of power even when it seems completely denied us.

II

Given this background of the specular, and our vexed relations to
it as feminists, what can the connection between gender and modes

---

[21]For an expression of this view, see Mark Seltzer, "The Naturalist Machine," in
Sex, Politics, and Science in the Nineteenth-Century Novel, Selected Papers from the
English Institute, 1983–84, n. s. 10, ed. Ruth Bernard Yeazell (1986), 116–47. The
ability to continue feminist criticism, given such assumptions, has plagued femi-
nists interested in Foucault. For some tentative suggestions about how to do so, see
Nancy Armstrong, *Desire and Domestic Fiction: A Political History of the Novel* (1987),
and *Foucault and Feminism: Reflections on Resistance*, ed. Irene Diamond and Lee
Quinby (1988).

[22]The best-known proponent of this more complicated reading of Lacan is Jane
Gallop; see her *Daughter's Seduction* and *Reading Lacan* (1985).

of literary representation add to this debate? Within literary representations, the evidence provided by seemingly insignificant details—the minutiae or innumerable particulars that make up the complexion of the larger text—has frequently been maintained as the guarantor of realism; a text's attention to detail is traditionally supposed to attest to its realism and is traditionally associated with the novel, not romance. Of course, as Naomi Schor suggests, a simple focus on the particular is different from the excessive heaping up of details, and an overabundance or excess of detail, although claimed by iconoclasts like Roland Barthes as representing precisely the "reality-effect," more conventionally has been seen as antirealistic.[23] Indeed the ornamentalism of schools like Orientalism have in literary history (in *Vathek* or even some of the works of Scott) been associated with (gothic) romance. Yet the association with realism of a certain moderated and controlled emphasis on detail continues to make sense despite the doubleness of detail—not because there is some kind of intrinsic and essential relation between whatever subjects hypothesize as reality and the particular or specific, but because realism asserts that relation in order to try to present itself *as* reality, not hypothesis. Such a maneuver denies its status as ideological production, screening as supposed fact the assumptions that govern it and screening too its own claims to govern that Foucault has suggested attend assertions of truth or knowledge. In order to make and mask such claims, realism claims a connection with detail because, as Foucault has also suggested, power invisibly infiltrates itself through details, through a multiplicity of small points of contact.[24]

Within literary texts, the motif of detail is consistently part of a more global metaphor of seeing. The critical argument that in a sense determined the modern importance of the novel and is most familiar to readers through James and Lubbock, the modern promoters of the form, is the argument for the effectiveness of the novelistic scene as *seen*, of what critics often call "showing" rather than "telling." The claim that in presenting a story "showing" is more dramatic and interesting because also more believable, more

[23]Roland Barthes, "The Reality Effect," trans. R. Carter, in *French Literary Theory Today: A Reader*, ed. Tzvetan Todorov (1982), 11–17.

[24]For a discussion of this kind of connection between details and the realistic novel, see Miller, *The Novel and the Police*, 17.

lifelike, more true suggests how writing aligns itself with the visual and does so to claim for itself the authority of the empirical. It is almost by now a truism of criticism that the classical realism of nineteenth-century novels especially draws on metaphors of sight for its effect. Critics of the novel, such as J. Hillis Miller, Elizabeth Ermarth, and Catherine Belsey, have discussed realism's presentation of itself as a transparent optic, its reliance on what Belsey calls "vivid description and close attention to realistic detail" as a way seemingly to ground itself empirically.[25] The rhetoric of the visual validates the form of realism by denying that it is a form. As Belsey suggests: "the term [realism] is useful in distinguishing between those forms which tend to efface their own textuality, their existence as discourse, and those which explicitly draw attention to it. Realism offers itself as transparent."[26] Realism's emphasis on seeing makes it hard to see. Even in works by an author like Eliot, who is often explicitly careful to distinguish between realism and reality, to remind the reader now and then that the optic changes the picture, realism still presents itself as an optic, implicitly retaining the very mode of presentation (and the possible access to reality) it may temporarily question.[27]

Realism borrows from the visual in order to seem not just real but also true; it relies on the authority the visual seems to provide, the way it naturalizes ideological constructions into universal and accepted truths. As Stephen Heath writes: "where a discourse appeals directly to an image, to an immediacy of seeing, as a point of its argument or demonstration, one can be sure that all difference is being elided, that the unity of some accepted vision is being re-

[25]Catherine Belsey, "Re-Reading the Great Tradition," in *Re-Reading English*, ed. Peter Widdowson (1982), 123. See also her *Critical Practice* (1980). For a further discussion of the visual metaphors that realism relies on, see J. Hillis Miller, "Character in the Novel: A 'Real Illusion,'" in *From Smollett to James: Studies in the Novel and Other Essays, Presented to Edgar Johnson*, ed. Samuel I. Mintz, Alice Chandler, and Christopher Mulvey (1981), 277–85, and Elizabeth Deeds Ermarth, *Realism and Consensus in the English Novel* (1983).

[26]Belsey, *Critical Practice*, 51.

[27]For just one instance of Eliot's careful distinguishing, see the passage in chapter 17 of *Adam Bede* (a passage I discuss later in another context): "I aspire to give no more than a faithful account of men and things as they have mirrored themselves in my mind. The mirror is doubtless defective" (George Eliot, *Adam Bede*, ed. Stephen Gill [1980], ch. 17, p. 222); all future references to this book (hereafter abbreviated *AB*) will appear in the text.

produced."[28] The techniques of realism—its omniscient all-seeing narrator, its emphasis on the particulars of that narrator's vision, the narrator's use of them to survey his world and detect and unravel its mysteries—are concerned "with seeing, with a seeing in detail," Mark Seltzer argues, to aid in our acceptance as subjects not just of one true unified vision but of an invisible supervision.[29] For the visual has also been posited as an effective medium for imposing and maintaining social control: Foucault has described how the surveillance of the panopticon is the essential mechanism of the self-regulating system of power relations. By aligning itself with the visual, the classical realism of nineteenth-century novels like Eliot's (as a whole school of critics including D. A. Miller along with Seltzer has argued) participates in and promotes this system by attempting to contain it in itself. Classical realism is actually both a document of and effective propaganda for the system of power in which all subjects are inscribed.

In the English tradition, George Eliot's works have become synonymous with classical realism, and the relation of realism to the authority of the visual is a consistent focus that they investigate as well as rely on. Like the other novelists I consider, Eliot uses romance to define her own realistic novels; in her novels, the claim of realism to the precision and clarity of specularity contrasts with a rhetoric associating the dizzying profusion of details, or their indistinctness, with romance. Yet, as for other novelists, Eliot's realism cannot keep separate from what it casts as its opposite. In The Mill on the Floss, describing Maggie "battling with the old shadowy enemies that were forever slain and rising again" (MF.7.5.644), Eliot describes too the struggle between the realism of her novels and an undispatchable romance within them. Eliot locates the terms of the dynamic I have been charting a little differently from the other novelists I have considered: between what critics call modes, not genres, attitudes or presentation rather than types or forms.[30] Eliot means for her dominant mode of presentation to ensure the primacy of her genre, the novel, but romance is a shadowy enemy, always rising again, because, in fighting it, realism is

[28]Stephen Heath, "Difference," Screen 19 (1978): 53.
[29]Seltzer, Henry James, 50.
[30]For a discussion of the difference between modes and genres, see Northrop Frye, Anatomy of Criticism: Four Essays (1957), 95–99, 246–326.

fighting its own shadow. Like all the heroines I have analyzed, Maggie embodies this struggle in herself: "her thoughts generally were the oddest mixture of clear-eyed acumen and blind dreams" (1.11.177). Yet, although the novel attempts to reproduce this as a battle, presenting the "sense of opposing elements, of which a fierce collision is imminent" (5.1.394), their mixture in Maggie also suggests their kinship: as the title to the chapter in which Maggie escapes to the gypsies ironically suggests, Maggie cannot run away from her shadow—the differences between realism and romance cannot be maintained. The struggle between a realism and a romance that are ultimately indistinguishable exposes how the fight between them, conducted on the site of the woman, is rigged. No matter which side wins, the struggle she embodies does not liberate but remains dangerous to her, ultimately deadly—the moral Maggie's end poses to her cautionary tale.

The investigation of this double bind seems central to Eliot's fiction, for she admits both warring factions easily into her work. Eliot's derision of romance is much less strict than (although often still as virulent as) that of the other novelists I have considered, and her definition of realism in her essays and letters outlines a mode of representation that is explicitly problematic and contradictory. *Adam Bede* and *The Mill on the Floss*—early novels in which Eliot maps out her realism—never completely dispel romance, although in them readers find Eliot's strongest disclaimers against it; by the end of her career, in *Daniel Deronda*, disclaimer has softened to conciliation: Eliot writes, for example, that although "to say that Deronda was romantic would be to misrepresent him," still, he has "a fervour which made him easily find poetry and romance among the events of everyday life. And perhaps poetry and romance are as plentiful as ever in the world. . . . They exist very easily in the same room with the microscope."[31] Romance, as present in the everyday life of her first fiction as it is in the later works, may be more intensely denied early on to deny the initial shock of disillusionment and frustration—and failure—in attempting to imagine an alternative to realism and the order it represents.

Eliot's reference to the microscope in the previous passage indi-

---

[31]George Eliot, *Daniel Deronda*, ed. Barbara Hardy (1967), ch. 19, p. 245. All further references to this book (hereafter abbreviated *DD*) will appear in the text.

cates the initial differences her fiction charts between realism and
romance. Her realism is based in an optic that focuses on "minute
reality."[32] In contrast, Eliot seems to imply (and critics have agreed),
romance lacks such minute particulars. R. E. Francillon, in an early
review of *Daniel Deronda*, writes:

> It is precisely in the detailed elaboration of the little, charac-
> teristic, everyday things which procure universal acceptance for a
> book at once that we are most conscious of an unusual want in
> *Daniel Deronda*. In this respect also it is distinctively of the nature
> of the Romance, which tends to bring universal and essential
> things into prominence, and to leave accidental and transitory
> things on one side. It will never require a department in the
> museum.[33]

The "unusual want" of details in romance may provide one way to
elude what Foucault might call the micro-optics of power—the
anonymous scrutiny of everyday things which objectifies and masters them—one way to escape being institutionally exhibited ("it
will never require a department in the museum")—exhibited, say,
through an institution of literary representation like realism (as
Eliot might hope that Dorothea's "indefiniteness" will keep her
from being exhibited to the male gaze in the Hall of Statues in the
Museum in Rome).

The traditional association of romance with the essential and
universal that we find in Francillon's review suggests that romance
too remains essentializing and dangerous. Romance's "want" is
just as dangerous as realism's completeness because it still accedes
to the same law, which sees only what it looks for or nothing at
all—which sees only itself and thereby makes itself universal. Romance remains connected to realism; it also "exists very easily in
the same room with the microscope." The microscope in its scrutiny of detail continues their connection for it also turns realism
into romance; it transforms "little, characteristic, everyday things"
into the whole field of vision, making the everyday seem un-
familiar, the little larger than life, magnifying—"bringing into

---

[32]"John Blackwood to George Eliot, Edinburgh, 31 March 1858," in vol. 2 of *The George Eliot Letters*, ed. Gordon S. Haight, 9 vols. (1954–78), p. 445.

[33]"George Eliot's First Romance," from the *Gentleman's Magazine*, in *George Eliot: The Critical Heritage*, ed. David Carroll (1971), 395.

prominence"—what is supposedly "essential," making it into the "universal." The general and particular remain inseparable in Eliot's fiction, for, as Eliot has Lydgate explain, "a man's mind must be continually expanding and shrinking between the whole human horizon and the horizon of an object-glass" (*MM*.63.690). This confusion of realism and romance—Eliot's hesitation between them—may suggest that there is no real choice.

Reviewing Ruskin's *Modern Painters* III, Eliot does seem to choose realism, to define it in a way that critics have aptly applied to her own novels: "The truth of infinite value that [Ruskin] teaches is *realism*—the doctrine that all truth and beauty are to be attained by a humble and faithful study of nature, and not by substituting vague forms, bred by imagination on the mists of feeling, in place of definite substantial reality."[34] In borrowing her idea of realism from a doctrine about painting, Eliot's verbal system is directly predicated on an analogy with a visual one—one that celebrates the definite, the detailed. Eliot's definition is also in keeping with the Victorian critical consensus on realism. That critic most important to Eliot, George Henry Lewes, similarly equates realism with descriptive detail. In a letter to Eliot's publisher, John Blackwood, about a story that she wrote not long after the essay on Ruskin, "Janet's Repentance." Lewes admits: "What you say about the hacknied nature of the clergyman's story is perfectly true; and it appears all the more hacknied because the rest of the tale is so entirely original; but the vaguer such a story, the *more* hacknied it would necessarily appear; details give an air of reality, and I could have wished G.E. had been more detailed."[35] Similarly, Edith Simcox, reviewing *Middlemarch,* assumes by "realism, the positive background of fact."[36]

[34][George Eliot], "Art and Belles Lettres," *Westminster Review* n.s. 9 (January and April 1856): 626.

[35]"George Henry Lewes to John Blackwood, Richmond, [23? August? 1857]," in *Letters,* 2: 378.

[36]H. Lawrenny [Edith Simcox], Review of *Middlemarch,* from the *Academy,* in Carroll, *George Eliot: The Critical Heritage,* 324. Modern literary critics assume the same equation, especially when distinguishing realism from romance. George Levine, like Lewes, uses detail in opposing realism to the vague and hackneyed. Victorian novelists, Levine writes, "seem to take pleasure in the details they invoke from outside the patterning conventions of romance. And the great realistic fictions are exuberant with details" (Levine, *The Realistic Imagination: English Fiction from Frankenstein to Lady Chatterly* [1981], 21). Levine goes on to suggest that realism, in

Yet these literary critics do not assert a simple connection between details and what Lewes calls the "air of reality"; Lewes
himself, for instance, is especially critical of what he terms the
"*detailism* which calls itself realism"—a false realism that has gone
too far, by piling up arbitrary details, and too many of them, at the
expense of meaning.[37] Like Eliot, he believes that "all Art depends
on Vision," but he goes on to elaborate that "the rage for 'realism,'
which is healthy in as far as it insists on truth, has become unhealthy, in as far as it confounds truth with familiarity, and predominance of unessential details," a predominance that ultimately
calls that realism into question.[38] Lewes finds especially unhealthy
and unessential those details taken from what he sees as low subjects; in an appeal to class-consciousness, he dismisses a realism
built on details that might delight tailors and upholsterers.[39] That

fact, makes use of detail in order to displace romance—one of its "major devices" is
"the reduction of the romantic to the banal by means of the translation of a rhetorically inflated cliche into a set of unattractive details" (281). Levine elsewhere particularly links Eliot's early realism to "confident empiricism," "assured rendering," and
"clear perception" (Levine, "George Eliot's Hypothesis of Reality," *Nineteenth-Century Fiction* 35 [June 1980]: 3). Lennard J. Davis also argues that "the romancer's view
of the world is thus based on the effacing of the offending or nonconforming fact or
event and the creation of the ideal, the paradigmatic, the traditional. The writer of
novels, on the other hand, sees narrative as more oriented to the specific, the
particular, the eccentric, the factual" (Davis, *Factual Fictions: The Origins of the English
Novel* [1983], 33). Jonathan R. Quick suggests that when Eliot intentionally strives
for romance, as in *Silas Marner,* she abandons "the sharp precision and fullness of
detail" of her realistic works for a "darkened, dreamlike atmosphere" (Quick, "Silas
Marner as Romance: The Example of Hawthorne," *Nineteenth-Century Fiction* 29
[December 1974]: 291). For Eliot's assumption of romance as visually obscure, see,
for instance, her criticism of the popular novelist Fredrika Bremer's "pink haze of
visions and romance," in "[Three Novels]," in *The Essays of George Eliot,* ed. Thomas
Pinney (1963), 332. This passage is interesting, for in it Eliot is discussing Bremer's
treatment of "the cause of women," which Eliot wishes had more "attention to
detail" and more "light of common day" than romantic haze.

[37]George Henry Lewes, *The Principles of Success in Literature,* ed. Fred N. Scott
(1891), 83. These essays were originally published in the journal Lewes edited, the
Fortnightly Review, from May through November of 1865, and were first published in
book form in 1885. For a discussion of Lewes's detailism, see Richard Stang, *The
Theory of the Novel in England, 1850–1870* (1959), 174.

[38]Lewes, *Principles of Success,* 84. He writes that "I wish to guard the Principle of
Vision from certain misconceptions which might arise on a simple statement of it.
The principle insists on the artist assuring himself that he distinctly sees what he
attempts to represent. *What* he sees, and *how* he represents it, depend on other
principles" (85).

[39]Lewes, *Principles of Success,* 84–85. Lewes writes: "The painter who devotes
years to a work representing modern life, yet calls for even more attention to a

Lewes felt he had to outline a suspect detailism somehow different from Eliot's use of detail, and that he did so in a rhetoric whose appeal to bias tried to mask the problems of its logic, indicate the difficulty of claiming "the truth of infinite value" that Eliot wants to ascribe to detail and reveal that such problems worried Eliot's circle. Yet the paradoxical status of detail, while it calls the certainties of realism into question, does not necessarily overturn the visual system; such contradictions may be what allow that system to flourish by retaining it as the standard, keeping all of us in it locked between alternatives of what we can or cannot see. Eliot's very difficulty is finding out how to negotiate these alternatives.

The validity of Eliot's realism is also uncertain because its own relation with visual detail is vexed—vexed by what Barbara Hardy has best described as Eliot's sense of the "disenchanted day-lit room," her discomfort with solid particulars.[40] The "definite substantial reality" that Eliot praises in Ruskin becomes "the dreary persistence of definite measurable reality" in "Janet's Repentance," with its "oppressive distinctness" of "details," and also becomes the "hard, inevitable reality" of *Adam Bede*, heavy too with the weight of "details" (*AB*.38.444).[41] Hardy suggests that it is only Eliot's characters who recoil from the "oppressive narrowness" (*MF*.4.1.363) of the world of Eliot's realism and that acceptance of this world is part of Eliot's moral for them. Yet surely Eliot herself

---

waistcoat than to the face of a philosopher, may exhibit truth of detail which will delight the tailor-mind, but he is defective in artistic truth, because he ought to be representing something higher than waistcoats. . . .if a man means to paint upholstery, by all means let him paint it so as to delight and deceive an upholsterer; but if he means to paint a human tragedy, the upholsterer must be subordinate" (84–85).

[40]Barbara Hardy, *The Novels of George Eliot: A Study in Form* (1959), 190. Eliot's reliance on but discomfort with descriptive detail may have been what kept her from writing for years. In "How I Came to Write Fiction," she records that although she felt at "ease in the descriptive parts of a novel," she realized that scene painting and detail were not groundwork enough for fiction ("George Eliot Journal, Richmond, 6 December 1857," in *Letters*, 2:406–7). Eliot uneasily proceeded to build her realism on the very quality she found troubling, and —although she admitted her doubts in her journal—she defended her emphasis on description against others. She wrote to Charles Bray about "Three Months in Weimar": "Don't say anything about it, for to people who do not enjoy description of scenery it will seem very tame and stupid, and I really think a taste for descriptive writing is the rarest of all tastes among ordinary people" ("George Eliot to Charles Bray, East Sheen, 12 May 1855," in *Letters*, 2:201).

[41]George Eliot, "Janet's Repentance," in *Scenes of Clerical Life*, ed. David Lodge (1973), ch. 16, p. 349.

recoils; her rebellion against that realism is responsible for the (realistically) implausible ending of *The Mill on the Floss*, for instance.[42]

Eliot had reason to be uneasy with detail, for although her books were immediately praised, by Blackwood for example, for the effect of their "minute touches," those touches could also backfire.[43] Blackwood first criticized her work because of its visual particularity; he found that in "Amos Barton" Eliot tried "too much to explain the characters of [her] actors by descriptions" and that she ruined the deathbed scene by "specifying so minutely."[44] None of Eliot's novels escaped criticism of this sort. Perhaps the best-known criticism in this vein is Henry James's, who found *Middlemarch* "a treasure-house of details, but it is an indifferent whole."[45] Ruskin, rather than recognizing his own realism in Eliot's project, found her details common and trashy, using against her both the class prejudice and the image of unhealthiness that Lewes associated with detailism—to Ruskin, her details were "the sweepings out of a Pentonville omnibus" and the "blotches, burrs and pimples" in a "study of cutaneous disease."[46] Rather than providing a solution to the very problems that Lewes outlined, Eliot's realism repeated those problems despite itself.

Coincident with Eliot's association of detail and realism is a competing association of detail and romance, drawn from another writer Eliot admired, Sir Walter Scott, whom Lewes called her "longest-venerated and best-loved Romancist" in his inscription in the set of

[42]For a feminist interpretation of that implausibility, see Nancy K. Miller, "Emphasis Added: Plots and Plausibilities in Women's Fiction," *PMLA* 96 (January 1981): 36–48, especially 44–47.

[43]"John Blackwood to George Eliot, Edinburgh, 3 November 1858," in *Letters*, 2: 492.

[44]"John Blackwood to George Henry Lewes, Edinburgh, 12 November 1856," in *Letters*, 2: 272.

[45]Henry James, Unsigned Review of *Middlemarch*, from the *Galaxy*, in Carroll, *George Eliot: The Critical Heritage*, 353.

[46]John Ruskin, from *Nineteenth-Century*, in Carroll, *George Eliot: The Critical Heritage*, 167. For more of such criticism of Eliot's novels, see, for example, the unsigned review of *The Mill on the Floss* from the *Dublin University Magazine*, which criticized its "photographic pettiness" and its "heaping-up of meaningless details" (in Carroll, *George Eliot: The Critical Heritage*, 145, 146). See also R. H. Hutton's unsigned review of *Felix Holt*, from the *Spectator*, which finds fault with its "overflowing affluence of lively and striking detail" (in Carroll, *George Eliot: The Critical Heritage*, 258).

Waverley novels he gave to her.[47] Scott writes in *Waverley*: "The most romantic parts of this narrative are precisely those which have a foundation in fact."[48] As Donald Stone tells us, "William Hazlitt said of Scott what later commentators observed of Dickens and George Eliot: 'Sir Walter has found out (oh, rare discovery) that facts are better than fiction; that there is no romance like the romance of real life.' "[49] From the first, critics did indeed observe this of Eliot; a reviewer of *Scenes of Clerical Life* approved its "just appreciation of the romance of reality."[50] Eliot was so influenced by this model that, while she was working on the book that she herself termed a romance, *Romola*, Lewes wrote to Blackwood: "when you see her, mind your care is to discountenance the idea of a Romance being the product of an Encyclopaedia."[51] This heaping up of everyday reality, facts, detail (a totalizing overabundance of it, as the reference to the Encyclopedia suggests), points to the way romance can also be determined by the empirical (even as it stretches its limits).

The title character of *Adam Bede* seems to provide the steadiest support for the empiricism of the novel, its plain, commonsensical realism; Adam is himself plain and commonsensical, at home with facts and the things of the world, "observant of the objects round him" (38.438). Adam's attention to detail, which directly aligns him with the specular law of realism, also aligns him with the legal system in the novel: Dinah sees him as a kind of patriarch (as his name suggests), and he is specifically like the lawyer in Hetty's case, who is also observant, "a cute fellow, with an eye that 'ud pick the needles out of the hay in no time" (42.473). But the law in this story is crucial in trying and condemning Hetty and, through this, the novel suggests that Adam's relation to the law is also double-edged. This law, in punishing Hetty, also contravenes his own desires. Her suffering calls his adherence to it into question, shows him his own inflexibility and culpability. Adam's pain is

[47]Quoted in Gordon S. Haight, *George Eliot: A Biography* (1968), 319.

[48]Sir Walter Scott, *Waverley*, vol. 2 of *The Large Paper Edition of the Works of Sir Walter Scott*, 50 vols. (1912–13), p. 311.

[49]Donald D. Stone, *The Romantic Impulse in Victorian Fiction* (1980), 13.

[50]Unsigned review of *Scenes of Clerical Life*, from the *Atlantic Monthly*, in Carroll, *George Eliot: The Critical Heritage*, 66.

[51]"George Henry Lewes to John Blackwood, London, [14 December 1861]," in *Letters*, 3:474.

Eliot's lesson for him—he must bend under the same inflexible rule that he has sanctioned for others, and, from his own suffering, he gains forbearance and sympathy for them. Yet Adam's moral lesson—that those who uphold the law are themselves guilty and must suffer under it—points to the doubleness within Eliot's realism and begins to put the idea of its law (as something a subject might be above or outside) into question.

It is not so much Adam's as Hetty's example that reveals as an illusion our hopes as subjects of maintaining the category of law as something we can either claim or transgress. " 'Law?' " asks Bartle Massey. " 'What's the use o' law when a man's once such a fool as to let a woman into his house?' " (21.284). Adam suffers at Hetty's expense; she becomes the little piece of trash discarded to save the rest. While comforting Adam in his sorrow over Hetty's crime, the rector, Mr. Irwin, suggests that " 'if the evidence should tell too strongly against her . . . we may still hope for a pardon' " (40.458). Critics have argued that the evidence tells too strongly indeed: the kind of detail associated with Adam and from which he draws strength explicitly becomes evidence, the circumstantial facts that convict Hetty at her trial and save Adam from her. Hetty falls victim to the war of detail fought between realism and romance. She is not pardoned but sacrificed, it seems, for nothing more than a handshake between two men; her death facilitates the Girardian reconciliation that takes place between Adam and Arthur at novel's end.[52]

The violence of Eliot's realism enacted on scapegoats like Hetty is meant to purge it of romance, which it depicts as deviant and onto which it projects (and hence denies) its own violence. Beginning with "Amos Barton," Eliot associates the romantic and the criminal: she builds her first story around a realistic, unheroic hero who is so partly because he "had no undetected crime within his breast."[53] *Adam Bede*'s narrator wryly suggests that that book is realistic too in part because "romantic criminals [aren't] half so frequent as your common labourer" (*AB*.17.225). In *The Mill on the Floss*, Aunt Moss's farm is Maggie's romantic retreat, her "Alsatia,

[52]For a discussion of the connection between men in this novel, see Eve Kosofsky Sedgwick, *Between Men: English Literature and Male Homosocial Desire* (1985), 134–60.

[53]George Eliot, "The Sad Fortunes of the Rev. Amos Barton," in her *Scenes of Clerical Life*, ch. 5, p. 80.

where she was out of the reach of the law" (MF.1.8.139), and the narrator suspects readers may find that the realism of the novel is "sordid" because it has none of "the dark shadows of misery and crime" they can find in romance (MF.4.1.362). Eliot uses this metaphor of the shadowy underworld to reiterate that romance is outside her work, eclipsed by her realism. Yet she has her own cast of romantic criminals, her ladies with daggers. They themselves remain marginal to her stories (as Madame Laure does), or their crimes remain indefinite and unacted (as Gwendolen's or Caterina's do), yet what she defines as romance invades Eliot's work nonetheless in their characterization. Whether the violence her book portrays is defined as legitimate—as in the court's penalty—or illegitimate—as in the women's revenge—it is violence all the same, putting into question the differences between the modes that practice it. That the violence ultimately rebounds onto women like Hetty and Maggie, killed off to resolve the impossible demands of their stories, suggests that their sacrifice is meant to hide the seamlessness of an order that wishes to appear divided. They supposedly perish because of their association with romance, but such violence is all that awaits them in the world of realism as well.

Hetty is expressly made to seem a romantic criminal; she kills her baby partly to preserve her vague romances about Arthur, to deny the reality of what has happened to her, and Eliot indicts such romance through the setting of Hetty's trial: the story pauses to tell us that the trial takes place in what was once a kind of Arthurian court (linking Hetty's dreams about her own particular Arthur and conventional Arthurian romances). But the court has been taken over by Eliot's realism, ironically transformed into a court of law (AB.43.476). Eliot seems, and has angered some readers by seeming, a firm supporter of the law that Hetty and the others violate, on the side of Adam and the order he claims.[54] Yet, as feminist

---

[54]At her most censorious, Eliot, in depicting Bartle Massey's dog's solicitude for her puppies, goes so far as to imply that Hetty's crime is against the law of nature as well as that of man—Hetty, Eliot suggests, is not after all so much like the cute little animal to which the narrator and characters have compared her and should therefore forfeit the small sympathy readers were allowed to give her for that similarity. But Eliot mitigates her disapproval a little by putting blame elsewhere than on these women. Grandcourt is the one who drives Gwendolen (almost) into crime. Readers can blame Caterina's passion on Wycroft and Cheverals, who aren't "romantic" enough to adopt her (George Eliot, "Mr. Gilfil's Love-Story," in her Scenes of Clerical

critics have pointed out, the idea of law itself also comes into question in Eliot's work: another set of villains in *The Mill on the Floss* are
the men of maxims, guided "solely by general rules, thinking that
these will lead them to justice by a ready-made patent method"
(*MF*.7.2.628).[55]

Questioning the law, however, does nothing to save Hetty. Eliot
may need to shatter Hetty's romance building in order to preserve
the very legend of George Eliot, a self carefully constructed through
her novels and other writings. In a letter written during her evan-
gelical period, the young Mariann Evans works out her relation to
writing by decrying the effects of fiction—both novels and romances—in language that foreshadows George Eliot's depiction of
Hetty and outlines the complications that inform her later work:

> The Scriptural declaration, "As face answereth to face in a glass,
> so the heart of man to man," will exonerate me from the charge of
> uncharitableness or too high an estimate of myself if I venture to
> believe that the same causes which exist in my own breast to
> render novels and romances pernicious have their counterpart in
> that of every fellow-creature.
>
> I am I confess not an impartial member of a jury in this case for I
> owe the culprits a grudge for injuries inflicted on myself. I shall
> carry to my grave the mental diseases with which they have con-
> taminated me. When I was quite a little child I could not be
> satisfied with the things around me; I was constantly living in a
> world of my own creation, and was quite contented to have no
> companions that I might be left to my own musings and imagine
> scenes in which I was chief actress. Conceive what a character
> novels would give to these Utopias. I was early supplied with
> them . . . and of course I made use of the materials they supplied
> for building my castles in the air.[56]

The wishful opening of this passage—"as face answereth to face in
a glass, so the heart of man to man"—exposes one anxiety of Eliot's

---

Life, ch. 3, p. 152). Readers can even recuperate Hetty and Madame Laure, by
discovering in them, as Gilbert and Gubar do with Eliot's other transgressors, her
own covert resistance to the constraints of the established system; see Sandra M.
Gilbert and Susan Gubar, *The Madwoman in the Attic: The Woman Writer and the
Nineteenth-Century Literary Imagination* (1979), 443–535, for a discussion of the image
of the veil in Eliot and of Eliot's veiled resistance to patriarchy.

[55]See Nancy K. Miller, "Emphasis Added," and Jacobus, *Reading Woman*, 62–79.
[56]"George Eliot to Maria Lewis, Griff, 16 [March 1839]," in *Letters*, 1: 22.

that aligns her with Hetty; the young writer here insists that *she* sees in the mirror more than just her own face—she exonerates herself from the "high estimate of self" of which Eliot later convicts Hetty. The mirror gives her that connection with others that becomes the moral law of Eliot's realism, a position of truth from which she can denounce other fiction. Yet the wishfulness suggests that Hetty's narcissism and her resulting delusive dreams, which Eliot outlaws from her fiction, are outlawed because Eliot believes them to be such present dangers. The "confession" of this letter suggests the writer's identification with Hetty, for whom confession is so important in *Adam Bede*—by confessing, that writer shows that she is the accused as well as the judge, as much in Hetty's position as the one who sets her up.

When judging, Eliot confesses that she "is not an impartial member of a jury" in her prosecution of fiction in this letter, nor is she later in prosecuting Hetty in *Adam Bede:* by denouncing romance in that novel, she hopes to protect her own realism from the "contamination" she notes in her letter; she would also like to believe that the realism of her novels is built not of air but of solid concrete detail. Yet she admits here that such a foundation is not enough, that she is drawn to her vapory imaginings—"I could not be satisfied with the things around me."

Hetty bears the brunt of her grudge; she is sacrificed, supposedly exorcising romantic influences and testifying to the preeminence and validity of realism, in order to create a world in which the hearts of men do answer to each other (as Adam's and Arthur's do), where men can be contented with their companions because such companionship does not enmire them in power relations. The desire for this utopia is supposedly common to every fellow creature but can be represented only as between fellows, as a world of *men:* this remains perhaps the most pernicious limitation of (Eliot's) fiction (although, in exposing this limit, Eliot also exposes that it is by no means uniquely hers). Eliot's authorial self gains the consolation of autonomy from a world of strife and waste only by identifying with the male order, becoming George Eliot.

Yet the author of *Adam Bede* is no more able, by embracing a powerful realism or subversive romance, to write herself out of the structures of representation than Hetty is able to transform her world to her desires. With its opening sentences, borrowing an image from the *Arabian Nights,* the book's endeavor is associated with Hetty: as critics have long remarked, the sorcerer's drop of ink (*AB*.1.49), in which the writer sees her visions, reappears as Hetty's "black pool" (37.435), in which she longs to end all vision. Even realism's manifesto in chapter 17, through its imagery, ties that realism to the romantic Hetty and back to the letter about the dangers of fiction. Eliot writes: "I aspire to give no more than a faithful account of men and things as they have mirrored themselves in my mind. The mirror is doubtless defective; the outlines will sometimes be disturbed; the reflection faint or confused; but I feel as much bound to tell you, as precisely as I can, what that reflection is, as if I were in the witness-box narrating my experience on oath" (17.221). The defective mirror of realism cannot be divorced from the spotty mirror before which Hetty looks at herself and dreams her romances (15.194–202). In speaking from "the witness-box," Eliot takes an oath that guarantees her "preciseness," her commitment to the detailed account of realism, just as the oaths of those in the witness-box in *Adam Bede* convict Hetty and dispel the romance she represents. But Eliot's oath has already been put into question by her earlier confession of partiality; because of Eliot's identification with Hetty, by convicting her, she convicts herself. She remains a culprit and a victim even as she tries to exercise power.

As Hetty's importance in the struggle of realism with romance suggests, woman's definition is a crucial issue in Eliot's work. As she began to prepare for writing fiction, Eliot thought constantly about the woman question, projecting more articles about it than she could write and reading and editing the articles of others, and her fiction expressly takes a woman's life as its starting point.[57]

Woman is more than just the basis for Eliot's stories, however; she also figures the problems of representation that are the focus of

[57]Eliot published the essays "Woman in France" (1854) and "Silly Novels by Lady Novelists" (1856), as well as reviews of women writers. She projected publishing "Ideals of Womankind" and "Women in Germany" (see "George Eliot to John Chapman, Berlin, 9 January [1855]," in *Letters*, 2: 190). She edited Chapman's 1855 article, "The Position of Women in Barbarism and among the Ancients." Lewes's "The Lady Novelists" was published in 1852. For examples of the explicit reliance of her fiction on women's stories, see the claim in *The Mill on the Floss* that it is grounding its tale in a woman's vicissitudes (6.3.494) or see, in *Middlemarch*, the narrator's comparison of herself to Herodotus, "who also, in telling what had been, thought it well to take a woman's lot for his starting-point" (11.123).

Eliot's work. In an early essay outlining the nature of realism, "The Natural History of German Life," in a vignette later echoed in *Adam Bede* (*AB*.19.253), Eliot emphasizes the importance of woman:

> Observe a company of haymakers. When you see them at a distance . . . you pronounce the scene "smiling," and you think these companions in labour must be as bright and cheerful as the picture to which they give animation. Approach nearer, and you will certainly find that haymaking time is a time for joking, especially if there are women among the labourers; but the coarse laugh that bursts out every now and then, and expresses the triumphant taunt, is as far as possible from your conception of idyllic merriment.[58]

Such scene painting, what Eliot calls in *Middlemarch* "that softening influence of the fine arts which makes other people's hardships picturesque" (39.429), hides that the relations between such "companions" are power relations. The introduction of gender—for Eliot, as for her culture, the differences of gender are represented by women—into the specular exposes the logic of the specular. Although it is unclear whether women give or receive the triumphant taunt, the implication is that gender differences introduce conflict, introduce the idea of triumph or defeat. Minute observation and women converge; woman becomes the telling detail that changes the picture from a vague idyll, viewed at a distance, to a rendering that can only be coarse in its accuracy and comes too close to us for comfort. Eliot's hesitation in aligning herself with either perspective is made explicit. The narrator here prefers only to gesture to but not examine this picture, only to shatter what might be vague romance while withholding scrutiny of what might be hardships—and, likely, women's hardships.

Yet, despite a reluctance to take sides, in exposing the attempt to claim and purge the specular order by scapegoating its problems onto women, Eliot's fiction repeats that scapegoating. *Adam Bede* deplores Hetty's narcissism, her posing before her mirror. But in admiring herself as a visual object and attempting to look like the portraits of ladies at the Chase, Hetty is only doing what the novel

---

[58]George Eliot, "The Natural History of German Life," in Pinney, *Essays of George Eliot*, 269.

itself does to her: it presents her as something to look at, a picture, an object—her trial reveals that she is rarely out of someone's sight. Blackwood's reaction to her is typical: "Hetty is a wonderful piece of painting. One seems to *see* the little villain."[59] The *novel's* association of women with the descriptive detail of its realism makes Hetty into a spectacle; in flaunting her looks, she only acts out its logic.[60]

Adam is the spokesman for the connection in the novel between woman and the naked fact. When Hetty puts a rose in her hair to imitate a picture, Adam explicitly formulates the place of woman in the specular economy: "Ah . . . that's like the ladies in the pictures at the Chase; they've mostly got flowers or feathers or gold things i' their hair, but somehow I don't like to see 'em; they allays put me i' mind o' the painted woman outside the shows at Treddles'on fair" (*AB*.20.269). Adam's equation exposes the logic of the specular order. Painted women (pictures) ultimately equal painted women (prostitutes). Although Adam hates to admit it of Hetty (yet it is what draws him to her), woman as object is inevitably a sexual object.

Woman's association with detail quickly becomes her reduction to anatomical detail, as the reaction of Eliot's contemporary critics to her minuteness indicates. Their criticism of what they saw as the excessive facts within Eliot's work frequently became criticism of what the *Examiner* called an "almost obstetric accuracy of detail," what they all felt was Eliot's overemphasis on the facts of life.[61]

[59]From a letter dated 4 October 1858, quoted in Haight, *George Eliot: A Biography*, 265.

[60]For Hetty as spectacle: see "Hetty was quite used to the thought that people liked to look at her" (*AB*.9.141); "She's like a pictur in a shop-winder" (36.423); and see also Arthur remembering Hetty as a "picture" (44.485). Hetty also regards herself from the position of "an invisible spectator" (15.195). Catherine Belsey argues that woman as spectacle, in the case of Gwendolen, grows from "the social production of femininity" as well as from the production of realism (Belsey, "Re-reading," 132). For the standard discussion of woman as spectacle, see John Berger (with Sven Blomberg, Chris Fox, Michael Dibb, Richard Hollis), *Ways of Seeing* (1972), 45–64.

[61]From the *Examiner*, quoted in Carroll, *George Eliot: The Critical Heritage*, 11. See also the unsigned review of *Scenes of Clerical Life*, from the *Saturday Review*, which finds that Hetty's story "read[s] like the rough notes of a man-midwife's conversations with a bride" (in Carroll, *George Eliot: The Critical Heritage*, 76); or the unsigned review of *The Mill on the Floss*, from the same journal, which says that Eliot and other women writers "linger on the description of the physical sensations that

That the facts of life the specular builds on are necessarily biological is implied in the assumptions informing Eliot's conception of
representation. The nineteenth-century positivism that ascribed its
authority to empiricism—to sensory data as the ultimate base of
observation—also, as recent critics have shown, legislated that
anatomy equals destiny, that "for women biology controlled social
destiny."[62] This hidden trap of essentialism, so inimical to women,
is built into Eliot's fiction; her realism seems to embrace it, and her
romance is unable to avoid or overturn it.[63]

---

accompany the meeting of hearts in love" (in Carroll, *George Eliot: The Critical
Heritage*, 188); or the unsigned review of *Silas Marner*, from the *Westminster Review*,
which criticizes Eliot's "somewhat objectionable use of physiological images" (in
Carroll, *George Eliot: The Critical Heritage*, 188). Critics still emphasize anatomical
detail in Eliot's fiction, as in Ellen Moers's discussion of the significance of the Red
Deeps (*Literary Women* [1976; 1985], 252–57) or the current debate over Daniel Deronda's circumcision (see Cynthia Chase, "The Decomposition of Elephants: Double-Reading *Daniel Deronda*," *PMLA* 93 [March 1978], 215–27; K. M. Newton,
"*Daniel Deronda* and Circumcision," *Essays in Criticism* 31 [October 1981]: 313–27;
and Mary Wilson Carpenter, " 'A Bit of Her Flesh': Circumcision and 'The Significance of the Phallus' in *Daniel Deronda*," *Genders* 1 [March 1988]: 1–23).

[62]Jill Conway, "Stereotypes of Femininity in a Theory of Sexual Evolution," in
Suffer and Be Still: Women in the Victorian Age, ed. Martha Vicinus (1972), 153. See
also, Sue V. Rossner and A. Charlotte Hogsett, "Darwin and Sexism: Victorian
Causes, Contemporary Effects," and Marie Tedesco, "A Feminist Challenge to Darwinism: Antoinette L. B. Blackwell on the Relations of the Sexes in Nature and
Society," both in *Feminist Visions: Toward a Transformation of the Liberal Arts Curriculum*, ed. Diane L. Fowlkes and Charlotte S. McClure (1984), 42–52, 53–65.

[63]As the focus of the *Examiner* on obstetrics suggests, one of the forms essentialism takes is maternity. *Adam Bede* suggests that realism enforces that vision of
women. Bartle Massey says: "The doctor's evidence is heavy on [Hetty]—is heavy"
(42.474). Within Eliot's realism, "heaviness," a conventional euphemism for pregnancy, substitutes equally for evidence; the two are almost equivalent. But Hetty's
abrupt termination of her maternity, as well as the Princess Halm-Eberstein's unconventional motherhood in *Daniel Deronda*, suggest Eliot's complex interpretation
of this supposedly essential role for women. Eliot may have complicated the question of maternity—seen it as more than simple essentialism—because for her it was
a question of representation; the role of maternity touched Eliot personally as a
(woman) writer. Lewes, in "The Lady Novelists," suggested that women writers
might stick to topics that they could treat better than men, and Eliot echoed his
thoughts: in "Woman in France," she argues that a woman writer has something to
contribute because "under every imaginable social condition, she will necessarily
have a class of sensations and emotions—the maternal ones—which must remain
unknown to man" ("Woman in France: Madame de Sablé," in Pinney, *Essays of
George Eliot*, 53). And yet, as a writer (who was not a mother), Eliot did not limit
herself to that class of sensations. Moreover, she disparaged silly lady novelists by
comparing their literary outpourings to a kind of maternal tic: she tells us that she
regards them in "a very different tone from that of the reviewers who, with a

One response to the phallocentrism built into realism is to exploit it—to compete with men on their own terms, to attempt to seize control of the structures of power by imitating them through the explicit visual metaphors of realism. One tendency within Eliot's work to accept the ruling order accounts for why feminist critics are sometimes angry at her.[64] But I would like to consider now, by turning from *Adam Bede* to *Middlemarch*, the way Eliot shows that we are all, whether or not we like it, part of that order. Her fiction stresses that to embrace explicitly the constraints of a method does not make them less constraining. Obedience to that order only gives the illusion of power, one that is, in Eliot's own derogatory sense of the term, a romantic illusion, the danger and ultimate emptiness of which she dramatizes in Maggie's unsuccessful adherence to Thomas à Kempis's lessons of submission and obedience. Yet romance offers no escape either; neither of the representative possibilities open to women transforms the problems of representation.

In *Middlemarch*, Eliot exposes how the ability to control and regulate the category of woman becomes the tactic by which the male order (unsuccessfully) hopes to shore itself up as an order and identify itself with the system of power entrapping us all.[65] If Eliot cannot write her way out of that trap, out of the constraints of representation, by highlighting the consolations of gender that privilege one group over another, she at least makes those consolations more difficult to come by.

III

Lydgate's story exemplifies how the specular defeats those who hope to gain from it. Lydgate, the scientist and doctor, is one of the

---

perennial recurrence of precisely similar emotions, only paralleled, we imagine, in the experience of monthly nurses, tell one lady novelist after another that they 'hail' her productions 'with delight' " ("Silly Novels by Lady Novelists," in Pinney, *Essays of George Eliot*, 322).

[64]For a different reading, and one with which I disagree, see Zelda Austin, "Why Feminist Critics Are Angry with George Eliot," *College English* 37 (February 1976): 549–61. This debate continues in Elaine Showalter, "The Greening of Sister George," *Nineteenth-Century Fiction* 35 (December 1980): 292–311.

[65]Brian Swann writes that, in *Middlemarch*, "George Eliot's perfect reader will force himself, like Dorothea after her interview with Ladislaw, 'to dwell on every detail and its possible meaning'" ("*Middlemarch*: Realism and Symbolic Form," *ELH* 39 [June 1972]: 305).

group Eliot calls "observers and theorizers" (*MM*.15.176), and the character in *Middlemarch* who trades most on observation. Eliot's metaphors of vision do not just assume but throughout the book refer insistently to the scientific method, its supposed objectivity, its transformation of empirical data into truth. Modeling himself on that "great seer" (15.177) Bichat (one of the scientists Foucault also discusses when elaborating the workings of the clinical gaze[66]), Lydgate's research quite literally relies on "careful observation" and "the use of the lens" (15.176). As his use of the microscope, that crucial image in Eliot's fiction, suggests, in his pursuit of scientific truth Lydgate holds up the smallest detail for scrutiny according to "the philosophy of medical evidence" (13.153). He believes, and Eliot seems to suggest, that such an emphasis, rather than resulting in the anarchy of Lewes's detailism, shores up the dominant order. The primitive tissue that Lydgate seeks is, as *Middlemarch* makes plain, another figure for the web that weaves together the novel and stands for the patterns of relations in which its characters are trapped. Lydgate hopes that his minute observations will chart

> subtle actions inaccessible by any sort of lens, but tracked in that outer darkness through long pathways of necessary sequence by the inward light which is the last refinement of Energy, capable of bathing even the ethereal atoms in its ideally illuminated space. . . . He wanted to pierce the obscurity of those minute processes which prepare human misery and joy, those invisible thoroughfares which are the first lurking-places of anguish, mania, and crime. (16.194)

Critics have noted that, in this passage, Lydgate's desire to expose what is to others hidden, ignored, or inaccessible echoes directly the novel's own definition of its representations (an emphasis on vision picked up in the other familiar self-referential moments of the book: the "optical selection" governing the pier-glass and candle [27.297], the "keen vision" against which people keep themselves "well wadded with stupidity" [20.226]). Eliot's description of Lydgate's method may not be directly essentializing—she may not really be implying that the origins of human misery and joy are

---

[66]Michel Foucault, *The Birth of the Clinic: An Archeology of Medical Perception*, trans. A. M. Sheridan Smith (1973), 124–48; 149–73.

biological—but, nevertheless, she implies that the microscope is an optic that wants to discover and control them: the mode it represents is identified with the desire for such knowledge and power.

When Rosamond thinks Lydgate's "preoccupation with scientific subjects . . . a morbid vampire's taste" (64.711), then, the reader cannot dismiss her entirely. The specular economy is just that: an *economy* in which power is gained by draining it from others—or, as several epigraphs in the novel suggest, "power is relative" (64.697), and "finds its place in lack of power" (34.357). That Lydgate's scientific speculations rest on gaining power over others is suggested by more than that he tortures frogs and rabbits in his research (15.180). Lydgate himself figures his own allegiance to scientific observation in terms of discipline and obedience. The reader is told that "fever had obscure conditions, and gave him that delightful labour of the imagination which is not mere arbitrariness, but the exercise of disciplined power—combining and constructing with the clearest eye for probabilities and the fullest obedience to knowledge" (16.193). His own obedience to a supposed ideal, Lydgate thinks, allows him to exercise its power, to raise him above the others around him; he assumes, without much consideration, that his mastery of the microscope will keep him from being in thrall to everyday details, that "the peculiar bias of medical ability . . . toward material means" (13.154) will keep the material, in the shape of jeweler's or butcher's bills, from having much effect on him. Even if Lydgate does not consciously expect to master his neighbors through his disinterested observations of truth and of them, he assumes at least that such "[noodles] could have no power over him" (15.179). The whole trajectory of Lydgate's plot, of course, is to catapult him out of such delusions. But in uncovering Lydgate's delusions, the novel repeats them. It blames him because he isn't disinterested—his spots of commonness (15.178–79), blotting his vision, are, like Hetty's or Casaubon's (42.456), the result of self-interested egoism—and thereby still maintains the ideal of disinterested observation. This ideal is manifested, perhaps, by the novel itself, with its narrator as nobody, as general consciousness, with no self to taint it with egoism.[67] Lydgate's failure attests to the novel's

[67]For the narrator as nobody, see Ermarth, *Realism and Consensus in the English Novel*, 65–92; for "the narrator as general consciousness," see J. Hillis Miller, *The Form of Victorian Fiction: Thackeray, Dickens, Trollope, George Eliot, Meredith, and Hardy* (1968), 53–90.

success; his lack of power to pierce obscurity perhaps is meant to expose its own power, for, as the novel claims in *Adam Bede*, unlike Lydgate's, its "imagination is a licensed trespasser"(*AB*.6.115).

The observer draining power from that which it observes becomes particularly a question of gender. Lydgate's peculiar power as a doctor might be described as "penetration" (*MM*.16.186), and is one that he thinks deserves female appreciation; he expects the ideal wife, mastered by it, to worship it as sublime (58.632). The scientific method is itself figured in gender terms; adopting one of the traditional metaphors of empiricism, Eliot refers (in one of the epigraphs she wrote herself) to Nature—the Nature Lydgate hopes to penetrate—as a seductive woman (15.170). The practical observations resulting from Lydgate's scientific speculations also revolve around gender. As a doctor, Lydgate prefers to treat the Elizabeths (15.174) partly because they seem easier to control. His "strictly scientific view of women" (15.183) sees them as docile bodies, and it is that which attracts him to Rosamond:

> Certainly, if falling in love had been at all in question, it would have been quite safe with a creature like this Miss Vincy, who had just the kind of intelligence one would desire in a woman—polished, refined, docile, lending itself to finish in all the delicacies of life, and enshrined in a body which expressed this with a force of demonstration that excluded the need for other evidence. (16.193)

The scientist's penetration of the obscurity of Nature hopes to attest to masculine superiority, or at least, for Lydgate, to his own particular superiority, figured in his gender.

Yet the ironic tone of the passage I have just quoted suggests that claims to superiority through the evidence of gender are also exposed and undercut in *Middlemarch*; the interplay of realism and romance is crucial in this critique of the consolation of gender. The power struggle that revolves around gender—especially the battle of wills between Lydgate and Rosamond—calls the authority of "the everyday details" of realism into question: with the triumph of Rosamond seems to come the triumph of romance, since she is insistently associated with the "airy conditions" of romance throughout the book (64.711). Lydgate's view of Rosamond's docility is all wrong; with a power Will Ladislaw also later comes to dread (82.861), Rosamond overmasters her lord and master. But the clash between Lydgate and Rosamond may be not so much a battle between modes, ending with one of them triumphant, as a means to (dead)lock those modes together and question their distinctness. Lydgate and Rosamond are much alike, as are the fictional options they represent; the metaphors representing those options keep slipping into each other. Despite Lydgate's supposedly disinterested optic, he is still blind about Rosamond; he sees in her only the reflection of his desires. Rosamond, on the other hand, is not simply a vague dreamer: the "basis for her structure had the usual airy slightness, [but] was of remarkably detailed and realistic imagination when the foundation had been once presupposed" (12.146). Lydgate's illusions about their relationship are "a mere negative, a shadow," compared to that relation seen and shaped "through [Rosamond's] watchful blue eyes" (27.305).

The interconnectedness of these figures may suggest the infiltrations of a system of relations so intimately binding that any shift in the distributions of power is only local and temporary. The power that men and women take from each other is an empty consolation, in service of an economy that benefits—by perpetuating—only itself. The horror of Rosamond's and Lydgate's story, and the great waste of their lives, is that they remain trapped together, in that bond of human relations the book symbolizes by marriage, neither ever free from or in control of the other. This waste is made to seem their fault rather than the fault of the system—made particularly to seem Rosamond's fault, so that, although she lives on after him, the moral triumph is actually Lydgate's, of course. Their story enacts the narrative's claim that "in these acts called trivialities . . . the seeds of joy are for ever wasted, until men and women look round . . . at the devastation their own waste has made" (42.462). Rosamond, in particular, is made to waste these almost seminal "seeds of joy"—the book implies that, in a sense, she destroys her (first) child, just as Hetty does. This recourse to yet another charge of infanticide, rather than indicting the sex in general, begins to recall a pattern I noted in an earlier chapter in *East Lynne*. The novel attempts to blame its victims, women, making into the cause of social ills what are really its effects. In its picture of the social workings of Middlemarch, this novel's blame begins to seem strained because part of what it shows is how hard it is to locate blame.

The whole web of social interdependence catches together even the most unlikely figures, charting similarly inescapable bonds between almost everyone. In another plot that is explicit about the battles for and the workings of power, Lydgate's destiny gets inextricably intertwined with Bulstrode's, for example. Bulstrode seems the perfect illustration of the suggestion that no one owns power; his claims to it in fact facilitate his loss of it, in Middlemarch's readiness to shrug off his yoke. Yet even this story, which seems to show that such traps exceed gender, is itself worked out around gender. Bulstrode's story, like the novel, takes a "woman's lot" for its starting point, outlining "the subtle movement . . . shifting the boundaries of social intercourse" (11.122–23): this story too rests on the question of woman visible or invisible, the question of the "particulars of [Will's] mother's family" (61.670) and Bulstrode's part in keeping Will's mother "out of sight" (61.665).

With Bulstrode, Eliot provides another vision of what she sketches with Lydgate. Lydgate's observations seem to reveal to him (and to us) the organic whole that connects and makes meaning, which he finds symbolized by "that agreeable after-glow of excitement when thought lapses from examination of a specific object into a suffusive sense of its connections with all the rest of our existence" (16.194), a totality that the book is meant to display and reflect. Bulstrode's story is about such connectedness too but shows the dark side of it, the "entanglements of human action" (45.481). These "various entanglements, weights, blows, clashings, motions, by which things severally go on" (31.328) reveal that people "mov[e] heavily in a dim and clogging medium" (50.535), an "embroiled medium . . . [a] troublous, fitfully-illuminated life" (MM.30.324). Bulstrode's power comes in recognizing and playing on such a dim web. As Eliot notes,

Mr. Bulstrode's power was not due simply to his being a country banker, who knew the financial secrets of most traders in the town and could touch the springs of their credit; it was fortified by a beneficence that was at once ready and severe—ready to confer obligations, and severe in watching the result. . . . [H]is private charities were both minute and abundant. He would take a great deal of pains about apprenticing Tegg the shoemaker's son, and he would watch over Tegg's churchgoing; he would defend Mrs. Strype the washerwoman against Stubb's unjust exaction on the score of her drying-ground, and he would himself scrutinize a calumny against Mrs. Strype. His private minor loans were numerous, but he would inquire strictly into the circumstances both before and after. In this way a man gathers a domain in his neighbours' hope and fear as well as gratitude; and power, when once it has got into that subtle region, propagates itself, spreading out of all proportion to its external means. It was a principle with Mr. Bulstrode to gain as much power as possible. (16.184–85)

This description of Bulstrode, coming as it does in the midst of the two chapters outlining Lydgate's empiricism, suggests that watchfulness and "scrutiny," rather than being objective, can be a ploy of the worst kind of egoism, a means of enforcing one's views on others.

Bulstrode, too, despite his claims to power and control, is hopelessly entangled in the same web. In the system of surveillance that maintains power, everyone is observed, no one can escape his own "shadowy monitor" (42.464), which is all the more effective in being unlocatable, dispersed throughout the system (similarly, the shadowiness of romance, rather than providing an alternative to realism, might simply provide a foil to enforce the assumptions implicit in them both). Those selfish monitors, the Featherstones, as they sit watching outside Peter Featherstone's sick room, may be in the book precisely to embody this philosophy: "there was a general sense running in the Featherstone blood that everybody must watch everybody else, and that it would be well for everybody else to reflect that the Almighty was watching him" (32.338). The Featherstones, by literally embodying this notion (it runs in their blood), suggest that this system is not controllable by human will or intention; the narration of Peter Featherstone's death and funeral ironically underscores that the pains he takes with his own will are an extreme and ill-fated reaction against, an attempt to bully away, his own ultimate powerlessness. The desire to seem in control, which both Featherstone and Bulstrode illustrate, is also one that we, as readers of the novel, share with them. The novel is able to set itself up as an ideal observer—in the position of the Almighty, the end of the chain of observers, capping and containing them—by appealing to that desire in its readers; the narrator consistently asks us to join in observing characters who cannot look back (11.122; 40.442–43), so that we seem to share this position of authority and autonomy. Yet our seeming autonomy is still entrapped in and determined by the specular, encoded in the naturalness with which the novel abjures us to monitor ourselves: to "set a watch over our affections and our constancy as we can over other treasures" (57.625). In Bulstrode's case, the very activity of observing overturns his claims to power: Raffles "thrust[s] himself on [Bulstrode's] unwilling observation" (60.657). The sudden vision of Raffles, and the details of his past that Bulstrode has deliberately suppressed and overlooked, do not disrupt the specular economy from which Bulstrode has profited, but they do disrupt his claims to it.

Neil Hertz suggests that Bulstrode's decrease of power seems to figure his wife's increase, an observation that points to some of the implications of gender in this economy.[68] In Bullstrode's story of reduplicating gazes, his wife seems to take the position of the (ultimate) observer. After his exposure, Bulstrode imagines confessing all his sins to his wife when she is a watcher at his deathbed (85.882). That neither Mrs. Bulstrode nor Rosamond suffer the same diminishment as their husbands, that the optic of the book, in fact, brings them into prominence while their husbands fade, does not, however, suggest the mutinous victory of romance over realism, of women over men. Mrs. Bulstrode, through her husband, is herself exposed and humiliated (74.806). No amount of Gilbertian and Gubarian reading against the grain can completely redeem Rosamond or completely turn the narrative's account of what it casts as an egoism so blamable that it ultimately kills Lydgate into a subversive story of feminist resistance. A misogynistic self-hatred that, like culture, indicts women for all our ills, remains part of Eliot's fiction, an indication of the way that it too cannot escape the very cycle it concerns itself with, no more than we, as readers or interpreters, can avoid being trapped within the structures we may wish to expose.

Dorothea's story suggests another approach to that inscription, however, one that does not attempt to deny or triumph over it. Dorothea's story is much like those stories I have been charting of

[68]Hertz, *The End of the Line,* 81.

other women; Hertz sees her, too, eclipsing a waning husband, Casaubon.[69] Dorothea, is, in a sense, Rosamond redeemed, as their similar plots—despite Dorothea's supposed extraordinariness, both are ultimately propelled along the same path of love and marriage—and their sympathetic coming together at the end suggest. It is Rosamond, in fact, whose supposedly false romances (her delusions about Lydgate first and then Will) enable her to see in Dorothea's story its similarity to her own and to alert readers to the degree of romance in Eliot's novel. She correctly outlines the plot of Dorothea's story, calling Casaubon's interdiction against Will " 'the most charming romance. . . . Mr. Casaubon jealous, and foreseeing that there was no one else whom Mrs. Casaubon would like so to marry. . . . [O]h, I have no doubt the end will be thoroughly romantic' " (59.646). Yet the airy vagueness of Rosamond's or Hetty's romances seems somehow transformed in Dorothea. In the Prelude to *Middlemarch*, discussing the "mere inconsistency and formlessness" (25) of the new Theresas (the original Theresa, we recall, having fed on romances), the narrator remarks:

> Some have felt that these blundering lives are due to the inconvenient indefiniteness with which the Supreme Power has fashioned the natures of women: if there were one level of feminine incompetence as strict as the ability to count three and no more, the social lot of women might be treated with scientific certitude. Meanwhile the indefiniteness remains, and the limits of variation are really much wider than any one would imagine from the sameness of women's coiffure and the favourite love-stories in prose and verse. (25–26)

Women's indefiniteness, originally the narrator's tongue-in-cheek borrowing from "some"-body else, from whom it distinguishes itself—presumably, the colon implies, the same fatuous somebody who would be relieved to fix a certain limit on, that is, to define, this indefiniteness—becomes by the end of the passage the narrator's own term and woman's very way to elude limits, especially those of "scientific certitude." Moreover, this indefiniteness aligns women with and characterizes a romance that is more than simply "the favourite love-stories." Dorothea's "Quixotic" character (76.820; see

[69]Hertz, *The End of the Line*, 81–82.

also 2.38) lies in her ability to elude the tyranny of speculation; no one ever quite knows what she will do, and this indefiniteness is reflected at the end of the novel by the emphasis of the story on the effectiveness of her "hidden life" (Finale.896). Her vagueness seems exactly what defeats male scrutiny; in posing her as a scientific puzzle, Mr. Brooke admits his inability to solve it: "in short, woman was a problem which, since Mr. Brooke's mind felt blank before it, could be hardly less complicated than the revolutions of an irregular solid" (4.65).

But is such indefiniteness any more helpful to Dorothea than it is to that "planless riddle" (MF.6.4.505), Maggie? Unlike Maggie, Dorothea does not die at the end of her story, and her indefiniteness throughout does seem, in fact, to be a way to elude attempts to define her that are violent or dangerous. Will (whose name connects him to those will makers Casaubon and Featherstone, so concerned with maintaining their own power even after death), on one level presents the most definite threat to Dorothea. Throughout, this artist manqué is "hungry" for a "vision" of Dorothea (MM.82.860), and he vows that "he would never lose sight of her: he would watch over her—if he gave up everything else in life he would watch over her, and she should know that she had one slave in the world" (37.396). Such a relation more explicitly enslaves Dorothea than it does Will, and Mr. Hawley's warning about him—"He'll begin with flourish about the Rights of Man and end with murdering a wench" (37.393)—suggests the danger of this slavery for Dorothea. Will's supposed enslavement to her ("I would rather touch her hand if it were dead, than I would touch any other woman's living" [78.836]) is chilling in its imagery and, through its language, again ties him to his relation, Casaubon, whose own dead hand attempts to control Dorothea (and suggests the way the male order attempts to circumvent its own vulnerabilities by projecting them onto women). Will's vision of Dorothea in the Hall of Statues acts out the reifying tendency of his impulses and places it within the novel's larger concern with the real; this careful observation of Dorothea is little different from the reader's, from the first pages of the novel, where the reader is asked to attend to the details of the picture of Miss Brooke, to focus on her "hand and wrist" (1.29), just as Naumann and Will later gaze at her.

Does Dorothea's hidden life at the end of the novel, then, present another perspective, a valid romance, somehow better than Hetty's or Rosamond's dreams? Eliot makes Dorothea obscure at the end of the novel (obscure both in her social world—she slips from gentility into the mass—and for Eliot's readers—we no longer minutely observe her) in a way that does not really seem to unsettle any limits; in fact, her effacement in aiding Will's career in government could be seen as the ultimate service to patriarchy.

Moreover, like Maggie (or Hetty, or Rosamond), Dorothea is not solely identified with the obscure or unrepresentable. As Virginia Woolf has written, the tragedy of all these women may be that they demand something "perhaps incompatible with the facts of human existence."[70] They are nonetheless firmly enmired in those facts. In the schoolroom—where, Mary Jacobus suggests, both characters and readers are being taught about women—Maggie is aligned with the particular: she brings on Mr. Stelling's observations about her sex in general by skipping the rules of Latin because the examples are so absorbing (MF.2.1.217).[71] For Dorothea, an attention to detail is exploded early by the novel, shown to be the very mechanism that delivers her over into patriarchy. Her misguided romance about Casaubon before their marriage sees that patriarch as a savior, one who will especially save her from the world of the everyday. Because Casaubon seems to her "unconscious that trivialities existed" (MM.3.55), she feels certain that their lives together will elude banality; she says that " 'there would be nothing trivial about our lives. Everyday-things with us would mean the greatest things' " (3.51). Instead, Dorothea's marriage makes her aware that she is inescapably part of the everyday: "that new real future which was replacing the imaginary drew its material from the endless minutiae by which her view of Mr. Casaubon and her wifely relation, now that she was married to him, was gradually changing

---

[70]Virginia Woolf, "George Eliot," in Women and Writing, ed. Michèle Barrett (1979), 159.

[71]Jacobus, Reading Woman, 69. Maggie, through her association with detail, joins a family of similar women in Eliot's early books: the sharp-eyed Mrs. Poyser, or her own mother, Mrs. Tulliver, whose household "objects" make life "comprehensible" to her (MF.4.2.368). Even Dinah, who, at the start of Adam Bede "seemed unobservant of all details" (AB.15.205), has, through her love for Adam, so changed by the end of the book that he can remark approvingly, "You're getting to be your aunt's own niece, I see, for particularness" (AB.50.536).

with the secret motion of a watch-hand from what it had been in her maiden dream" (20.226). Rather than a life of transcendence, Dorothea finds herself forced to dwell within the endless minutiae of a reality that dispels her dreams.

Mutual surveillance is what binds Dorothea with Will; both long for the sight of the other. Although he is wrong to ascribe to Dorothea lack of sympathy and individual malevolence, Casaubon is not far wrong when he suspects her as a "spy watching everything with a malign power of inference" (20.232–33). The book suggests that even the best of us are defined by and vehicles for an impersonal field of control. For all of Dorothea's short-sightedness and abstraction (" 'Dodo, how very bright your eyes are!' " Celia at one point exclaims, " 'And you don't see anything you look at' " [77.833]), for all her disclaimers about being unable to understand paintings (9.105; 21.238; 62.678), the implication throughout the book is that she does see, although perhaps in a way different from the others. Celia consistently disparages "the strange coloured lamps by which Dodo habitually saw" (84.878); she tells her that " 'you always see what nobody else sees . . . you never see what is quite plain' " (4.59). Yet Dorothea's vision, like vision throughout the novel, still causes other pain: her "way of looking at things" is like "spilt needles, making one afraid of treading, or sitting down, or even eating" (2.43).

When Will first meets Dorothea, he recognizes her as "one of Nature's inconsistencies" (9.105), and, as Eliot tells us in an epigraph from *Rasselas*, "Inconsistencies . . . cannot both be right, but imputed to man they may both be true" (61.660). Unlike Dr. Johnson, Eliot imputes them to women. For Lydgate, what is most damning about Dorothea's view (and perhaps about her having a view at all) is that it is not from "the proper feminine angle" (11.122). Dorothea's characterization engages our feminist sympathies precisely because her vision seems to refuse what has been decreed as proper to it. Yet what may be ultimately most attractive about Dorothea is not that she is an impossible rebel but that she is so ordinary, torn between the desire to be different from her world and her recognition of the impossibility of being so. Dorothea may be distinctive in this novel because she accepts her ordinariness. Her view is different from others because, as another Eliot epigraph suggests, "[she] seeth only that [she] cannot see" (20.224).

The novel may emphasize that famous climax of Dorothea at the window (in chapter 80) not for its reclaimed faith in what is actually the empty consolation of human activity but because it accepts that that activity is inescapably embroiled in a system outside our control. Through Dorothea, the book suggests that none of us, least of all women, is outside the gaze, nor can we control it:

> She opened her curtains, and looked out towards the bit of road that lay in view, with fields beyond, outside the entrance-gates. On the road there was a man with a bundle on his back and a woman carrying her baby; in the field she could see figures moving—perhaps the shepherd with his dog. Far off in the bending sky was the pearly light; she felt the largeness of the world and the manifold wakings of men to labour and endurance. She was part of that involuntary, palpitating life, and could neither look out on it from her luxurious shelter as a mere spectator, nor hide her eyes in selfish complaining. (80.846)

The emphasis on labor and endurance, the inevitability, the involuntariness of our position as subjects within both sides of the specular, our unchangeable position in a double bind—this is all the resolution of Eliot's novel. And the bind comes partially because our very exposure of the system simply continues the mechanism that constructs and furthers it in the first place. Farebrother's suggestion that "the stronger thing is not to give up power, but to use it well" (52.554) may be the closest the book comes to a solution, but it is one still trapped in the logic it questions, within a tautology where, in questions of power, the good must be the strong.

Eliot's fiction suggests that women are also part of the power system that constrains them. To see women implicated in that inequitable system within which they suffer, too, bespeaks the same kind of ambivalence or deadlock that we have been discussing between realism and romance—and perhaps resolves itself into the same ultimate deployment of and subordination to that system. Although feminists often gesture to Eliot's unconventional life as evidence of her true insubordination, there are daunting indications enough of capitulation in Eliot's private writings, as well as in her novels; Eliot seems ready enough to blame women for the ills of the world in which she operates while according the power of that world to men. She tells one female correspondent that "woman does not yet deserve a much better lot than man gives her," and similar statements run throughout her letters, all resulting from what she tells another female friend: that, for Eliot, men somehow "always eclipse the female—pardon the word."[72]

Yet "eclipse" (if that is the word we are to pardon), by pointing to Eliot's dissection of the specular, also allows us to pardon this attitude in Eliot (or, rather, to see that we are in no position to pardon her), to see that attitude as what even that literary patriarch, Leslie Stephen, recognized as "bitterness . . . a kind of misgiving"—one that colored Eliot's view of women.[73] This *jeu de melancolie* (what Eliot called *The Lifted Veil*) comes from the recognition that everyone is enmired in a system that lays everything to waste, whether we ignore or dwell on that sight.[74] This is the horrid picture of *The Lifted Veil*, what Latimer comes to learn, for when the veneer of life is "seen as if thrust asunder by a microscopic vision, [it] showed all the intermediate frivolities, all the suppressed egoism, all the struggling chaos of puerilities, meanness, vague capricious memories, and indolent make-shift thoughts, from which human words and deeds emerge like leaflets covering a fermenting heap."[75] That the inescapable structure of sight reveals this fermenting heap as the only available site—the site on which those of us hoping for better must found a sympathetic construction of woman and of the social change that might benefit her—explains Eliot's bitterness. Like Gwendolen Harleth, Eliot may feel "a sort of terror: it was as if some ghastly vision had come to her in a dream and said, 'I am a woman's life' " (*DD*.14.190). To keep from denying this vision, as

---

[72]The first reference is "George Eliot to Mrs. Peter Alfred Taylor, London, 1 February 1853," in *Letters*, 2: 86; the second, "George Eliot to Sara Sophia Hennell, [London, 25 June 1852]," in *Letters*, 2:38.

[73]"Unsigned Obituary Article," from Stephen's journal *Cornhill*, in Carroll, *George Eliot: The Critical Heritage*, 483. Stephen goes on to write: "We must admit that there is something rather depressing in the thought of these anonymous Dorotheas feeling about vaguely for some worthy outlet of their energies . . . wishing ardently to reform the world, but quite unable to specify the steps to be taken, and condescending to put up with a very commonplace life in a vague hope that somehow or other they will do some good" (Carroll, *George Eliot: The Critical Heritage*, 483).

[74]"George Eliot to John Blackwood, [Wandsworth] 31 March [1859]," in *Letters*, 3: 41.

[75]George Eliot, *The Lifted Veil* (1985), 19–20.

Gwendolen does, Eliot may embrace it with a vengeance that turns on women—herself included.

Although Eliot cannot imagine a way of salvaging this waste, she holds open the possibility that her sifting through it may ultimately provide a clue; she conjectures that a piece of debris, unremarked by us now "may end by letting us into the secret of usurpations" (*MM*.41.448). Her writing becomes a kind of stop-gap, whose ultimate effectiveness lies not with Eliot but, perhaps, with some future reader: "a bit of ink and paper which has long been an innocent wrapping or stop-gap may at last be laid open under the one pair of eyes which have knowledge enough to turn it into the opening of a catastrophe" (*MM*.41.448). Eliot's writing becomes what she later says about the laws to help women, of which she earlier seemed skeptical: "one round of a long ladder stretching far beyond our lives."[76] To gesture provisionally to some possible change, despite the present impossibility of such changes—despite her recognition of the inevitable self-defeat of such gestures—seems wishful in Eliot, but if we as her critics are to accuse her for it, we align ourselves with (the old) Adam in our lack of fellow-feeling, for he too cannot accept "the weakness that errs in spite of foreseen consequences" (*AB*.19.255).

By placing woman within the specular, then, Eliot does not completely cut the ground out from under feminism; her work instead suggests that locating claims for power solely in terms of the male (as one side of the dispute about the male gaze and feminist directions wishes to do) risks supplying feminists with our own gender consolation that allows us to ignore our own implication in dominant systems—an ignorance that impedes, if not undoes, our investigations. It bears repeating what feminism already knows well but often wishes, understandably and even of necessity, to overlook: that a critique is not (nor does it need to be) a solution; that simply to expose a strategy as male does not undo it; that our investigations must repeat on some level the very mechanism we are analyzing; and that just to recognize our implication—a currently overmystified tactic of post-structuralism—is not necessarily subversive, because our recognition does not somehow mag-

[76]"George Eliot to Sara Sophia Hennell, Richmond, [28 January 1856,]" in *Letters*, 2: 227.

ically free us from it. Eliot's novels show that she does not advocate, on the other hand, that we stop critiquing, exposing, investigating, and recognizing our position in the power struggles played out in gender relations—by no means—for to do so is just the flip side of the same old thing, one of those delusive opposites everyone oscillates between.

That such crucial recognitions are all our lot offers us may in fact correspond with Freud's recognition that the best he could offer his patients was an informed self-recognition that translated their misery into common unhappiness.[77] What seems the pessimism of George Eliot's fiction, and the real reason that feminists are often angry at her, may reflect the concentration of her fiction on the limits of the possibilities for directly willed feminist change. But rather than being antifeminist, her fiction enables our feminist struggle by highlighting that that struggle is necessarily interminable and that it must go on despite the absence of a clear goal or reward. The much-discussed loss of faith fueling Eliot's fiction may well be another version of the way the very issue of the doubtfulness of our endeavors provides the focus that fuels and justifies them. Eliot's peculiar double vision about feminism—that her works seem caught between a clarity of vision and a willful blindness when it comes to the causes of gender inequities—exposes the contradictions within feminism rather than dispensing with it. Her novels, in attempting both to establish and to question their

[77]Sigmund Freud, "The Psychotherapy of Hysteria," *SE,* 2: 305. It is intriguing that Freud makes this suggestion especially when he is discussing problems peculiar to gender division (which, feminists might argue, come to seem women's problems), as he does in this essay, and later, when the impossibility of a cure becomes the very focus of "Analysis Terminable and Interminable" (*SE,* 23: 209–53). In that pessimistic essay, he suggests that gender division itself leads to the problems that cannot be cured and the unhappiness that cannot be alleviated: "At no other point in one's analytic work does one suffer more from an oppressive feeling that all one's repeated efforts have been in vain, and from a suspicion that one has been 'preaching to the winds,' than when one is trying to persuade a woman to abandon her wish for a penis on the ground of its being unrealizable or when one is seeking to convince a man that a passive attitude to men does not always signify castration and that it is indispensable in many relationships in life" ("Analysis," in SE, 23: 252). The underlying biologism of Freud's claim (he writes that, with such essential sexual differences, "we have penetrated through all psychological strata and have reached bedrock" ["Analysis," in SE, 23: 252]) suggests not only his wish to locate the source of our unhappiness but also the way he reaffirms the particular bedrock that will support his approach.

own authority, interrogate the question of gender within the metaphor of vision that underwrites them—a metaphor that they, too, do not just adopt but investigate. Their examination provides a kind of admonitory vision, which suggests the necessity of keeping the limits on us as subjects from letting us as feminists settle for a complacent pessimism, of continuing instead the necessary process of self-examination. Like Dorothea, Eliot may yearn "after order and a perfect rule" (*MM*.9.98); with an "eagerness for a binding theory" (10.112), she may impatiently identify herself with the very authority she cannot escape, but she nowhere settles long for it, nor for easy answers.

Conclusion

Throughout this book, I have linked romance with consolation, but perhaps the greatest consolation is to cast romance—other people's romance—that way. It has become almost a post-structuralist truism that we are not so different from other people; the kind of insight that pretends to expose the illusions of others can operate only by being on some level blind to its own. Yet even this recognition of and gesture to our blindness—at least *we* can see it—can be just a more ingenious way to ignore it or cover it over. Recent theory reminds us that we can't ever know exactly what it is that we don't know. Indeed; but to remind us of that may be only one more attempt to manage that ignorance, somehow to know it after all.

I want to fight the temptation to use this conclusion as just such a talisman to ward off gaps or implications within my study that I can't begin to account for. Instead I shall consider how the implicit attempts throughout this study to work such a countercharm have been perhaps its own consolation. My adherence to a post-structuralism that emphasizes its own implication in the structures it examines has also contained an implicit reassurance, a reliance on a theoretical self-sufficiency that tries to cover all the angles paradoxically by asserting that it cannot. Such gestures to totalization are all the more encompassing especially because my particular interest is in a post-structuralism that is also post-Foucault, one that questions our ability deliberately (or perhaps ever) to deviate from the forces that create us as subjects—an approach that can be said to result in a determinism even more emphatic and implacable than that of most critical methods. One effect in particular of such an approach is to imply that it actually does account for everything, if only because it always points to an englobing, infinitely connected network in which everything is comprised. It also incorporates as a basic principle what is usually seen as a problem of methodology: that our discourse inevitably determines the problems we see and the answers we find.

By attending to the appearance of just this determinism in fiction, in this conclusion I want to examine how constructing such a vast matrix can itself be a consolation that enables and bolsters my critical practice. The critical practice inherited from Foucault's notions of power—in which a complex of forces outside human agency is so immitigable that reaction against these forces may simply accommodate them and make more predictable their outcome—is itself a peculiar construction. Those attentive to culture and history might see it as a construction peculiarly French, manifesting itself about a century before Foucault in the French realist and naturalist novelists whose own internalization and critique of Enlightenment notions form a philosophical and aesthetic background to Foucault's thought.[1]

For my purposes, the English novelists who placed themselves in this tradition found themselves defensive of, but also somewhat discomfited by, its way of patterning the world (and in this way they are much like some current English-speaking critics, influenced by but wary of Foucault). Their pictures of grim destiny—personified variously as the meshwork of fate, the embrace of nature, or the iron chain of evolution—were seen by their critics as growing out of the same kind of pessimism with which I have charged George Eliot (and with which my own readings might be

[1]See, for example, Foucault's early essay on Flaubert, "Fantasia of the Library," in his *Language, Counter-Memory, Practice: Selected Essays and Interviews*, ed. Donald F. Bouchard, trans. Donald F. Bouchard and Sherry Simon (1977), 87–109. Of Zola, he is less respectful. He writes: "Zola . . . is the type of the 'universal' intellectual, bearer of law and militant of equity, but he ballasts his discourse with a whole invocation of nosology and evolutionism, which he believes to be scientific, grasps very poorly in any case, and whose political effects on his own discourse are very equivocal" (Michel Foucault, "Truth and Power," in his *Power/Knowledge: Selected Interviews and Other Writings, 1972–1977*, trans. Colin Gordon, Leo Marshall, John Mepham, and Kate Soper, and ed. Colin Gordon [1980], 129). Interestingly, criticism of Foucault has occupied itself with saying very similar things about him.

charged). Certainly fine distinctions may be drawn between the philosophies of determinism, naturalism, and pessimism, but in the complex of attitudes within such fiction, there is an implicit slide: from the idea that various interdependent conditions necessitate certain effects, through the idea that everything is comprised within a regulating but indifferent natural law, to the idea that the world is patterned in the worst possible way. Because their vision embraced all these ideas at once, writers such as Thomas Hardy or Arnold Bennett found themselves in an uneasy position. They denied that they were pessimistic at the very same time that they asserted that, anyway, such a view of life was true: that our experience might be explained by an inexorable arrangement in which people were not central but only a small part of a consuming and indifferent pattern—this may seem like the worst view of things, but it was also (they said) seeing things as they were.[2] It is in just this pessimism, this attitude that posits and responds to an inexhaustible, devouring network, that I see a kind of consolation, gloomy as it seems. In locating it there, I hope to reflect a bit on the way my own study hedges around similar reassuring totalizations.

Arnold Bennett, whose career was much influenced by French ideas and who yet maintained withal a solid English skepticism about them (a tension reflected in a work such as *The Old Wives' Tale*), was one of those to defend naturalism from the charge of pessimism. Countering such a response to George Gissing's fiction, for instance, Bennett insists that Gissing's world view is not discolored by bitterness or in any way idiosyncratic; it is simply true: "Mr. Gissing has often been called a pessimist: he is is not one. He paints in dark tints, for he has looked on the sum of life, and those few who have done this are well aware that life is dark."[3] The "dark" view and the "sum of life" are connected. Bennett implies that Gissing's critics do not see the world so comprehensively because they cannot stand the vision. Gissing's distinctiveness lies in his ability to see the world wholesale: "he sees

[2]See, for example, Thomas Hardy's "General Preface to the Wessex Edition of 1912," reprinted in various Penguin editions of his work, as in *Tess of the D'Urbervilles: A Pure Woman*, ed. David Skilton (1978), 491–96, especially 495–96.

[3]Arnold Bennett, "George Gissing," in *The Author's Craft and Other Critical Writings of Arnold Bennett*, ed. Samuel Hynes (1968), 164.

the world not bit by bit—a series of isolations—but broadly, in vast wholes."[4] These vast wholes embody the pattern determining existence, and Gissing's dark picture of them becomes a kind of heroic fatalism for Bennett: "he has seen, he knows, he is unmoved; he defeats fate by accepting it."[5]

In his own artistic practice, Bennett especially concerned himself with vast wholes. His best-read novel, *The Old Wives' Tale*, literally embodies its own fatalism in such engrossing figures. Margaret Drabble, as Bennett's biographer, points out that *The Old Wives' Tale* is preoccupied with massive entities—"balloons, elephants, and fat old ladies"—that recur in a pattern of repetitions that carries the book to its prearranged conclusion.[6] I might argue that it is this very vastness that is meant to dispel illusions, to blot out a radiant romance that paints life in its own soft shades. One of Bennett's heroines, Sophia, is taught such knowledge through a lesson in reading:

> The broad corridor was lighted by a small, smelling oil-lamp with a crimson shade. That soft, transforming radiance seemed to paint the whole corridor with voluptuous luxury. . . . Under the lamp lay Madame Foucault on the floor, a shapeless mass of lace, frilled linen, and corset. . . . At the first glance, the creature abandoned to grief made a romantic and striking picture, and Sophia thought for an instant that she had at length encountered life on a

[4]Bennett, "George Gissing," 162. In another essay, Bennett makes this connection when ventriloquizing the average reader: "the 'tone' of the book should be serious and even staid, but not pessimistic; pessimism connotes lack of faith; it also saddens. 'Is not life sad enough already?' This protesting query, so often heard, means that our novel must not embrace the whole of life" (Arnold Bennett, "The 'Average Reader' and the Recipe for Popularity," in Hynes, *The Author's Craft,* 59).

[5]Bennett, "George Gissing," 164. Bennett in fact locates in Gissing an attitude similar to that I located in Eliot. He quotes with approval from *The Nether World:* "to both was their work given. . . . Sorrow certainly awaited them, perchance defeat in even the humble aims that they had set themselves; but at least their lives would remain a protest against those brute forces of society which fill with wreck the abysses of the nether world" ("George Gissing," 164). Yet notice how his very characterization of Gissing—"he has seen, he knows, he is unmoved"—begins to make him over into the very indifferent fate he is supposed to just accept and suffer.

[6]Margaret Drabble, *Arnold Bennett* (1974), 148. For a discussion of how such patterns of recurrence make this book parallel its own conception of life, see John Wain's Introduction to *The Old Wives' Tale*, by Arnold Bennett, ed. John Wain (1983), 7–25, especially 16–17; all future references to this book (hereafter abbreviated *OWT*) will appear in the text.

plane that would correspond to her dreams of romance. . . . But when Sophia bent over Madame Foucault, and touched her flabbiness, this illusion at once vanished; and instead of being dramatically pathetic the woman was ridiculous. . . . Then she was amazingly fat; her flesh seemed to be escaping at all ends from a corset strained to the utmost limit. And above her boots—she was still wearing dainty, high-heeled, tightly laced boots—the calves bulged suddenly out. (*OWT*.3.5.389)

The vastness this Foucault suddenly obtrudes on Sophia overwhelms her romance; the ample outlines of this figure, like the ample outlines of Bennett's determinism (he criticizes his other heroine, Constance, because "she did not see the cosmic movement in large curves" [4.5.608]), seems meant to insist on a darker picture. This creature's sufficiency of fat absorbs "the vast structure of make believe" (3.5.391) that had characterized Sophia's earlier relations with her. It is replaced by what Bennett calls elsewhere a sense of "the vast inherent melancholy of the universe" (for Sophia and Constance both learn—though they often ignore—that "the vast inherent melancholy of the universe did not exempt [them]" [2.2.197]). Sophia comes to see Madame Foucault for what Bennett's novel shows her to be, for what Madame Foucault in her grief tells her she is, an aging prostitute who is on her way to becoming a charwoman. Although Sophia finds herself "irritated by the unrelieved darkness of the picture drawn by Madame Foucault" (3.5.394), the novel notes that "doubtless Madame Foucault fulfilled her own prediction as to her ultimate destiny"(3.6.418).

"The Foucault" (3.5.404), as Sophia's friend Chirac calls her, seemingly a minor character appearing midway through the story, actually is central to the book. Part of his emphasis on her monumentalness comes from how large the idea she figured bulked in Bennett's own imagination. His inspiration for *The Old Wives' Tale* came when he was eating in his favorite restaurant (an institution that he described to his mother in one of his daily letters to her as "enormous").[7] There, he is nearly displaced from his usual seat by a "fat, shapeless, ugly, and grotesque" old woman, whose re-

---

7 "(*To Sarah Ann Bennett*), [4, rue de Calais], [Paris], [postmarked 10-12-03]" in vol. 4 of *The Letters of Arnold Bennett*, ed. James Hepburn, 4 vols. (1966–86), p. 7.

pulsive dimensions, he writes, obtrude her on the notice of the restaurant, which finds her ridiculous (Preface.31).[8] Rather than sharing in their laughter, Bennett thinks: " 'her case is a tragedy. One ought to be able to make a heart-rending novel out of the history of a woman such as she' . . . there is an extreme pathos in the mere fact that every stout ageing woman was once a young girl with the unique charm of youth in her form and movements and in her mind" (Preface.31–32). Bennett's stout woman, like Madame Foucault who comes to stand in for her, represents the very culmination of the particularly tragic pattern that for Bennett makes up a novel.

As in so many of the other novels I have discussed, woman's flesh figures as the shapeless matter out of which the author shapes his story; in Bennett's case in particular, a story about how life actually is shaped, part of an immense and appalling whole. In his idea for his novel, he pictured two such women, sisters, one of whom—Sophia—was originally meant to wind up, as Madame Foucault, a fat and failed prostitute.[9] In retaining this figure, he is able to retain the traditional scapegoat for anxieties about corporality and mortality, and part of Sophia's response to her is to linger on the details of the supposed loathsomeness of female flesh—to anatomize her corpulence in just the way the novel repeatedly anatomizes various corpses. Perhaps Bennett locates that loathsomeness in corpulence out of another anxiety, too; part of the cruel humor directed at big women in general has to do with how their very bulk threatens the idea that men's greater size and strength clinch their superiority.

The story of Bennett's life frames his own anxieties in figures of vast corporality. While writing *The Old Wives' Tale*, he was haunted by visions of overconsumption. He records in his journal various

[8]For his reaction to her supposed repulsiveness, see also Bennett's description of this event in vol. 1 of *The Journal of Arnold Bennett*, 3 vols. (1932–33), pp. 131–32. Note here and in the Preface how the pair of waitresses at this restaurant—the fat, maternal waitress who manages Bennett and whose neurotic sexual possessiveness of him sends him fleeing, and the young, slim, beautiful and unattainable waitress who winds up serving the repulsive old woman—parallel neatly the structure (the movement from youth to age) and concerns (youth ultimately in thralldom to age, the bulk of age overwhelming this author who wishes for escape from it) of the novel.

[9]Bennett, *Journal*, 1: 132; see also "(To Frank Harris), Villa des Néfliers, 30th Nov 1908," in *Letters*, 2: 238–39.

images and anecdotes: peasant women "deformed, chiefly by vast deposits of flesh"; provincial gluttons who would eat so much on occasion that they would need to be plunged naked into muck heaps, enveloped in manure up to the neck to promote digestion; famous painters who would vie in their greed to monopolize the dishes at a *table d'hôte*; an avaricious old lady who would starve herself one day to have twice the mutton the next.[10] Such preoccupations may seem in part a readily understandable response to having to conjure in his novel the starvation of the siege of Paris, a way of countering and managing those imaginative horrors. But they also seem partly to have to do with other more general worries about Bennett's own self-integrity and his relation to a larger system that blots out and absorbs him.

Bennett's journals show that his particular kind of naturalism arose not just from the physical determinism of nineteenth-century theories of evolution, with the biological and social consequences that so fascinated the French novelists who influenced him; they also came from the logical determinism of Stoic philosophy. While writing *The Old Wives' Tale*, in an apparent attempt to control and regulate himself, Bennett read Stoic philosophy every morning, especially Marcus Aurelius.[11] Yet his endeavors were unsuccessful: "it is humiliating," he writes, "that I cannot get through one single day . . . without yielding to appetites that I despise!"[12] His discomfort with sexual appetite in particular hints at the anxiety prompting fears of consumption; of sexual relations with women he writes: "I do not like to think that I am not absolutely complete and sufficient in myself to myself."[13] Yet the vast wholeness Bennett longs for also disturbs him, and this conflicted desire is perhaps best characterized in the title of a book he was drawn to years later when he tried to diet, *Eat and Grow Thin*.[14] Bennett's attitude

---

[10]Bennett, *Journal*, 1: 238, 239, 245, 269.

[11]And the Stoic assumption that men may have no power to alter their circumstances explains why Marcus Aurelius interested Foucault as well as Bennett. See Foucault's references to him in *The Care of the Self*, trans. Robert Hurley, vol. 3 of *The History of Sexuality* (1986), and "Technologies of the Self," in *Technologies of the Self: A Seminar with Michel Foucault*, ed. Luther H. Martin, Huck Gutman, and Patrick Hutton (1988), 16–49.

[12]Bennett, *Journal*, 1: 299–300.

[13]Bennett, *Journal*, 1: 300–301.

[14]"(*To Edward Knoblock*), 75, Cadogan Square, 16-7-26," in *Letters*, 3: 271.

may be double because his fears of his own appetite point to fears of other appetites that might consume him.

That some larger determining totality may eclipse his own absoluteness gets translated into Bennett's worry about the relation of his work to the tradition that formed him. He stresses that *The Old Wives' Tale* had two heroines in order to swamp Guy de Maupassant's *Une Vie* (as well as to surpass the work of women novelists, such as Mrs. W. K. Clifford) (*OWT*.Preface.32–33); it is perhaps the strain of trying to swallow up such large reputations with his own work that makes Bennett bilious while writing his novel.[15] That novel, which he refers to consistently as his *big* book, is perhaps a way to establish his completeness and self-sufficiency (and perhaps also a compensation for whatever impulse made him later sign himself "Little" in his letters to the mother of his child, Dorothy Bennett). At any rate, his achievement was received that way by his literary circle. H. G. Wells, for whom *The Old Wives' Tale* is also "a great book and a big book," tells Bennett "it at least doubles your size in my estimation."[16] André Gide, who admits that he didn't initially think much of Bennett, is overwhelmed by *The Old Wives' Tale*, because he finds it an enormous novel with a prodigious force of penetration.[17]

Bennett responds to a perceived threat of displacement by himself incorporating the threatening object; his heroine Sophia follows the same pattern. Her judgment of Madame Foucault is partly so harsh because Madame Foucault has earlier so entirely taken her over. In a scene that parallels Bennett's inspiration for the novel, a younger, naive, and impressionable Sophia is struck by the appearance of this then unknown woman in a restaurant. The formidable self-sufficiency of this figure—as indifferent to the curiosity she excites as Freud's narcissistic woman—intimidates Sophia, who is not yet experienced enough to see, as the novel does, that Madame Foucault's charm is just that of "the excessive ripeness of a blonde who fights in vain against obesity" (*OWT*.3.2.331). Years later, by the

---

[15]Bennett, *Journal*, 1: 297. For Bennett's use of images of consumption in his relations to other novelists, see his description to Frank Harris of reading one of his books: "To my regret I have already swallowed the book. . . . I read it greedily" ("[*To Frank Harris*], Hotel Belvédere, Mont Pélerin, Sur Vevey, Switzerland, 13 Dec 1908," in *Letters*, 2: 242).

[16]Quoted by Drabble, *Arnold Bennett*, 156.

[17]Bennett, *Letters*, 1: 401 n432; *Letters*, 3: 136 n143.

workings of fate, a delirious Sophia is given over to Madame Foucault, and part of the illusion Sophia attempts to dispel by her emphasis on the vastness of Madame Foucault's corruption is the "immense devotion" with which Madame Foucault has cared for her in her illness (3.5.381). The defeat of Sophia's romance shifts the figurative meaning of Madame Foucault's enormous bulk, changes her from mother to prostitute.[18] That bulk symbolizes the way Madame Foucault has (like Constance, who "folded [her infant] in an immense tenderness" [2.3.211]) overwhelmed and overpowered Sophia—given her life, a "rebirth" she has neither requested nor desired (3.5.380).[19] Sophia's response to Madame Foucault's power is characteristically like her response to her own mother. Mrs. Baines, who has seemed not just to recognize but herself to preordain ends, has her omnipotence shown up by her daughter. Similarly, Sophia overmasters and displaces Madame Foucault, taking over her furniture, tenants, and lodgings—and by taking over her space perhaps strives to occupy her self-sufficiency. Yet, although Madame Foucault vanishes from the novel, what Sophia takes over leaves her no more complete than before.

In this dynamic of incorporation and displacement, Sophia becomes what she fears, but just how she is like it is part of the ironic humor of the book. Rather than assuming some kind of lasting self-completeness that she mistakenly once attributed to Madame Foucault, Sophia becomes like her in turning old and fat instead; she ultimately dies, given up at the end to the vast wholeness that

[18]As I argued in conclusion to the chapter on Dickens, it is these easy swings from one avatar of woman's construction to another that keep her caught in the network scapegoating her. Mothers and prostitutes, along with madwomen—and the old woman in the restaurant, along with the fat waitress who tends him, seems to Bennett hysterical (*Journal*, 1: 131–32)—recur in this study because, as Bennett's work makes clear, they, rather than Freud's triad in "The Theme of the Three Caskets," have been the three fates sketched out for women in our culture, any of which can substitute for another and still enforce its burden of ideology. See Sigmund Freud, "The Theme of the Three Caskets," vol. 12 of *The Standard Edition of the Complete Psychological Works of Sigmund Freud*, trans. James Strachey, 24 vols. (1953–74), pp. 289–301.

[19]Madame Foucault, along with her housemate Laurence, quite literally overpowers Sophia in order to submerge her in life-giving baths, that traditional symbol for the mother's oceanic engulfment of the child. That these are cold baths, which, like Bennett's irony, actually dispel Sophia's embrace of disease and clear her mind, simply continues the identification of Madame Foucault with the motive force of the novel (*OWT*.3.5.378–79).

then seems to be represented by *The Old Wives' Tale* itself, the plot of which stands in for the inexorable pattern of life.

This is the dynamic I have considered throughout this study: woman is made to figure the system of power—for Bennett, as for Gerald in the novel, it seems as if "she, and not he, stood for destiny" (3.1.315)—but only so that through a chain of displacements he can actually seem to assume her place. It is just this kind of dynamic that the Foucault-inspired critic Mark Seltzer, in discussing the role of women in the American naturalist novel, has also outlined: he argues that naturalist themes, and the form of naturalism itself, on one level work through an anxious male response to what it casts as generative female power.[20] Yet to cast this pattern of incorporation simply in terms of threat and anxiety is also to simplify, if not misread, a more complex dynamic. Bennett is interesting to me as I analyze my own approach in this book because of the way he emphasizes self-analysis: he doesn't just wishfully transfer this power to his creation; he also questions the consolations of doing so.

Bennett implies that the dark picture inscribed by the sum of life is itself an illusion. Since his earliest responses to literature, Bennett admits that he has been drawn to such a picture: "I was six or so when The Ugly Duckling aroused in me the melancholy of life, gave me to see the deep sadness which pervades all romance, beauty, and adventure."[21] Yet such deep sadness is aligned with romance, part of a fairy tale. Although Bennett finds in his own fledgling literary endeavors "a remorseless naturalism that even thus early proclaimed the elective affinity between Flaubert and myself," he later in life asserts that "the notion that 'naturalists' have at last lighted on a final formula which ensures truth to life is ridiculous. 'Naturalist' is merely an epithet expressing self-satisfaction."[22] That this pretense of self-satisfaction has to do with illusions of self-sufficiency, of vastness and completeness, may have to do with the way Bennett locates romance in the impulse to sum up and connect. Writing about the attractions of the theater, his desire

[20]Mark Seltzer, "The Naturalist Machine," in *Sex, Politics, and Science in the Nineteenth-Century Novel*, Selected Papers from the English Institute, 1983–84, n.s. 10, ed. Ruth Bernard Yeazell (1986), 116–47.

[21]Arnold Bennett, *The Truth about an Author* (1911), 10.

[22]The first phrase is from Bennett, *Truth*, 14; the second is from Bennett, "The Author's Craft," in Hynes, *The Author's Craft*, 23.

to see what drives it behind the scenes, Bennett admits that the fitting together of things can be a romance: "After all," he writes, "the romance of the organization of these affairs interests me. . . . certainly what interests me is organization."[23] What interests him above all is the organization of what he knows to be an illusion.

The englobing organization of *The Old Wives' Tale* may thus also be a kind of theater, the dark picture it paints a kind of romantic effect. Bennett does in fact suggest a link between his novel and the romantic pathos embodied by a figure like Madame Foucault. Sophia thinks she is seeing a true picture when she learns to see Madame Foucault as not "dramatically pathetic" but ridiculous. Yet in his inspiration for the novel, Bennett sees beyond such scornful reactions by the other restaurant patrons and recognizes instead "extreme pathos" in the story he wants to tell of the fat woman. Rather than dispelling the romance of Madame Foucault, *The Old Wives' Tale* is in this sense actually predicated on it. Moreover, Bennett uses Sophia's experience in Madame Foucault's chamber to teach his readers another lesson. Gaining what seems for a moment the novel's own objective and comprehensive vision, she looks out from her high window and sees the melancholy "spectacle of existence," the sweep of life around her. Lost in the embrace of this melancholy, Sophia's response, the novel observes, is actually a kind of abandonment in which "sadness became a voluptuous pleasure" (3.5.384).

Women—fat women—may not just be decoys, meant to be displaced; they may really be the novel's figures for its determinism. Bennett may emphasize them in their corpulence, fix them as figures in their very predominance and solidity, to make that identification with the vast sum of life stick. What a figure like Madame Foucault perhaps best embodies in the novel is actually the artificiality of this engulfing pattern and the way it gives us as readers some kind of pleasure or solace. Sophia is able to see through Madame Foucault's romance because she has earlier peeped behind her dressing screen to discover the filthy secrets of her toilette, to see through the artifice that makes her seem so charming (3.5.385–86). And the artifices of the prostitute are not much different from the artifices of the mother; the conceit that Mrs.

---

[23]Bennett, *Journal*, 1: 303, 304.

Baines or Constance can enwrap their children and somehow determine their fate, provides only another illusory pleasure. As
readers we may not be meant to glimpse, behind the screen of
these large women, the artifices of Bennett's own totalizing novel;
we may not even want to question the charms of its melancholy
and the pleasures its way of accounting for everything gives us. Yet
Bennett himself was ready enough to draw a connection between
himself and women, telling one correspondent, "I am partly a
woman, *à mes heures.*"[24] The identification of women and the vast
consuming whole we call fate, power—whatever impulse prompts
and determines us as subjects—may not be meant to scapegoat but
to comfort and to reassure, allowing the ultimate consolation of
authorial omnipotence, authorial narcissism.

In his reading of the naturalist novel, Seltzer argues that naturalism itself incorporates the mechanics of power, makes its relentless network of forces both its subject and technique.[25] I would
argue that recent Foucault-inspired approaches, such as Seltzer's or
my own, are interested in naturalism because of the neat fit between it and their own assumptions.[26] That is, Foucauldian criticism also identifies with and incorporates the network of forces it
describes; it imitates the vast and totalizing system it theorizes. Just
as in Bennett's naturalism, this inexhaustible and inexorable vision
can be its most radical consolation, not least because it allows such
criticism circularly to be able to account for everything. Because it
incorporates everything as a product of its own totalizing system,
even what seem reactions to it, it becomes nonfalsifiable. As Bennett tells us about his Foucault, such criticism fulfills its own prediction as to its ultimate destiny.

If that consolation is to any degree disturbed in my study, it is
perhaps through the agency of feminism. In his reading of the use
of women in naturalism, Seltzer argues that gender difference—
although an important political distinction he himself makes

---

[24]James Hepburn, Introduction to *Letters*, 4: xxxviii.

[25]Seltzer, "Naturalist Machine," 141–42.

[26]In addition to Seltzer's forthcoming book *Bodies and Machines*, parts of which he
has published as the essays "The Naturalist Machine" and "Statistical Persons"
(*Diacritics* 17 [Fall 1987]: 82–98), see also Walter Benn Michaels, *The Gold Standard and
the Logic of Naturalism* (1987).

throughout the essay—is actually also (and perhaps, given the relentless machinery of the logic of his essay, ultimately) specious, a strategic way of imposing regulation while preserving the illusion of opposition. Seltzer's theoretical premises parallel neatly here the naturalist techniques he discusses: the gender inequalities he has earlier attended to in the "rivalry between 'male' and 'female' forces" disappear into "a more general economy of bodies and powers."[27] Specific local differences become incorporated in a totalizing scheme.

My own reliance on similar critical models in this book has meant that it, too, has often followed this dynamic; it does seem to me important to question the way gender division can be a ploy. Yet, despite the force of such theoretical premises, I can't so easily give up the distinctions between genders. Interrupting the sweep of this study's consuming abstractions, perhaps to the sacrifice of theoretical consistency (what I have been arguing in this conclusion might be a good thing), has been an insistence on the way gender divisions resist the forces of incorporation annulling them— even when those forces reside in my own argument.

The obstinate refusal of theory's coherence that an emphasis on women may play in my study is perhaps figured in studies like Seltzer's—and in Foucault's own work from which it draws—by a particularly rich and wayward emphasis on the stories of history, on anecdotes that go beyond the readings of them in these works. These historical details are not part of the influence of such works on this study, but, despite my inability to store up such anecdotes

---

[27]Seltzer, "Naturalist Machine," 120. After exposing the explicit tension in naturalism between female and male—the way naturalism attempts to coopt the generative power it locates in the mother by shifting it onto male technologies—Seltzer argues that female and male actually exist in naturalism as "a set of exchanges" rather than as oppositions (137). He writes: "The naturalist machine operates through a double discourse by which the apparently opposed registers of the body and machine are coordinated within a single technology of regulation" (142). But although his point is about gender, the language and particulars of gender drop out of his argument. Rather than demonstrating how this ploy of specious opposition works in particular in relation to gender, he relies at this point in his argument on his earlier book and past demonstration of this ploy; yet this earlier work has even less to say about gender. One wonders if, rather than simply being absorbed into a system that seems to account for everything, a careful attention to gender might to some degree complicate if not undo the general argument about the breakdown of opposition.

myself and despite some abiding questions I have about the pro-
cedures of thinking historically, such details are what seem to me
most exciting in such work. That I have, in fact, been much more
informed by the large theoretical outlines of Foucault's work rather
than by its historical focus could be charged against me as precisely
missing the point of that work, exemplifying the response that
made Foucault refuse explicitly to codify his work into a consistent
theory, to call it a theory at all. I might counter that such a refusal
was itself a ploy, to hide the theoretical overconsistency that his
works actually rely on. But what seems to me more useful is to
emphasize the tension between these different responses to Foucault's work, a debate between formalism and history encoded in
that work itself. This debate is perhaps the most hotly contested in
criticism right now not because it is located in Foucault-inspired
reactions to earlier post-structuralism but because it resides irre-
solvably in Foucault's work itself. At any rate, such debate makes
consolations more elusive for everyone.

The importance of historical specificity and contextualization
matched by a skepticism that questions the assumptions of history
has been crucial in work on women, taking the form of a tension
between the facts prompting her representation and the demands
of that representation itself. Woman's greatest oppression has lain
perhaps in the way that her construction has been whipsawed
between reality and representation, history and ideology, the way
that the forces of oppression have resorted to either angle when
their purposes demanded. Perhaps by emphasizing the irrecon-
cilableness of these approaches, feminist dialogue has disturbed
the ready oscillations of this dynamic. My study, in it polemics and
refusals, has tried to be part of the ongoing debate that keeps
gender central.

Yet, at the end of this book, what marks the debate between
history and formalism most for me is a sense that *its* problematiza-
tion may no longer be central. Perhaps when our forms are different and our history has changed—however slightly—we will see
another issue emerge, another tension informing our construction
as subjects. Perhaps in this study there are already insights that
resist, or just simply ignore, the conclusions preordained by this
debate and my reaction to it. That new tension may not be manifest

until it, too, is beside the point, another consoling illusion that only seems as crucial as the debate between form and history has seemed to me in this study. After all, Bennett tells us, we are able to see that "the romance of life has gone" only after it has left; "until it has gone it is never romance" (*OWT*.1.3.86–87).

Works Cited

Abrams, M. H. "The Deconstructive Angel." *Critical Inquiry* 3 (1977): 425–38.

Annan, Margaret. "The *Arabian Nights* in Victorian Literature." Ph.D. diss., Northwestern University, 1945.

Armstrong, Nancy. *Desire and Domestic Fiction: A Political History of the Novel.* New York: Oxford University Press, 1987.

Attridge, Derek, Geoff Bennington, and Robert Young, eds. *Post-Structuralism and the Question of History.* New York: Cambridge University Press, 1987.

Austin, Zelda. "Why Feminist Critics Are Angry with George Eliot." *College English* 37 (February 1976): 549–61.

Baker, Ernest. *The Age of Romance: From the Beginnings to the Renaissance.* Vol. 1 of *The History of the English Novel.* 10 vols. London: H. F. and G. Witherby, 1924–39.

Barrett, Michèle. "Ideology and the Cultural Production of Gender." In *Feminist Criticism and Social Change: Sex, Class, and Race in Literature and Culture.* Ed. Judith Newton and Deborah Rosenfelt, 65–85. New York: Methuen, 1985.

Barthes, Roland. "The Reality Effect." Trans. R. Carter. In *French Literary Theory Today: A Reader,* ed. Tzvetan Todorov, 11–17. New York: Cambridge University Press, 1982.

——. *S/Z.* Trans. Richard Miller. New York: Hill and Wang, 1974.

Baym, Nina. "The Madwoman and Her Languages: Why I Don't Do Feminist Literary Theory." In *Feminist Issues in Literary Scholarship.* Ed. Shari Benstock, 245–61. Bloomington: Indiana University Press, 1987.

Beach, Joseph Warren. *The Concept of Nature in Nineteenth-Century English Poetry.* New York: Russell and Russell, 1936.

Beer, Gillian. *Darwin's Plots: Evolutionary Narrative in Darwin, George Eliot, and Nineteenth-Century Fiction.* Boston: Routledge and Kegan Paul, 1983.

——. *The Romance*. London: Methuen, 1970.

Belsey, Catherine. *Critical Practice*. New York: Methuen, 1980.

——. "Re-Reading the Great Tradition." In *Re-Reading English*. Ed. Peter Widdowson, 121–35. New York: Methuen, 1982.

Bennett, Arnold. "The Author's Craft." In *The Author's Craft and Other Critical Writings of Arnold Bennett*. Ed. Samuel Hynes, 3–50. Lincoln: University of Nebraska Press, 1968.

——. "The 'Average Reader' and the Recipe for Popularity." In *The Author's Craft*, 51–60.

——. "George Gissing." In *The Author's Craft*, 159–65.

——. *The Journal of Arnold Bennett, 1896-1910*. Vol. 1 of *The Journal of Arnold Bennett*. 3 vols. New York: Viking, 1932–33.

——. *The Letters of Arnold Bennett*. 4 vols. Ed. James Hepburn. New York: Oxford University Press, 1966–86.

——. *The Old Wives' Tale*. Ed. John Wain. New York: Penguin, 1983.

——. *The Truth about an Author*. New York: George H. Doran, 1911.

Bennington, Geoff. "Not Yet." *Diacritics* 12 (1982): 23–32.

Benston, Alice N. Review of *The Political Unconscious*, by Fredric Jameson. *Sub-stance* 41 (1983): 97–103.

Berger, John (with Sven Blomberg, Chris Fox, Michael Dibb, Richard Hollis). *Ways of Seeing*. New York: Penguin Books, 1972.

Bloom, Harold. *The Anxiety of Influence: A Theory of Poetry*. New York: Oxford University Press, 1973.

Boose, Lynda E. "The Family in Shakespeare Studies; or, Studies in the Family of Shakespeareans; or, The Politics of Politics." *Renaissance Quarterly* 40 (Winter 1987): 707–42.

Boswell, James. *Life of Johnson*. Ed. George Birkbeck Hill, and revised and enlarged by L. F. Powell. 6 vols. Oxford: Clarendon Press, 1934–50.

Bové, Paul A. *Intellectuals in Power: A Genealogy of Critical Humanism*. New York: Columbia University Press, 1986.

Breuer, Josef, and Sigmund Freud. "On the Psychical Mechanism of Hysterical Phenomena: Preliminary Communication." In vol. 2 of *The Standard Edition of the Complete Psychological Writings of Freud*. Trans. James Strachey, 1–17. 24 vols. London: Hogarth Press, 1953–74.

Brontë, Charlotte. *Shirley*. Ed. Andrew and Judith Hook. New York: Penguin, 1974.

Brooks, Peter *Reading for the Plot: Design and Intention in Narrative*. New York: Knopf, 1984.

Brownlee, Kevin, and Marina Scordilis Brownlee, eds. *Romance: Generic Transformation from Chrétien de Troyes to Cervantes*. Hanover, N.H.: University Press of New England, 1985.

Carpenter, Mary Wilson. "'A Bit of Her Flesh': Circumcision and 'The Significance of the Phallus' in *Daniel Deronda*." *Genders* 1 (March 1988): 1–23.

Carroll, David, ed. *George Eliot: The Critical Heritage*. London: Routledge and Kegan Paul, 1971.

250   Works Cited

Chase, Cynthia. "The Decomposition of Elephants: Double-Reading *Daniel Deronda.*" *PMLA* 93 (March 1978): 215–27.

Cixous, Hélène, and Catherine Clément. *The Newly Born Woman.* Trans. Betsy Wing. Minneapolis: University of Minnesota Press, 1986.

Cohn, Carol. "Sex and Death in the Rational World of Defense Intellectuals." *Signs* 12 (1987): 687–718.

Collins, Jerre, J. Ray Green, Mary Lydon, Mark Sachner, and Eleanor Hong Skoller. "Questioning the Unconscious: The Dora Archive." *Diacritics* 13 (Spring 1983): 37–42.

Collins, Philip, ed. *Dickens: The Critical Heritage.* London: Routledge and Kegan Paul, 1971.

Collins, Wilkie. *The Woman in White.* Ed. Julian Symons. New York: Penguin, 1985.

Congreve, William. "The Preface to the Reader." In his *Incognita; or, Love and Duty Reconcil'd,* 107–53, vol. 1 of *The Complete Works of William Congreve.* Ed. Montague Summers, 4 vols. New York: Russell and Russell, 1964.

Conway, Jill. "Stereotypes of Femininity in a Theory of Sexual Evolution." In *Suffer and Be Still: Women in the Victorian Age.* Ed. Martha Vicinus, 140–54. Bloomington: Indiana University Press, 1972.

Creech, James, Peggy Kamuf, and Jane Todd. "Deconstruction in America: An Interview with Jacques Derrida." *Critical Exchange* 17 (Winter 1985): 1–33.

Culler, Jonathan. "Semiotics and Deconstruction." *Poetics Today* 1 (1979): 137–41.

Davis, Lennard J. *Factual Fictions: The Origins of the English Novel.* New York: Columbia University Press, 1983.

de Beauvoir, Simone. Introduction to *The Second Sex.* Trans. and ed. H. M. Parshley, xiii–xxix. New York: Knopf, 1968.

Derrida, Jacques, and Christie V. McDonald. "Choreographies." *Diacritics* 12 (1982): 66–76.

——. "The Law of Genre." Trans. Avital Ronell. *Glyph* 7 (1980): 202–29.

——. *Margins of Philosophy.* Trans. Alan Bass. Chicago: University of Chicago Press, 1982.

——. *Positions.* Trans. Alan Bass. Chicago: University of Chicago Press, 1981.

——. "Women in the Beehive: A Seminar with Jacques Derrida." In *Men in Feminism.* Ed. Alice Jardine and Paul Smith, 189–203. New York: Methuen, 1987.

Derrida, Jacques, and Christie V. McDonald. "Choreographies." *Diacritics* 12 (1982): 66–76.

Diamond, Irene, and Lee Quinby, eds. *Feminism and Foucault: Reflections on Resistance.* Boston: Northeastern University Press, 1988.

Dickens, Charles. *Bleak House.* Ed. Norman Page. New York: Penguin, 1971.

——. *Great Expectations.* Ed. Angus Calder. New York: Penguin, 1965.

——. "The Holly-Tree." In his *Christmas Stories,* 113–54, vol. 31 of *The Gadshill Edition of the Works of Charles Dickens,* Ed. Andrew Lang. 33 vols. New York: Scribner's, 1897–99.

——. *The Letters of Charles Dickens.* Edited by Madeline House, Graham Storey, and Kathleen Tillotson. 6 vols. to date. Oxford: Clarendon Press, 1965–.

——. "Mugby Junction." In his *Christmas Stories,* 127–204, vol. 32 of *The Gadshill Edition.*

——. *The Mystery of Edwin Drood.* Ed. Arthur J. Cox. New York: Penguin, 1974.

——. "Nurse's Stories." In his *The Uncommercial Traveler,* 174–86, vol. 29 of *The Gadshill Edition.*

——. *The Old Curiosity Shop.* Ed. Angus Easson. New York: Penguin, 1972.

——. *Oliver Twist.* Ed. Peter Fairclough. New York: Penguin, 1966.

——. *The Posthumous Papers of the Pickwick Club.* Ed. Robert L. Patten. New York: Penguin, 1972.

——. "A Preliminary Word." In his *Miscellaneous Contributions.* 3–4, vol. 19 of *The Standard Edition of the Works of Charles Dickens.* 22 vols. London: Gresham, n.d.

Dinnerstein, Dorothy. *The Mermaid and the Minotaur: Sexual Arrangements and Human Malaise.* New York: Harper and Row, 1976.

Doane, Janice, and Devon Hodges. *Nostalgia and Sexual Difference: The Resistance to Contemporary Feminism.* New York: Methuen, 1987.

Doane, Mary Ann. *The Desire to Desire: The Woman's Film of the 1940s.* Bloomington: Indiana University Press, 1987.

Dobson, Austin. *Eighteenth-Century Vignettes.* London: Chatto and Windus, 1892.

Donoghue, Denis. "A Criticism of One's Own." In *Men in Feminism.* Ed. Alice Jardine and Paul Smith, 146–152. New York: Methuen, 1987.

Drabble, Margaret. *Arnold Bennett.* New York: Knopf, 1974.

Dyson, A. E., ed. *Dickens's "Bleak House": A Casebook.* Nashville, Tenn.: Aurora, 1970.

Eagleton, Terry. "Fredric Jameson: The Politics of Style." *Diacritics* 12 (1982): 14–22.

Elam, Diane. " 'We Pray to Be Defended from Her Cleverness': Conjugating *Diana of the Crossways.*" *Genre* 21 (Summer 1988): 179–201.

Eliot, George. *Adam Bede.* Ed. Stephen Gill. New York: Penguin, 1980.

[——]. "Art and Belles Lettres." *Westminster Review* n. s. 9 (January and April 1856): 625–50.

——. *Daniel Deronda.* Ed. Barbara Hardy. New York: Penguin, 1967.

——. *The George Eliot Letters.* Ed. Gordon S Haight. 9 vols. New Haven: Yale University Press, 1954–78.

——. *The Lifted Veil.* New York: Penguin, 1985.

——. *Middlemarch.* Ed. W. J. Harvey. New York: Penguin, 1965.

——. *The Mill on the Floss*. Ed. A. S. Byatt. New York: Penguin, 1979.

——. "The Natural History of German Life." In *The Essays of George Eliot*. Ed. Thomas Pinney, 266–99. London: Routledge and Kegan Paul, 1963.

——. *Scenes of Clerical Life*. Ed. David Lodge. New York: Penguin, 1973.

——. "Silly Novels by Lady Novelists." In *The Essays of George Eliot*, 300–324.

——. "[Three Novels]." In *The Essays of George Eliot*, 325–34.

——. "Woman in France: Madame de Sable." In *The Essays of George Eliot*, 52–81.

Ermarth, Elizabeth Deeds. *Realism and Consensus in the English Novel*. Princeton: Princeton University Press, 1983.

Ferguson, Frances. "Rape and the Rise of the Novel." *Representations* 20 (1987): 88–112.

——. "Wollstonecraft Our Contemporary." In *Gender and Theory: Dialogues on Feminist Criticism*. Ed. Linda Kauffman, 51–62. New York: Basil Blackwell, 1989.

Fielding, Henry. "*The Covent Garden Journal*, No. 24." In *The Criticism of Henry Fielding*, Ed. Ioan Williams, 191–94. London: Routledge and Kegan Paul, 1970.

Finke, Laurie. "The Rhetoric of Marginality: Why I Do Feminist Theory." *Tulsa Studies in Women's Literature* 5 (Fall 1986): 251–72.

Firmat, Gustavo Pérez. "The Novel as Genres," *Genre* 12 (Fall 1979): 269–92.

Flieger, Jerry Aline. "The Prison-House of Ideology: Critic as Inmate." *Diacritics* 12 (1982): 47–56.

Forster, John. *The Life of Charles Dickens*. 3 vols. Boston: Estes and Lauriat, 1872.

Foucault, Michel. *The Birth of the Clinic: An Archeology of Medical Perception*. Trans. A. M. Sheridan Smith. New York: Pantheon, 1973.

——. "Body/Power." In his *Power/Knowledge: Selected Interviews and Other Writing, 1972–77*. Trans. Colin Gordon, Leo Marshall, John Mepham, and Kate Soper, and ed. Colin Gordon, 58–59. New York: Pantheon, 1980.

——. *The Care of the Self*. Vol. 3 of *The History of Sexuality*. Trans. Robert Hurley. New York: Vintage, 1986.

——. *Discipline and Punish: The Birth of the Prison*. Trans. Alan Sheridan. New York: Vintage, 1979.

——. "Fantasia of the Library." In his *Language, Counter-Memory, Practice: Selected Essays and Interviews*. Ed. Donald F. Bouchard, trans. Donald F. Bouchard and Sherry Simon, 87–109. Ithaca: Cornell University Press, 1977.

——. *The History of Sexuality: An Introduction*. Vol. 1. Trans. Robert Hurley. New York: Vintage, 1980.

——. "Technologies of the Self." In *Technologies of the Self: A Seminar with Michel Foucault*. Ed. Luther H. Martin, Huck Gutman, and Patrick Hutton, 16–49. Amherst: University of Massachusetts Press, 1988.

——. "Truth and Power." In his *Power/Knowledge*, 109–33.

——. *The Use of Pleasure*. Vol. 2 of *The History of Sexuality*. Trans. Robert Hurley, New York: Vintage, 1986.

Fraser, Nancy. "Foucault's Body-Language: A Post-Humanist Political Rhetoric?" *Salmagundi* 61 (Fall 1983): 55–70.

Freud, Sigmund. "Analysis Terminable and Interminable." In volume 23 of *The Standard Edition of the Complete Psychological Works of Sigmund Freud*. Trans. James Strachey, pp. 209–53. 24 vols. London: Hogarth Press, 1953–74.

——. "Constructions in Analysis." In vol. 23 of *The Standard Edition*, pp. 255–69.

——. "Creative Writers and Daydreaming." In vol. 9 of *The Standard Edition*, pp. 141–53.

——. "Female Sexuality." In vol. 21 of *The Standard Edition*, pp. 223–43.

——. "Fragment of an Analysis of a Case of Hysteria." In vol. 7 of *The Standard Edition*, pp. 1–122.

——. "Medusa's Head." In vol. 18 of *The Standard Edition*, pp. 273–74.

——. "Negation." In vol. 19 of *The Standard Edition*, pp. 235–39.

——. "Psycho-Analytic Notes on an Autobiographical Account of a Case of Paranoia." In vol. 12 of *The Standard Edition*, pp. 1–82.

——. "The Psychotherapy of Hysteria." In vol. 2 of *The Standard Edition*, pp. 253–305.

——. "Some Psychical Consequences of the Anatomical Distinction between the Sexes." In vol. 19 of *The Standard Edition*, pp. 243–58.

——. "The Theme of the Three Caskets." In vol. 12 of *The Standard Edition*, pp. 289–301.

Froula, Christine. "When Eve reads Milton: Undoing the Canonical Economy." *Critical Inquiry* 10 (December 1983): 321–47.

Frye, Northrop. *Anatomy of Criticism: Four Essays*. Princeton: Princton University Press, 1957.

——. *The Secular Scripture: A Study of the Structure of Romance*. Cambridge, Mass.: Harvard University Press, 1976.

Gallagher, Catherine. "George Eliot and *Daniel Deronda*: The Prostitute and the Jewish Question." In *Sex, Politics, and Science in the Nineteenth-Century Novel*, Selected Papers from the English Institute, 1983–84, n. s. 10, Ed. Ruth Bernard Yeazell, 29–62. Baltimore: Johns Hopkins University Press, 1986.

Gallop, Jane. *The Daughter's Seduction: Feminism and Psychoanalysis*. Ithaca: Cornell University Press, 1982.

——. "Psychoanalytic Criticism: Some Intimate Questions." *Art in America* 72 (November 1984): 9–15.

——. *Reading Lacan*. Ithaca: Cornell University Press, 1985.

Gardiner, Judith Kegan, Elly Bulkin, Rena Grasso Patterson, and Annette Kolodny. "An Interchange on Feminist Criticism: On 'Dancing through the Minefield.'" *Feminist Studies* 8 (1982): 629–75.

Gilbert, Sandra M. "What Do Feminist Critics Want? A Postcard from the

Volcano." In *The New Feminist Criticism: Essays on Women, Literature, and Theory*. Ed. Elaine Showalter, 29–45. New York: Pantheon Books, 1985.

Gilbert, Sandra M., and Susan Gubar. *The Madwoman in the Attic: The Woman Writer and the Nineteenth-Century Literary Imagination*. New Haven: Yale University Press, 1979.

———. "The Man on the Dump versus the United Dames of America; or, What Does Frank Lentricchia Want?" *Critical Inquiry* 14 (Winter 1988): 386–406.

Gissing, George. *Charles Dickens: A Critical Study*. Vol. 20 of *The Standard Edition of the Works of Charles Dickens*. 22 vols. London: Gresham, n.d.

Godwin, William. *Memoirs of Mary Wollstonecraft*. Ed. W. Clark Durant. New York: Greenberg Publisher, 1927.

Greimas, A. J., and F. Rastier. "The Interaction of Semiotic Constraints." *Yale French Studies* 41 (1968): 86–105.

Haight, Gordon S. *George Eliot: A Biography*. New York: Oxford University Press, 1968.

Hansen, Miriam, "Pleasure, Ambivalence, Identification: Valentino and Female Spectatorship." *Cinema Journal* 25 (Summer 1986): 6–57.

Hardy, Barbara. *The Novels of George Eliot: A Study in Form*. London: University of London, Athlone Press, 1959.

Hardy, Thomas: "General Preface to the Wessex Edition of 1912." In his *Tess of the D'Urbervilles: A Pure Woman*. Ed. David Skilton, 491–96. New York: Penguin, 1978.

Hawkins, Sir John. *The Life of Samuel Johnson, LL.D.* 1787, Reprinted as vol. 20 of *Johnsoniana*. 25 vol. New York: Garland, 1974.

Heath, Stephen. "Difference." *Screen* 19 (1978): 51–112.

———. "Male Feminism." In *Men in Feminism*. Ed. Alice Jardine and Paul Smith, 1–32. New York: Methuen, 1987.

Hertz, Neil. *The End of the Line: Essays on Psychoanalysis and the Sublime*. New York: Columbia University Press, 1985.

Homans, Margaret. *Bearing the Word: Language and Female Experience in Nineteenth-Century Women's Writing*. Chicago: University of Chicago Press, 1986.

Horney, Karen. "The Dread of Woman." *International Journal of Psychoanalysis* 13 (1932): 348–60.

Hyder, Clyde K. "Wilkie Collins and *The Woman in White*." *PMLA* 54 (1939): 297–303.

Irigaray, Luce. "Commodities among Themselves." In her *This Sex Which Is Not One*. Trans. Catherine Porter, with Carolyn Burke, 192–97. Ithaca: Cornell University Press, 1985.

———. *Speculum of the Other Woman*. Trans. Gillian C. Gill. Ithaca: Cornell University Press, 1985.

———. "Women on the Market." In her *This Sex Which Is Not One*, 170–91.

Jacobus, Mary. "Freud's Mnemonic: Women, Screen Memories, and Feminist Nostalgia." *Michigan Quarterly Review* 26 (1987): 117–39.

——. "In Parenthesis: Immaculate Conceptions and Feminine Desire." In *Body/Politics: Women and the Discourses of Science.* Ed. Mary Jacobus, Evelyn Fox Keller, and Sally Shuttleworth, 11–28. New York: Routledge, 1990.

——. "The Law of/and Gender: Genre Theory and *The Prelude.*" *Diacritics* 14 (1984): 47–57.

——. *Reading Women: Essays in Feminist Criticism.* New York: Columbia University Press. 1986.

Jameson, Fredric. "Cognitive Mapping" and subsequent "Discussion." In *Marxism and the Interpretation of Culture.* Ed. Cary Nelson and Lawrence Grossberg, 347–57. Urbana: University of Illinois Press, 1988.

——. "Imaginary and Symbolic in Lacan: Marxism, Psychoanalytic Criticism, and the Problem of the Subject." *Yale French Studies* 55/56 (1977): 338–95.

——. "Interview: Fredric Jameson." *Diacritics* 12 (1982): 72–91.

——. *The Political Unconscious: Narrative as a Socially Symbolic Act.* Ithaca: Cornell University Press, 1981.

Jardine, Alice A. *Gynesis: Configurations of Woman and Modernity.* Ithaca: Cornell University Press, 1985.

——. "Men in Feminism: Odor di Uomo Or Compagnons de Route?" In *Men in Feminism.* Ed. Alice Jardine and Paul Smith, 54–61. New York: Methuen, 1987.

Jardine, Alice, and Paul Smith. "A Conversation: Alice Jardine and Paul Smith." In *Men in Feminism,* 246–51.

Johnson, Barbara. *A World of Difference.* Baltimore: Johns Hopkins University Press, 1987.

Johnson, Edgar. *Charles Dickens: His Tragedy and Triumph.* 2 vols. New York: Simon and Schuster, 1952.

Johnson, Samuel. *The Rambler.* Vol. 4 of *The Yale Edition of the Works of Samuel Johnson.* Ed. Walter Jackson Bate and Albrecht B. Strauss. 15 vols. to date. New Haven: Yale University Press, 1969–.

Jones, Ann Rosalind. "Julia Kristeva on Femininity: The Limits of a Semiotic Politics." *Feminist Review* 18 (November 1984): 56–73.

Kamuf, Peggy. "Replacing Feminist Criticism." *Diacritics* 12 (1982): 42–47.

——. "Writing Like a Woman." In *Women and Language in Literature and Society.* Ed. Sally McConnel-Ginet, Ruth Borker, and Nelly Furman, 284–300. New York: Praeger, 1980.

Kaplan, Cora. *Sea Changes: Essays on Culture and Feminism.* London: Verso, 1986.

Kaplan, E. Ann. "Is the Gaze Male?" In *Powers of Desire: The Politics of Sexuality.* Ed. Ann Snitow, Christine Stansell, and Sharon Thompson, 309–27. New York: Monthly Review Press, 1983.

Kaplan, Fred. *Dickens and Mesmerism: The Hidden Springs of Fiction.* Princeton: Princeton University Press, 1975.

Klein, Melanie. "Early Stages of the Oedipal Conflict." *International Journal of Psychoanalysis* 9 (1928): 167–80.

Klein, Richard. "In the Body of the Mother." *Enclitic* 7 (Spring 1983): 66–75.

Kolodny, Annette. "Dancing between Left and Right: Feminism and the Academic Minefield in the 1980s." *Feminist Studies* 14 (Fall 1988): 453–66.

——. "Dancing through the Minefield: Some Observations on the Theory, Practice and Politics of a Feminist Literary Criticism." *Feminist Studies* 6 (1980): 1–25.

——. "A Map for Rereading; or, Gender and the Interpretation of Literary Texts." *New Literary History* 11 (Spring 1980): 451–67.

Kristeva, Julia. *Desire in Language: A Semiotic Approach to Literature and Art.* Ed. Leon S. Roudiez and trans. Thomas Gora, Alice Jardine, and Leon S. Roudiez. New York: Columbia University Press, 1980.

——. *Powers of Horror: An Essay on Abjection.* Trans. Leon S. Roudiez. New York: Columbia University Press, 1982.

Kucich, John. *Excess and Restraint in the Novels of Charles Dickens.* Athens: University of Georgia Press, 1981.

Lacan, Jacques. "The Agency of the Letter in the Unconscious or Reason since Freud." In his *Ecrits: A Selection,* Trans. Alan Sheridan. 146–78. New York: Norton, 1977.

——. "Aggressivity in Psychoanalysis." In his *Ecrits,* 8–29.

——. "The Direction of the Treatment and the Principles of Its Power." In his *Ecrits,* 226–80.

——. "The Freudian Thing." In his *Ecrits,* 114–45.

——. "God and the *Jouissance* of The Woman." In *Feminine Sexuality: Jacques Lacan and the école freudienne.* Trans. Jacqueline Rose and ed. Juliet Mitchell and Jacqueline Rose, 137–48. New York: Norton, 1982.

——. "The Meaning of the Phallus." In *Feminine Sexuality,* 74–85.

——. "The Mirror Stage as Formative of the Function of the I." In his *Ecrits,* 1–7.

LaCapra, Dominick. *History and Criticism.* Ithaca: Cornell University Press, 1985.

——. "Ideology and Critique in Dickens's *Bleak House.*" *Representations* 6 (Spring 1984): 116–23.

Lennox, Charlotte. *The Female Quixote; or, The Adventures of Arabella.* Introduction by Margaret Dalziel; Appendix by Duncan Isles. New York: Oxford University Press, 1970.

Lentricchia, Frank. "Andiamo!" *Critical Inquiry* 14 (Winter 1988): 407–13.

——. "Patriarchy against Itself—The Young Manhood of Wallace Stevens." *Critical Inquiry* 13 (1987): 742–86.

Levine, George. "George Eliot's Hypothesis of Reality." *Nineteenth-Century Fiction* 35 (June 1980): 1–28.

——. *The Realistic Imagination: English Fiction from Frankenstein to Lady Chatterly.* Chicago: University of Chicago Press, 1981.

Lewes, George Henry. *The Principles of Success in Literature.* Ed. Fred N. Scott. Boston: Allyn and Bacon, 1891.

Lovell, Terry. *Consuming Fiction.* London: Verso, 1987.

[McCarthy, Justin]. "Novels with a Purpose." *Westminster Review* n. s. 26 (July and October 1864): 24–49.

McKeon, Michael. *The Origins of the English Novel, 1600–1740*. Baltimore: Johns Hopkins University Press, 1987.

MacPike, Loralee. " 'The Old Cupiosity Shape': Changing Views of Little Nell, Part I." *Dickens Studies Newsletter* 12 (June 1981): 33–38.

Marcus, Jane. " 'Clio in Calliope': History and Myth in Meredith's *Diana of the Crossways*." In her *Art and Anger: Reading Like a Woman*, 20–48. Columbus: Ohio State University Press, 1988.

Martin, Biddy. "Feminism, Criticism, and Foucault." In *Feminism and Foucault: Reflections on Resistance*. Ed. Irene Diamond and Lee Quinby, 3–19. Boston: Northeastern University Press, 1988.

Marx, Karl. *Capital: A Critique of Political Economy*. Ed. Frederick Engels. New York: Modern Library, 1906.

——. *The Economic and Philosophic Manuscripts of 1844*. Trans. Martin Milligan and Dirk J. Struik. In *Marx and Engels: 1843–44*, 229–346. Vol. 3 of *Collected Works*, by Karl Marx and Frederick Engels. 50 vols. projected. New York: International Publishers, 1975–.

Meisel, Martin. "Miss Havisham Brought to Book." *PMLA* 81 (June 1966): 278–85.

Meredith, George. *Diana of the Crossways*. Vol. 16 of *The Memorial Edition of the Works of George Meredith*. 29 vols. New York: Scribner's, 1910–12.

——. *The Egoist*. Vols. 13 and 14 of *The Memorial Edition*.

——. "Essay on the Idea of Comedy and the Uses of the Comic Spirit." In his *Miscellaneous Prose*, pp. 3–55. Vol. 23 of *The Memorial Edition*.

——. *The Letters of George Meredith*. Ed. C. L. Cline. 3 vols. London: Oxford University Press, 1970.

Michaels, Walter Benn. *The Gold Standard and the Logic of Naturalism*. Berkeley: University of California Press, 1987.

Miller, D. A. *Narrative and Its Discontents: Problems of Closure in the Traditional Novel*. Princeton: Princeton University Press, 1981.

——. *The Novel and the Police*. Berkeley: University of California Press, 1988.

——. "Under Capricorn." *Representations* 6 (Spring 1984): 124–29.

Miller, J. Hillis. "Character in the Novel: A 'Real Illusion.' " In *From Smollett to James: Studies in the Novel and Other Essays, Presented to Edgar Johnson*, Ed. Samuel I Mintz, Alice Chandler, and Christopher Mulvey, 277–85. Charlottesville: University Press of Virginia, 1981.

——. "The Critic as Host." *Critical Inquiry* 3 (1977): 439–47.

——. *The Form of Victorian Fiction: Thackeray, Dickens, Trollope, George Eliot, Meredith, and Hardy*. Notre Dame: University of Notre Dame Press, 1968.

——. "A Guest in the House: Reply to Shlomith Rimmon-Kenan's Reply." *Poetics Today* 2 [1980/81]: 189–91.

——. " 'Herself against Herself': The Clarification of Clara Middleton." In *The Representation of Women in Fiction*, Selected Papers from the English Institute, 1981, n.s. 7. Ed. Carolyn Heilbrun and Margaret Higonnet, 98–123. Baltimore: Johns Hopkins University Press, 1983.

Miller, Nancy K. "Emphasis Added: Plots and Plausibilities in Women's Fiction." *PMLA* 96 (January 1981): 36–48.

——. "Reading as a Woman: The Body in Practice" In *The Female Body in Western Culture: Contemporary Perspectives.* Ed. Susan Rubin Suleiman, 354–62. Cambridge, Mass.: Harvard University Press, 1986.

——. "The Text's Heroine: A Feminist Critic and Her Fictions." *Diacritics* 12 (1982): 45–53.

Mitchell, Juliet. "On Freud and the Distinction between the Sexes." In her *Women: The Longest Revolution,* 221–32. New York: Pantheon, 1984.

Modleski, Tania. *Loving with a Vengeance: Mass-Produced Fantasies for Women.* Hamden, Conn.: Archon, 1982, Reprint. New York: Methuen, 1984.

Moers, Ellen. "*Bleak House:* The Agitating Women." *The Dickensian* 69 (January 1973): 13–24.

——. *Literary Women.* New York: Doubleday, 1976, Reprint. New York: Oxford University Press, 1985.

Morris, Meaghan. "in any event . . . " In *Men in Feminism.* Ed. Alice Jardine and Paul Smith, 173–81. New York: Methuen, 1987.

Mulvey, Laura. "Afterthoughts on Visual Pleasure and the Narrative Cinema Inspired by 'Duel in the Sun.' " *Framework* 15/16 (1981): 12–15.

——. "Visual Pleasure and the Narrative Cinema." *Screen* 16 (1975): 6–18.

Mykyta, Larysa. "Jameson's Utopias." *New Orleans Review* 11 (Spring 1984): 46–51.

Newsom, Robert. *Dickens on the Romantic Side of Familiar Things: 'Bleak House' and the Novel Tradition.* New York: Columbia University Press, 1977.

Newton, Judith. "History as Usual?: Feminism and the 'New Historicism.' " *Cultural Critique* 9 (Spring 1988): 87–121.

Newton, K. M. "*Daniel Deronda* and Circumcision." *Essays in Criticism* 31 (October 1981): 313–27.

Oliphant, Margaret. *The Literary History of England in the End of the Eighteenth and the Beginning of the Nineteenth Century.* 3 vols. London: Macmillan, 1882.

Owens, Craig. "Outlaws: Gay Men in Feminism." In *Men in Feminism.* Ed. Alice Jardine and Paul Smith, 219–32. New York: Methuen, 1987.

Parker, Patricia. *Inescapable Romance: Studies in the Poetics of a Mode.* Princeton: Princeton University Press, 1979.

Paulson, Ronald. *Satire and the Novel in Eighteenth-Century England.* New Haven: Yale University Press, 1967.

Pease, Donald E. "Patriarchy, Lentricchia, and Male Feminization." *Critical Inquiry* 14 (Winter 1988): 379–85.

Polan, Dana. *Power and Paranoia: History, Narrative, and the American Cinema: 1940–50.* New York: Columbia University Press, 1986.

Polwhele, Richard. *The Unsex'd Females.* New York: Cobbett, 1797.

Poovey, Mary. *The Proper Lady and the Woman Writer: Ideology as Style in the Works of Mary Wollstonecraft, Mary Shelley, and Jane Austen.* Chicago: University of Chicago Press, 1984.

——. *Uneven Developments: The Ideological Work of Gender in Mid-Victorian England.* Chicago: University of Chicago Press, 1988.

Porter, Carolyn. "Are We Being Historical Yet?" *South Atlantic Quarterly* 87 (Fall 1988): 743–86.

Quick, Jonathan R. "Silas Marner as Romance: The Example of Hawthorne." *Nineteenth-Century Fiction* 29 (December 1974): 287–98.

Rabine, Leslie W. *Reading the Romantic Heroine: Text, History, Ideology.* Ann Arbor: University of Michigan Press, 1985.

Radford, Jean, ed. *The Progress of Romance: The Politics of Popular Fiction.* New York: Routledge and Kegan Paul, 1986.

Radway, Janice A. *Reading the Romance: Women, Patriarchy, and Popular Literature.* Chapel Hill: University of North Carolina Press, 1984.

Reeve, Clara. *The Progress of Romance through Times, Countries, and Manners.* 2 vols. London: Constable, 1785, Reprint. New York: Garland, 1970.

Reiss, Timothy J. "Revolution in Bounds: Wollstonecraft, Women, and Reason." In *Gender and Theory: Dialogues on Feminist Criticism.* Ed. Linda Kauffman, 11–50. New York: Basil Blackwell, 1989.

Rose, Jacqueline. *Sexuality in the Field of Vision.* London: Verso, 1986.

Rosmarin, Adena. *The Power of Genre.* Minneapolis: University of Minnesota Press, 1985.

Ross, Andrew. "Viennese Waltzes." *Enclitic* 8 (Spring/Fall 1984): 71–82.

Rossner, Sue V., and A. Charlotte Hogsett. "Darwin and Sexism: Victorian Causes, Contemporary Effects." In *Feminist Visions: Toward a Transformation of the Liberal Arts Curriculum.* Ed. Diane L. Fowlkes and Charlotte S. McClure, 42–52. University: The University of Alabama Press, 1984.

Rubin, Gayle. "The Traffic in Women: Notes on the 'Political Economy' of Sex" in *Toward an Anthropology of Women.* Ed. Rayna R. Reiter, 157–210. New York: Monthly Review Press, 1975.

Sadoff, Dianne F. *Monsters of Affection: Dickens, Eliot and Brontë on Fatherhood.* Baltimore: Johns Hopkins University Press, 1982.

Said, Edward. "Traveling Theory." *Raritan* 1 (Winter 1982): 41–67.

Schaum, Melita. " 'Ariel, Save Us': Big Stick Polemics in Frank Lentricchia's *Ariel and the Police.*" *Genders* 4 (March 1989): 122–29.

Scholes, Robert. "Reading Like a Man." In *Men in Feminism,* Ed. Alice Jardine and Paul Smith, 204–18. New York: Methuen, 1987.

Schor, Naomi. *Breaking the Chain: Women, Theory, and French Realist Fiction.* New York: Columbia University Press, 1985.

——. "Dreaming Dissymmetry: Barthes, Foucault, and Sexual Difference." In *Men in Feminism.* ed. Alice Jardine and Paul Smith, 98–110. New York: Methuen, 1987.

——. "*Eugénie Grandet:* Mirrors and Melancholia." In *The (M)other Tongue: Essays in Feminist Psychoanalytic Interpretation.* Ed. Shirley Nelson Garner, Claire Kahane, and Madelon Sprengnether, 217–37. Ithaca: Cornell University Press, 1985.

——. *Reading in Detail: Aesthetics and the Feminine.* New York: Methuen, 1987.

Scott, Sir Walter. "An Essay on Romance." In *Chivalry, Romance, the Drama*. Vol. 6 of his *The Miscellaneous Prose Works*, 153–256. 6 vols. Edinburgh: Cadell, 1827.

——. *Waverley.* Vol. 2 of *The Large Paper Edition of the Works of Sir Walter Scott*. 50 vols. New York: Houghton Mifflin, 1912–13.

Sedgwick, Eve Kosofsky. *Between Men: English Literature and Male Homosocial Desire*. New York: Columbia University Press, 1985.

Seltzer, Mark. *Henry James and the Art of Power*. Ithaca: Cornell University Press, 1984.

——. "The Naturalist Machine." In *Sex, Politics, and Science in the Nineteenth-Century Novel*. Selected Papers from the English Institute, 1983–84, n.s. 10. Ed. Ruth Bernard Yeazell, 116–47. Baltimore: Johns Hopkins University Press, 1986.

——. "Statistical Persons." *Diacritics* 17 (Fall 1987): 82–98.

Showalter, Elaine. "Critical Cross-Dressing: Male Feminists and the Woman of the Year." In *Men in Feminism*. Ed. Alice Jardine and Paul Smith, 116–32. New York: Methuen, 1987.

——. "The Greening of Sister George." *Nineteenth-Century Fiction* 35 (December 1980): 292–311.

——. "Guilt, Authority, and the Shadows of *Little Dorrit*." *Nineteenth-Century Fiction* 34 (1979): 20–40.

——. *A Literature of Their Own: British Women Novelists from Brontë to Lessing*. Princeton: Princeton University Press, 1977.

Silverman, Kaja. *The Acoustic Mirror: The Female Voice in Psychoanalysis and Cinema*. Bloomington: Indiana University Press, 1988.

Small, Miriam Rossiter. *Charlotte Ramsay Lennox: An Eighteenth-Century Lady of Letters*. New Haven: Yale University Press, 1935. Reprint. Hamden, Conn.: Archon, 1969.

Snitow, Ann Barr. "Mass Market Romance: Pornography for Women is Different." *Radical History Review* 20 (Spring/Summer 1979): 141–61.

Spender, Dale. *Mothers of the Novel: One Hundred Good Women Writers before Jane Austen*. New York: Pandora, 1986.

Spivak, Gayatri Chakravorty. "Displacement and the Discourse of Woman." In *Displacement: Derrida and After*. Ed. Mark Krupnick, 169–95. Bloomington: Indiana University Press, 1983.

——. *In Other Worlds: Essays in Cultural Politics*. New York: Methuen, 1987.

——. "Love Me, Love My Ombre, Elle." *Diacritics* 14 (1984): 19–36.

Stang, Richard. *The Theory of the Novel in England, 1850–1870*. New York: Columbia University Press, 1959.

Stanton, Domna C. "Difference on Trial: A Critique of the Maternal Metaphor in Cixous, Irigaray, and Kristeva." In *The Poetics of Gender*, Ed. Nancy K. Miller, 157–82. New York: Columbia University Press, 1986.

Steig, Michael. "The Central Action of 'The Old Curiosity Shop,' or Little Nell Revisited Again." *Literature and Psychology* 15 (Summer 1965): 163–70.

Stevenson, Lionel. *Darwin among the Poets.* Chicago: University of Chicago Press, 1932.

——. *The Ordeal of George Meredith: A Biography.* New York: Scribner's, 1953.

Stone, Donald D. *The Romantic Impulse in Victorian Fiction.* Cambridge, Mass.: Harvard University Press, 1980.

Stone, Jennifer. "The Horrors of Power: A Critique of 'Kristeva.'" In *The Politics of Theory: Proceedings of the 1982 Essex Conference.* Ed. Frances Barker, Peter Hulme, Margaret Iversen, and Diana Loxley, 38–48. Colchester: University of Essex Press, 1983.

Sunstein, Emily W. *A Different Face: The Life of Mary Wollstonecraft.* New York: Harper and Row, 1975.

Swann, Brian. "*Middlemarch:* Realism and Symbolic Form." *ELH* 39 (June 1972): 279–308.

Tedesco, Marie. "A Feminist Challenge to Darwinism: Antoinette L. B. Blackwell on the Relations of the Sexes in Nature and Society." In *Feminist Visions: Toward a Transformation of the Liberal Arts Curriculum.* Ed. Diane L. Fowlkes and Charlotte S. McClure, 53–65. University: University of Alabama Press, 1984.

Thackeray, William Makepeace. "De Juventute." In his *Roundabout Papers,* 68–83. Vol. 22 of *The Charterhouse Edition of the Works of William Makepeace Thackeray.* 26 vols. Philadelphia: Lippincott, 1901.

Todd, Janet, ed. *A Wollstonecraft Anthology.* Bloomington: Indiana University Press, 1977.

Todorov, Tzvetan. "The Origin of Genres." Trans. Richard M. Berrong. *New Literary History* 8 (1976): 159–70.

Tompkins, J. M. S. *The Popular Novel in England, 1770–1800.* Lincoln: University of Nebraska Press, 1961.

Trevelyan, George Macauley. *The Poetry and Philosophy of George Meredith.* London: Archibald Constable, 1906.

Unsigned review of *The Female Quixote,* by Charlotte Lennox. *Monthly Review* 6 (April 1752): 249–62.

Van Ghent, Dorothy. *The English Novel: Form and Function.* New York: Harper and Row, 1953.

Waller, Marguerite. "Academic Tootsie: The Denial of Difference and the Difference It Makes." *Diacritics* 17 (1987): 2–20.

Warren, Leland E. "Of the Conversation of Women: *The Female Quixote* and the Dream of Perfection." In *Studies in Eighteenth Century Culture,* vol. 11, Ed. Harry C. Payne, pp. 367–80. Madison: American Society for Eighteenth-Century Studies/University of Wisconsin Press, 1982.

Watt, Ian. *The Rise of the Novel: Studies in Defoe, Richardson and Fielding.* Berkeley: University of California Press, 1957.

Weed, Elizabeth. "A Man's Place." In *Men in Feminism.* Ed. Alice Jardine and Paul Smith, 71–77. New York: Methuen, 1987.

White, Hayden. "Getting out of History." *Diacritics* 12 (1982): 2–13.

Williams, Carolyn. "Natural Selection and Narrative Form in *The Egoist.*" *Victorian Studies* 27 (1983): 53–79.

Williams, Ioan, ed. *Meredith: The Critical Heritage.* New York: Barnes and Noble, 1971.

Willis, Sharon. "A Symptomatic Narrative." *Diacritics* 13 (Spring 1983): 46–60.

Wilson, Edmund. "The Two Scrooges." In his *The Wound and the Bow: Seven Studies in Literature,* 1–104. Cambridge, Mass.: Riverside Press, 1947.

Wilson, Elizabeth. "Psychoanalysis: Psychic Law and Order?" *Feminist Review* 8 (1981): 63–78.

Wilt, Judith. *The Readable People of George Meredith.* Princeton: Princeton University Press, 1975.

Wollstonecraft, Mary. *Collected Letters of Mary Wollstonecraft.* Ed. Ralph M. Wardle. Ithaca: Cornell University Press, 1979.

——. *Letters Written during a Short Residence in Sweden, Norway, and Denmark.* Ed. Carol H. Poston. Lincoln: University of Nebraska Press, 1976.

——. *Mary, A Fiction.* In *Mary and The Wrongs of Woman.* Ed. James Kinsley and Gary Kelly, 1–68. New York: Oxford University Press, 1976.

[——]. Review of *The Evils of Adultery and Prostitution. Analytical Review* 14 (September 1792): 100–102.

——. *A Vindication of the Rights of Woman.* Ed. Miriam Brody Kramnick. New York: Penguin, 1975.

——. *The Wrongs of Woman; or, Maria, A Fragment.* In *Mary and The Wrongs of Woman,* 68–204.

Wood, Mrs. Henry. *East Lynne.* Ed. Sally Mitchell. New Brunswick, N. J.: Rutgers University Press, 1984.

Woolf, Virginia. "George Eliot." In *Women and Writing.* Ed. Michèle Barrett. New York: Harcourt Brace Jovanovich, 1979.

Index

Abjection, 172–73
Abrams, M. H., 52n–53n
Althusser, Louis, 30, 38
Amazons, 88–91
Arabian Nights, The, 136–38, 156, 211–12
Armstrong, Nancy, 12n, 21n, 197n
Aurelius, Marcus, 239
Austen, Jane, 26–28; *Emma*, 174n
Austin, Zelda, 216
Author, as whore, 113–14. *See also* Prostitute; Woman: writers; Writing
Autobiography, 95, 102
Autonomy. *See* Subject

Baker, Ernest, 17n
Balzac, Honoré de, 34n, 35–39
Barbauld, Mrs., 72
Barrett, Michèle, 6n
Barthes, Roland, 134–36, 157, 190n–91n, 198
Baym, Nina, 180n
Beach, Joseph Warren, 41
Beauvoir, Simone de, 2
Beckford, William: *Vathek*, 198
Beer, Gillian, 17n 18n, 41n
Belsey, Catherine, 199
Bennett, Arnold, 235–47
Bennett, Dorothy, 240
Bennington, Geoff, 31n
Benston, Alice N., 35n
Berg, Margaret, 149n
Berger, John, 214n
Birth, 56, 102, 120–22
Blackwood, John, 203, 206–7, 214
Bloom, Harold, 29–30, 34, 38
Body, 10, 27, 39, 105–26, 177–78, 214–16; collapse with, 44–55, 105–26; as figurative, 107–8; hysteric's, 159–60, 169; inscription upon, 53–55, 121–25, 161, 169–70; as the material, 44–46, 107–9; maternal, 101; and meaning, 123–26; prostitute's, 109, 118; sacrifice of to male order, 123; woman's, 10, 44–55, 107–26, 237–39; and writing, 113–26, 237–40. *See also* Essentialism
Boose, Lynda, 185
Boswell, James, 82
Bové, Paul, 184
Bulkin, Elly, 179n–180n
Burney, Fanny, 82
Bray, Charles, 205n
Bremer, Fredrika, 204n
Breuer, Josef, 164
Brontë, Charlotte, 110–12; *Jane Eyre*, 174n; *Shirley*, 110–11
Brooks, Peter, 116n
Brownlee, Kevin, 18n
Brownlee, Martha Scordilis, 18n

Calprenade, 90
Capitalism, 28, 114 16
Carlyle, Thomas, 41, 59
Carpenter, Mary Wilson, 215n
Carter, Mrs., 82
Castration, 25, 28, 54, 86, 88, 101, 106, 197
Cervantes, Miguel de, 78; *Don Quixote*, 62, 72
Character, 48–49, 119–26; construction of, 4, 43; woman's, 48, 53–55, 57. *See also* Construction; Self; Subject
Charcot, Jean-Martin, 160

263

Library of Congress Cataloging-in-Publication Data

Langbauer, Laurie.
  Women and romance : the consolations of gender in the
English novel / Laurie Langbauer.
    p.   cm.—(Reading women writing)
  Includes bibliographical references (p.).
  ISBN 0-8014-2421-6 (alk. paper). —ISBN 0-8014-9692-6
(pbk. : alk. paper)
  1. English fiction—Women authors—History and
criticism. 2. Dickens, Charles, 1812-1870—Characters—
Women. 3. Women and literature—Great Britain—
History. 4. Romanticism—Great Britain. 5. Sex role in
literature. 6. Women in literature. I. Title. II. Series.
PR830.W6L36 1990
823.009'9287—dc20   90-55116